TRUE
TO
LIFE

TRUE TO LIFE

Janet L. Folger

Loyal Publishing
www.loyalpublishing.com

Cover photo by Kelly Rusin.

Cover design by David Uttley Design

True to Life

To my parents, Jim and Beth Folger, who gave me Life, Love, and the Support and Encouragement that made every story in this book possible.

Table of Contents

Table of Contents

Foreword

Ihave been involved in a leadership role in the pro-life movement, nationally and internationally, for three decades. I mention this only to point out that during this time I've had the privilege of meeting and working with almost every major, and many lesser, pro-life leaders in the United States and abroad. After this length of time one gains a certain perspective, and I draw upon this in writing this foreword.

If I were to think of a single young person who, in effect, came up out of nowhere, plunged into the pro-life movement and has become a star, I certainly would rank Janet Folger near, or at the top of, this list.

My dear wife Barbara and I first encountered her as a student at Cleveland State University. She was then, as she has remained since, an activist leader. I don't know all of the chemistry that brought her to the fore, but there she was, a pretty, blonde student with an effervescent personality that she has carried with her ever since.

I was still president of the National Right to Life Committee when she joined the staff at Ohio Right to Life in Columbus, Ohio. Coming from Cincinnati, I had, from 1975 to 1980, been president of that organization and remained on its board. Naturally, I kept a close eye on the happenings in Ohio, even though, during the decade of the '80s I was president of the National Right to Life Committee.

Janet is the sort of person who catches your eye. First of all, she's an attractive young woman, but entirely natural. There's nothing artificial about her. She makes friends instantly and in a very genuine fashion. She is concerned about you in a very genuine personal sense.

There's no question but that she cut her teeth as a lobbyist while with the Ohio Right to Life Society. She quickly, not merely became known, but got to know members of the House and Senate. A quick study, she knew what had to be known about legislation, but added her very personal friendly touch. As I would walk through the halls of the State Capitol, it was typical that we would meet an assemblyman. Naturally, we would stop to say hello, but Janet would have further conversation. "Jimmy, how'd your boy do at the soccer game last Saturday?". . . and . . . "I missed you at the meeting the other night, but I heard that you. . . ." And on it would go. Her contacts were on a first-name basis, with a personal touch of family, church, and professional details. This is the best kind of lobbying, and she is a master at it.

From here she branched into writing, into lecturing, and into a radio interview program of her own.

All in all, she was too good to keep, and in due time Dr. D. James Kennedy lured her away from us in Ohio. She has left a gap that has not been filled, but then it probably never will be in kind. There is only one Janet Folger—a deeply dedicated pro-lifer, a warm friend, an attractive and effervescent Christian, and all of this wrapped up in an intelligent young woman who I am proud to say has been for many years now a close personal friend to both Barbara and me.

J. C. Willke, M.D.
President
Life Issues Institute

Acknowledgments

*Let this be written for a future generation, that a people
not yet created may praise the LORD.*
—Psalm 102:18 (NIV)

The God of the Universe—who worked through every detail of this book and every detail of my life that brought it about. He gets credit for every idea, course of action, and every result.

Clark Hollingsworth—former Executive Vice President of Coral Ridge Ministries. The best boss I ever had. Thank you for your faith in me and for the freedom to dream, attempt, and witness God-sized things.

Greg Hoadley—who traveled all the way from California to attend the 1998 Reclaiming America For Christ Conference. He asked what he could do for the pro-life cause and I hired him. Greg is a brilliant writer whose hard work and research helped make possible the writing, editing, and typesetting of this book in less than a month. Greg does the research and the majority of the writing for the Reclaiming America Commentaries now heard on 300 radio and nearly 50 television stations.

In his office hangs a picture of what he considers the most beautiful place in all the world: the Foroyar Islands near Iceland, where the buildings are covered in sod. He was less than appreciative, however, when we tried to make his *work environment* just as lovely by covering his desk, computer, bookshelves, chair, window sill, garbage can and everything in his office with sod!

xi

Rich DeFilippo—Rich supervised the dissemination of all information via the computer and created the computer files that housed this book in progress. His folder labels included, "Book," "New Book," "REALLY NEW BOOK," "Final Book," and "NEW FINAL BOOK," and the "ALMOST DONE BOOK" and "MILLENNIUM BOOK." Rich is a talented field representative at the CENTER, who worked like a maniac while still maintaining a positive attitude, no matter what was coming at him. When I informed him of the discovery that we lost two days work by working from the wrong files, he just said, "We'll just redo it." Yeah, just redo it—that's all.

Rachel Gaines—oversaw the documentation process for this book. In addition to spending hours on the phone updating materials, she made sure we had all the sources for the endnotes that she kept closely guarded with warning signs and penalties that paralleled touching the Ark of the Covenant. She had to decipher my descriptions of resources like, "It's a white paper with yellow highlights in the right hand corner." Sure, that narrows it right down. She maintained a positive attitude even though she didn't quite see the project as I had described it: "It'll be fun—*like a scavenger hunt!*"

Carol Krpata—worked long and late hours running the office while I was out writing, in addition to making sure everything was moving forward on the book. She also handled all of the stress-related issues that came up in putting a project of this magnitude together in a month—including talking employees down from the ledges—that just wouldn't *look good* for a pro-life book! An incredible administrator, Carol kept my calls and interruptions to a minimum by posting signs, "Shhh! Janet is working!" on every door in the building.

Angela Guerrera—has the difficult task of trying to keep everything I'm doing straight. She is always willing to go the extra ten miles—even when it means driving to my house to get my computer cord that I left at home. In the midst of late hours, Saturdays, and a great deal of pressure, she still always had an encouraging word. She has also become my "fashion consultant," generation X focus group member and personal administrator.

Chris Gorbey—I discovered just how talented our new field representative was when I asked him to read a chapter of the book and make suggestions. I liked them so much I had him edit the rest of the book. I was encouraged by reports of Chris sitting in his office reading drafts of chapters laughing—hopefully at the content, rather than at the writing itself. Even in the midst of it all, he talked about how much he was "enjoying the process," but we all think he was just saying that because he's new on staff.

Christine Sneeringer—When I say that she was a *direct* answer to prayer, I mean a direct answer. On one occasion when I was putting my laptop in my bag to go and write at the beach, it fell out on the floor. When I turned it on, smoke came out. I'm not a computer technician, but I was pretty sure that wasn't a good thing. The very minute after praying, "God, if you want this book, you're going to have to help me," that prayer was answered by the sound "Ding! Dong!" It was Christine, who didn't know why she felt the need to stop by at that moment, "but just did."

She was not only the technical support, but an incredible encourager. The "verse of the book" was from her message on my answering machine, "Let this be written for a future generation that a people not yet created may praise the Lord" (Psalm 102:18 NIV). She kept me well nourished, and laughing, and was my reminder to give thanks—even in the midst of mishaps of spiritual proportions. She also mentioned that in the acknowledgements she would like the title of "Champion of the World." Also, the word "chided" found in chapter 7 was from Christine.

Barry Kase—the CENTER's Director of Media Relations tracked down all the rights and permissions to use resources in the book, including that nifty chart in chapter three. He also surfaced in a brainstorming session with the name for the sub-title. He helped keep everyone in good spirits—especially with his updates on how the "Yes, I Believe in God" song was making its way up the charts—and made the top ten by the time we went to press!

Soraya Rodriguez—"the keeper of the files" who gave honest feedback like, "don't you think you're overworking everybody?" Thanks for *your overwork* that helped to bring this together.

Jim Carter—the CENTER'S Communication Director, who took on all of the responsibilities of the Communication Department when everyone else was pulled away from him. Jim does an outstanding job writing for the *Impact* newsletter, overseeing the Web page, commentaries, and written resources. Jim enlarged one of my book-covers and put it on a 20-pound dictionary for me to deliver to the executive staff as my "completed book."

Barbara Collier—the CENTER'S Field Director offered extra insight on how to get Christians involved in the fight with her favorite word of all time, "grassroots!" She used her connections to track down critical information and held down the fort when I took people from her department to help out.

Maxine Makas—was a source of encouragement and insight. She also pitched in and found the "missing book" we thought was lost forever.

Nancy Britt—for her prayers, encouragement, and final editing of this book. A very talented woman who, thankfully, doesn't need a lot of sleep.

John Aman—The Head Book Honcho. Anyone who can harass us with so many unreasonable deadlines and still be our friend must be an incredible human being. He's also president of Fort Lauderdale's Broward County Right to Life.

Dr. and Mrs. Jack Willke—for their leadership and willingness to go anywhere and speak to anyone on this issue. Two years ago at the D.C. March for Life I ran into some pro-life friends standing in the roped off section for the V.I.P.'s. They were giving me a hard time for being on "the wrong side of the rope." From there the one-upmanship grew to the pinnacle of pro-life achievement: who knew the Willkes the best. One man said, "Oh yeah? I stayed across the hall from the Willkes in Moscow!" Not to be outdone, another woman said, "Oh, yeah? I rode on the same cable car with them in Bulgaria." They both looked triumphantly at me standing on the other side of the rope, when I replied, "I stayed at their house last night." Thanks to the Willkes for making me look so cool. I "love them both"—why can't I?

Jim, Tim and Todd Folger—for helping to "fine tune" my debating skills. A belated Merry Christmas—this is your "made gift."

Christine Breighner—who along with Christine Sneeringer provided hours of extra writing time for me that would have otherwise been spent finding what I was going to wear—by cleaning out my closet while I was out of town. The way I see it, if somebody does that for you, they deserve a mention in your book.

Katheryn Pina—whom I met at a "Teens for Life" rally in Traverse City, Michigan, and later became one of our staff interns over the past two summers. Thanks for giving up the beach to help out. Hurry up and graduate so we can hire you.

Ohio Right to Life—Thanks, especially, to Mark Lally, Lorraine Schmidt, Judy Gregory, Ben Gessler, Nichole Stoke, Becky Cain, Dorothy Mozzetti, Tim Welsh, Kathy Malott, the board members, and chapters that made Ohio a pro-life leader in the nation.

Tom Zabor—for speaking to my 10th grade class.

Cass Zabor—for training me in the pro-life speaker's bureau—and passing me.

Doug Johnson—Legislative Director, National Right to Life Committee for the original idea to ban partial birth abortions.

The Ohio Pro-Life Legislators—who gave the legislative chapters happy endings.

Teri Honaker, Uri Katz, and Bill Backman—for their prayers and encouragement.

Jim Nelson Black, for believing in me and for your encouragement, advice and direction.

Terry Shawn of the U.S. House Judiciary Committee and **Caryn Collier** of Family Research Council for your aid and persistence.

Mickey Caruana—for his prayers, dinners, and 4,357 rides to and from the airport, and who, with the help of Andy Piccolo, rearranged my furniture and redecorated my house while I was gone. I still think the toaster on the ceiling decor is sure to catch on.

Luc Nadeau and Carlos Velazquez—for all your help with "everything that could possibly go wrong with a computer."

Jerry and Kirsti Newcombe—My author friends—for their advice and wealth of information.

Don and Carol Van Curler—as far as I'm concerned, anyone who prays for me everyday should be in the book.

Everyone on our e-mail prayer list.

Matt Giambrone—for his early research and for sharing the vision long ago.

Matt and Cindy Krepcho—for giving me the lounge chairs by my pool that I used to write the last few chapters.

Thanks to all the people and organizations who were so helpful in putting up with our many calls and requests for assistance: National Right to Life, Brad Mattes and Life Issues Institute, Michigan Right to Life, Gayle Atteberry and Kay Estes and Oregon Right to Life, Minnesota Right to Life, Media Research Center, Rob Regier and Family Research Council, Donald Wildmon and the American Family Association, Keith Fournier, Mark Crutcher, Bill Johnson of the American Decency Association, Wallbuilders, Mary Anne Bunker, Rita Marker and the International Anti-Euthanasia Task Force, Linda Harvey and Mission America, Joleigh Little, Courtney Urbanek, John Quarquesso, Lisa Velazquez, John Sorenson, Clay Brasington, Randy Tavlin, and Stacy Mossop.

Rick Cataldo—for staying up all night to read this—twice, and for selecting this book cover despite how our restaurant focus group voted.

And Jim Weber: who helped me on a report in the fifth grade.

1

Why Read This Book?

Ｎew to the pro-life debate? No matter where you've come from, whether you've had an abortion, performed them, or are just now finding out the truth, I welcome you to the "human rights" movement of our time.

This is a book about life, but it's not about statistics. There are plenty of those. This is *not* a book about how abortions are being done and who is doing them. You probably already know that. Newcomer? Abortions are done mostly by dismemberment . . . and mostly by Planned Parenthood. There. That takes care of that.

If you're like many, you may be feeling overwhelmed. Feeling like what you do doesn't make a difference. Maybe you're afraid to speak up. That's exactly where I was twenty years ago. This book is about how, if you will trust God and step out in faith and in obedience to Him—He will use you in ways that are exceedingly greater than you can think or imagine. He did it for me, and I want to tell you how.

First, let me tell you where we are in this debate.

If you're like me you've been in the pro-life battle for years. January 22, 1973, means something to you—the date of the decision that has become synonymous with death: *Roe v. Wade.* Maybe you remember when seven men on the Supreme Court imposed their immorality on every child waiting to be born in this nation. And maybe you've been involved since then. If so, you have probably already read everything that's been written; you've attended all the conventions, the dinners, the protests, the marches, and the debates. If that's the case, why read another book?

Well, if you've done all that, I'm guessing that maybe you're tired. We're now in the twenty-first century and, well, it wasn't supposed to take this long. We were going to see children protected again and go back to our lives. All we needed was for a Human Life Amendment to be added to the Constitution, and that would be it. When that didn't happen, the war on abortion shifted to 50 separate state battlegrounds.

They *said* abortion was only going to be for the "hard cases"—for rape, incest, and the life of the mother. The pro-lifers predicted that if abortion were legalized, it would become commonplace, be used as a method of back-up birth control and, yes, even as the primary method of birth-control. But the reality was even more devastating than anyone could have predicted. Now *nearly 50 percent* of all abortions performed are on women for their second, third, fourth, and fifth abortion; 47 percent of them have had at least one previous abortion and 55 percent have had a previous birth.[1]

And why are women getting these abortions? Contrary to what the pro-aborts would have you believe, *only 1 percent of all abortions are for pregnancies caused by rape or incest!* The other 99 percent of all abortions are for mostly social reasons like: she felt she was not ready for the responsibility (21 percent); she had concerns for how it would change her life (16 percent); she had relationship problems (12 percent); she felt she wasn't mature enough (11 percent); she has all the children she wants (8 percent); she felt she couldn't afford a baby (21 percent). Only 3 percent of women getting an abortion did so for their own health. Another 3 percent because the baby may have health problems.[2]

No, abortion is *not* about rape and incest, the so-called "hard cases." It has become a routine method of birth control.

They targeted the disabled in the womb. And then they targeted the disabled out of the womb. Baby Doe was born in Bloomington, Indiana, in 1982 with a minor birth defect. He was starved to death while couples were standing in line to adopt this handicapped baby. Why? Because it was the parent's "right to choose," after all.

And then babies who are four-fifths born became the target in what they call "partial-birth abortion."

Following closely behind that they started selling the body parts of aborted babies. Price lists have been released showing the following: brains — $999; eyes — $75; livers — $150; ears — $75; skin — $100; spinal cords — $325 and complete baby bodies — $500–$600! It seems that these so-called blobs of protoplasm are in high demand.[3]

And then it was the adults—Jack Kevorkian, referred to as "Doctor Death." Then Oregon—targeting the terminally ill, the frail, and the elderly—just like the pro-life movement predicted back in 1973.

Nearly 40 million innocent children slaughtered . . . in our country, in our lifetime.

A bit overwhelming—wouldn't you say? Enough to make a person want to give up and go crawl in that same hole the rest of the country has

We ran this ad in *The Washington Times* in 1998—on the 25th anniversary of *Roe v. Wade* to show the "Permanent reminders that choices have consequences."

been hiding in—the same hole much of the Church has been hiding in. After all, you can't talk about abortion in church—it's a political issue. And you can't talk about abortion in politics—it's a religious issue. It's easy to see why so many have stayed on the sidelines with stellar logic like that.

And then there are the courts: the tyrannical rule of "unelected" judges overriding the rule of the people by overturning existing laws and making up their own laws from the bench—all while appointed for life.

And don't forget about the White House. With a stroke of a pen, President Bill Clinton wiped out every pro-life executive order issued by the Reagan and Bush administrations. He also vetoed the Partial-Birth Abortion Ban (twice as of this writing)—the law that would have protected children who are four-fifths born from having their brains sucked out. Then he turned around and told everyone how he wants to make abortion "rare."

In 1996, the American people re-elected him, and he has continued to do everything in his power to make sure there are *more—not less*—abortions. He has pushed to have abortions funded with our tax dollars, to be included in our healthcare, and he has done everything in his power to increase the funding available for abortions overseas.

And then there's Hollywood—we have all seen the stars at the abortion marches in Washington. (And isn't it amazing how the vast majority of these famous celebrities favor the killing of unborn humans, yet go out of their way to stand up for animal rights?)

And let's not forget the media. In case you couldn't guess it by the coverage, over 97 percent identify themselves as pro-abortion.[4]

And don't forget about the influence Planned Parenthood has over sex education in government schools. It looks like the odds are stacked against us pretty high—right?

The Truth

And all we have is the truth.

Imagine a scale. On one side of the scale are the courts, the White House, Congress, Hollywood, The National Education Association, the media, and a whole lot of money. And on the other side of the scale, there's just one thing—the truth. Want to know which side *I* would pick? That's easy. The truth. Why? Because everything else is temporary, but the truth will prevail.

I saw a young teenager a few years ago at the pro-life march in Washington on January 22—the anniversary of the bloody decision that started it all. He held a very straightforward sign I will never forget: "Call me an extremist, but I think dismembering children is wrong." We have the truth.

The harsh truth of abortion has really manifested itself in the debate over partial-birth abortion. Back when I was lobbying for the nation's first partial-birth abortion ban, it wasn't even called that yet. No one had ever heard of this horrible procedure. But my colleagues and I at the Ohio Right to Life Society (where I served as legislative director from 1988-1997) knew there was an Ohio abortionist committing this infanticide. He was pulling infants out of the womb feet first; grabbing their legs, torso, arms and neck until they were outside the womb, with only the child's head remaining in the mother's body. He then jammed a pair of scissors into the back of the child's neck and inserted a suction catheter to suck the baby's brains out. That's why the Ohio Legislature called it "brain-suction abortion."

How did we know this was going on? We knew because the abortionist told us. Actually, he told the National Abortion Federation about his wonderful new method of killing kids, and we found out because he put it in writing. So I approached the legislature with this information, and a surprising thing happened. Legislators—powerful people in both the House and Senate—including some in leadership, broke down and cried in front of me when they found out what was happening to children in our state.

Their reactions gave me hope because it showed me that the conscience of our nation was not already so seared that it couldn't be reached. That bill—and the one like it that followed in Washington—reached people like nothing else could. In all other abortion procedures, you can't see the baby. And if you can't see him, it's a whole lot easier to pretend he doesn't exist.

Virtually every independent opinion poll conducted since the partial-birth abortion debate has shown an 8–10 percent shift in the pro-life direction. On January 21, 1998, *USA Today* said, "Abortion rights support-ers say the issue has put them on the defensive. . . ."[5]

When the American people were forced to look at the truth of what happens in an abortion, they didn't like what they saw. That gives me hope.

Persistence

But step back from the overwhelming statistics for a moment. Step back from all the defeats, setbacks, and disappointments and look at a very basic fact. Abortion has been legal for nearly 30 years now—and yet it remains *the* most divisive, *most controversial* issue in our nation.

Do you know what that means? That means the pro-lifers have the single most important factor in winning this battle. That's persistence. That is something the pro-aborts never counted on. You see, we were supposed to have given up by now. The Ohio National Abortion and Reproductive Rights Action League (NARAL) director told the *Los Angeles Times,* "No one could have realized that the anti-choice people are never going to give up . . . the average member of the public doesn't understand the significance of the threat that is out there from people like Janet."[6] And that includes people like *you.*

What they didn't know is, once you know the truth about abortion, you can't walk away from it. Poll after poll proves it. This issue is *far* more important to the pro-life side—than the pro-abortion crowd. If you don't believe me, check the exit polls. Even though "the economy" tragically car-ried the day in the last two presidential elections, on the issue of abortion, George Bush *won* in 1992, and Bob Dole *won* in 1996.

For example, in the 1996 election, 12 percent of all voters polled in the Wirthlin Poll (11/5/1996)[7] cited abortion as one of the two most important issues in determining their vote. Fifty-four percent (54 percent) of those who cited abortion as one of their top two issues voted for pro-life can-didates. Fourteen percent (14 percent) of all those who voted for Dole voted for him because of his pro-life stance.[8] That's because to a "pro-choicer," this issue is just one of the "rights" they're concerned about. To pro-lifers, abor-tion is the ultimate in child abuse. The fact of the matter is, pro-lifers cannot, and *will not*, walk away until children are protected again. Life is of the utmost importance, and persistence wins.

Chinese Bamboo

In the Far East, people plant a tree called the Chinese Bamboo. During the first four years they water and fertilize the plant with seemingly little or no results. But during the fifth year they again water and fertilize—and in *five weeks* time the tree grows 90 feet in height!

The question: Did the bamboo tree grow 90 feet in five weeks or five years? Answer: It grew 90 feet in five years, because if at any time the people had stopped watering and fertilizing the tree, it would have died.

You don't always see results right away. By the third or fourth year, if I were the one watering the bamboo tree, I'd be pretty discouraged. But just because you don't always see the results of what you are doing right away, it doesn't mean what you are doing isn't making a difference.

St. Albert the Great

In college I would sometimes cut classes to give pro-life speeches in high schools. After all, that is where *I* was reached with the truth. On January 11, 1987, while I was in graduate school, I gave a pro-life speech to a group of teens at St. Albert the Great Church. Not the kind of event you'd like to focus on to keep you going—I was nervous, had trouble with the slides, and hardly anybody came to hear me. The next year I graduated and got a job two-and-one-half-hours away in Columbus at Ohio Right to Life. What made St. Albert the Great a more significant event was the fact that on my way to see my family from Columbus to Cleveland, I would have to drive past that church.

Every single time I saw that place I felt pangs of regret. I felt I had done a lousy job—and they had never asked me back. I would often get thoughts like, "What do you think you're doing in this business anyway? You are not a speaker, and you never were." You get the idea. This went on for five years—every time I drove home to see my parents.

Fast-forward to 1992. Bill Clinton is elected. I was scheduled to give about a dozen motivational talks and I just didn't have it in me. I wanted to give up. I remember going to the Bahamas and considering a promising career in braiding hair on the beach. (I thought it would be easier to learn to drive on the left side of the road than be ruled by the "left.") When I came back, I went to a pro-life dinner in Wisconsin with about 500 other people.

A guy I had never met recognized my name and introduced himself, saying that he lived in Texas. He said, "I know you must speak at a lot of places, and you're not going to remember this, but about five years ago my parents brought you in to speak at a church called St. Albert the Great." He had my attention. He said, "There was a girl there who didn't abort her baby because you came and spoke that day."

Wow! It's not about how eloquent you are. It's not about how many people show up. It's about being faithful. That's all God wants from us.

I wonder what the odds are that in a crowd of 500 people I would run into a guy who remembers the name of a speaker his parents (in another state) brought to their church five years prior—at precisely the time I needed it most? I think God only gives us a *glimpse* of what He is doing through us just to keep us going. If He showed us everything He was accomplishing through each of us, we would probably start to think that all those good things were happening because of how great *we* were.

If we are faithful to water and fertilize, the results and the victory *will* come! Persistence wins.

With all the things we have stacked against us, pro-lifers should have been obliterated by now. The pro-aborts now have the courts, the White House, Hollywood, the media, and public education. But with all of this control, and no matter how many decisions they hand down, no matter how many bills they veto, no matter how many bad movies they make, or how blatantly they slant the news and education, they can't make the issue go away. The truth will prevail. Persistence wins. And, thirdly, we are going to win this battle because love conquers all.

Love

Two years ago I was scheduled to debate an abortion clinic director who also happened to be a homosexual activist. (I get all the *easy* jobs at the

CENTER FOR RECLAIMING AMERICA.) It was the best debate I ever had. There were *no flaws* in my presentation. In fact, I didn't say *a thing* wrong in the entire debate . . . because it was *cancelled*.

As I prepared to fly to Pennsylvania to take on this flamboyant abortion director who operated several clinics, I got word that the plans had changed. The debate was cancelled. Why? I was pretty sure this guy wasn't intimidated by me. Eric Harrah—the abortion clinic director/homosexual activist—cancelled the debate because he gave his life to Jesus Christ. I love it when that happens! Turns out, a Christian layman, Steve Stupar, befriended him and led him to Christ.

The fact of the matter is that Jesus Christ died for that abortionist. He was nailed to the Cross for the person who has committed the worst sin imaginable—that's an incredible amount of love. And if we share that love, we *will* see results. Showing love to people opens their hearts so that the Holy Spirit can break through. And when that happened to Eric, the killing stopped. I recently did a radio show with him—only this time, we were both on the same side!

About three years ago I debated the executive director of NARAL at Ohio Wesleyan University. I made a pretty bold statement: "The *only* choice those in the abortion movement offer women is the choice of a dead child." I then backed that up with a show of hands, asking, "Does anyone know of a *single* home for unwed mothers run by the National Abortion and Reproductive Rights Action League? Planned Parenthood? The National Organization for Women (NOW)? Anyone? Anyone? Didn't think so."

Let me repeat that: The *only* choice those in the abortion movement offer women is the choice of a dead child—*if* they have the money to pay them. While they wear the "Choice" buttons and carry the "Choice" banners, the only "choice" they really care about is abortion—and they're not doing them for free.

What about us? That's what my opponent asked me: "Well, are *you* giving to the pregnancy centers?"

"Yes, I just did a fundraiser for them last week."

Not satisfied, she demanded, "Is *your organization* doing anything for the pregnancy centers?"

"Yes, they just bought a table for the Pregnancy Distress Center banquet." (Debate lesson number one: Never ask a question in a debate when you don't know the answer.) Pro-life pregnancy help centers offer women a choice that *both* they *and* their child can *live* with—free of charge (but at great personal expense). I think that speaks volumes about who really *cares* about women.

You see, I happen to think that women deserve more of an answer to their untimely pregnancy than the solution of a dead child. We can do better than that. And we must. And in nearly 3,400 pregnancy help centers nationwide, we are!

The media love to pit mother against child. They love to ask questions like, "what side are you on—the side of the woman or (by the much less affectionate Latin term) the fetus?"

My answer? "Why can't we love them both?" You see, no one *has* to die. We really can love and help *both* the mother *and* the child.

Keep Walking (But Let's Look at a Map)

Question: How do you get to the Promised Land? Answer: Keep walking. After 30 or so years into the journey, I wonder if Aaron or Joshua asked Moses if they might have a look at the map! (Or perhaps Moses' wife suggested they should stop and ask for directions.)

Yes, persistence wins, the truth prevails, and love conquers all—but we will win *sooner* if we act smarter. We need to keep walking, but we need to be sure we're headed in the right direction. We need to look at the map and share what we find. If we are to win sooner, we need to do better.

Pro-life activists are hardworking people who've been persevering against enormous odds, doing thankless tasks for many years, in being a voice for the voiceless. If that has been you, on behalf of the children you and your work has saved, and the women your work has spared, I thank you. I also thank you for the hope your work has given us as a nation.

But even though we are caring people who work hard, that does not guarantee we won't spend 40 years wandering around in the wilderness before we reach our desired goal of returning protection to children. To prevent this, we must work *smarter* and make sure we're *all* walking in the *right direction*. We must regroup and reevaluate what we've been doing—look at the mistakes we've made in order to show us how to alter our course. We must share the roads to victory we have discovered.

When I first began, I just knew they were killing children; it was wrong, and I had to do *something* to try and stop it. I just didn't know what . . . and I certainly didn't know how long it would take. Frankly, I'm not sure I would have enlisted in this battle if I had known it would take this long.

I've been told that I'm not the most patient person in the world. In my interview for legislative director at Ohio Right to Life, I told them, "Look, I'm going to be pro-life and involved no matter what I do. I don't need to be employed by you to do that." I had plans for my life that didn't include full-time pro-life work. After much deliberation, I committed to join them with this enthusiastic response, "I'll give you *one year*." It was *nine* years later that I finally moved on to Florida to work with Dr. D. James Kennedy and the CENTER FOR RECLAIMING AMERICA. If I knew I had to commit nearly a decade of my life to that task, I might not have signed up.

I was the kid who was afraid to give a speech in front of the class— who didn't even know what abortion *was* until the 10th grade. But, sometimes God uses the most unlikely people to accomplish His goals so that everyone will know it's Him at work—not the extraordinary talents of gifted people. Take a look at David. When it came time to anoint the next king, his own father forgot about him. After all, he was just a shepherd boy. Moses? He stuttered and was afraid to speak—yet God used him mightily.

All I know is, I have learned a lot of lessons and seen a lot of victories—including some "impossible ones" in my short lifetime. The bad news is that much of what I have learned was by making mistakes and stumbling around in the dark until I found the way out. I would have liked to have saved that time, trouble, and humiliation, and used it to advance our goals a lot further. That's why I'd like to share some of what I have learned through my true "life" stories.

2

Getting Out of the Desert

To get to the Promised Land where children are again protected, we must keep walking. And apart from the truth, persistence, and love, we need some additional things to get us out of the wilderness sooner, and the first one is God. I have always spoken on this issue from a scientific, logical, and legal perspective, but I'm here to tell you that we're not going to win it from those perspectives alone. Without seeking God's wisdom, direction, and power, and having faith in what He is able to do, we can forget about it. And with that comes our secret weapon to success: a mobilized Church engaged in the culture—being salt and light in this very dark world.

An Active Church

The very first step is to get on our knees and pray. I believe 2 Chronicles 7:14 says it best:

> If My people who are called by My name will humble them-selves, and pray and seek My face, and turn from their wicked ways, then I will hear from heaven and will forgive their sin and heal their land.

Pray as if millions of lives depend on it—because they do. Pray as if our country depends on it—because it does. Pray every day that the killing will stop. That is the *starting* point—and that is the one thing pro-lifers don't always seem to grasp. Prayer is the first step—it is not our only step. When I extend invitations for help, there are always people who say, "I'll pray about it." That's like telling the hungry to be warm and well fed while you whistle on your merry way (James 2:15-16). *Actions* are what you believe—everything else is just religious talk.

But what is keeping the Church trapped behind the stained glass windows? The biggest fraud of the 20th century—the supposed "constitutional separation of church and state"—which has been repeated loudly enough and often enough that almost everyone in America believes it. Let me tell you the secret to uncovering this fraud. What I am going to tell you could change your life and release you from the prison of censorship and passive subservience (that alone should be worth the price of this book!).

That supposed constitutional "gag rule" called the "separation of church and state" that has been used to silence Christians for decades? Well, it doesn't exist. But how can you be *sure* this "separation" isn't in our Constitution? I've discovered a foolproof way of reaching that conclusion: Read it. See for yourself—*it is not there*!

The much referred to "establishment clause" of the First Amendment says: "*Congress* shall make no law respecting *an establishment* of religion, *or prohibiting the free exercise* thereof." Not only is there no reference to the phrase "separation of church and state," note that there is no reference to what the *Church* shall *not* do. It refers *only* to restrictions on *Congress*. It doesn't tell Johnny he can't pray in school or that a nativity scene can't be displayed in a public park; it restrains the power of the *federal government* from infringing on the religious freedoms of the people!

But, it's easier to believe it than read it, and so we remove our nativity scenes from the courthouse and put them where no one can see them, and we retreat all too willingly into the closet, where modern society has told us we belong. I am confident of one thing—if we stay in that closet, very soon there will be a padlock on the outside of that door, not to just keep us from working in the pro-life arena, but from even sharing our faith with those around us.

The Answer

So the media isn't paying attention to you? Your elected officials aren't giving you the time of day? Don't feel respected or effective? There is one very simple answer to all of those problems: register, inform, and turn out the pro-life vote. If we do that, ALL of those problems go away. After we get up off our knees, this is our most significant action step. I believe it must begin in the pro-life, Bible-believing churches in every single community in America.

As I write this, I must admit that I am fearful of what will happen if we *don't* do this in the next election. There may be as many as three seats on the Supreme Court of the United States, which will be ultimately determined by what happens this November.[1] As you know, it's the President who gets to pick who they are. Those selections will, in a very real way, determine how long we stay in the desert where children are not protected. After prayer, there is nothing more significant the pro-life community can do than get out of the wilderness, register every single pro-life person they know to vote, and then inform them of all the candidates' positions. If you are not sure where the candidates stand on abortion, your local Right to Life chapter can inform you (as well as all the other candidates in your area), or you can call the CENTER FOR RECLAIMING AMERICA. If you do nothing else . . . do this. I cannot emphasize this enough.

We also must groom good pro-life candidates for local, state, and federal office who share our beliefs. And who knows? That just might be what God is calling you to do. When John Hostettler came to our annual Reclaiming America For Christ Conference in Fort Lauderdale, Florida, back in 1994, he attended a session that challenged Christians to run for Congress. So what did he do when he went back home to Indiana? He ran for Congress—and won! Sometimes people just need to be asked.

But for those of us who don't run, it's up to us to support those who do. In 1998 a conservative Christian ran for the Florida State Legislature. As it turns out, he belonged to a large church and 1,100 of his fellow church members lived in the district he would have represented—if only they had bothered to vote. About 600 of those who could have made a difference didn't even vote, and he lost in the primary by 675 votes! That's not the media's fault, and we can't blame it on the courts. We are the ones responsible—but the good news is that we can do something about it!

One of my all-time favorite legislators is a brilliant pro-life leader named Ed Kasputis. Ed was never supposed to win his Ohio House seat. In fact, I couldn't find a single incumbent who gave this newcomer a chance. He was running against the county chairman's son—some would say not a very bright move. He told me when he was looking for his Christian friends to help, he often heard, "I can't. I have Bible study," "I can't—prayer group." Granted, those are good and necessary things to do. But I thought Ed's perspective was very insightful: "We're in the Super Bowl and they're still doing push-ups."

If only the Christians *were* preparing themselves to enter the game! But the problem is that most of the Church is perfectly content to stay on the sidelines. In fact, many on the sidelines aren't even watching the game! This is our greatest hurdle: Christians who are living in a separate world. They go to church on Sunday, and maybe even Wednesday night; listen to Christian radio; take their kids to a Christian school; and attend Bible studies—all within the four walls of a church—while the nation crumbles around them.

When you have a light—what's the best thing to do? Hide it "under a basket?" In the Gospel of Matthew 5:14–15, Jesus clearly declared:

> You are the light of the world. A city that is set on a hill cannot be hidden. Nor do they light a lamp and put it under a basket, but on a lampstand, and it gives light to all who are in the house.

We are to let the light of Christ shine in and through us before men. We must be as a city on a hill, a shining example of truth for all the world to see.

Creativity

Another critical element to get us out of the desert is creativity. We all know we don't have the money, and I won't go over all the things stacked on the other side of the scale against us, but we have an incredibly effective and under-utilized tool that I have seen overcome all of that: *creativity.* I want to show you how, when we didn't have money or time, creativity more than made up for it. I hate to say it, but some of the hurdles we face are our own fault. While we whine and cry about how the media doesn't cover our "candlelight vigils" every year, it's not only because the media is biased against us; it's because we haven't taken the time and effort to come up with something different, creative, and more newsworthy.

Believe me, I'm angry at what they are doing to children, too. But when we talk about this on the news, to our friends, and in debates, even our well-placed anger is often misinterpreted as "mean-spiritedness." They need to know we're *not* angry with them—if they are pro-abortion, they are *deceived*—we're angry at the shedding of innocent blood. As the Bible says, we must be angry and sin not (Psalms 4:4 and Ephesians 4:26). I would say that probably most of my letters to the editor were fueled by anger. Use that energy. After all, God gave it to you. But, form your words in a constructive way and let people see that you are rational, logical, and loving.

Humor

This may surprise you, but something else I believe is essential in this battle is humor. Yes, we are facing a horrific issue, and celebrations are sometimes few and far between. But we must find a way to enjoy the journey— even though it often takes a concerted effort. Some of the most effective things I've done have played on the hypocrisy of the other side in a fun way where people couldn't help but laugh. The good news is that when their arguments aren't based in truth—as none of them are—inconsistencies abound. Just take your pick. My favorite times are when we can show this in a fun way—it helps make us likable to the outside world, and it uplifts and inspires pro-lifers who have had their share of letdowns.

And while we must strategize, learn, and persevere, I believe we should, whenever possible, make this fun. We have life, we have hope. And in the battle to give that to others, we must have joy, even in the midst of tragedy—because we know the outcome, because we're doing what's right, and because we're making our life count to help others have that chance.

Along with the truth, persistence, and love, if we are to get out of this wilderness, we *must* allow God to use us, and activate the Church—first by getting the members registered to vote and informing them of where the candidates stand on abortion. And when there is no pro-lifer to vote for, we should find someone—even if that's by looking in the mirror! I also believe we can get farther faster if we utilize creativity and humor while working together. We have to be sure that we share the information we find on the map with everyone else so we are all walking in the same direction toward the Promised Land of victory.

3

A Simple Issue

It was a dark and stormy night as the *U.S.S. Iowa* sailed the high seas. Suddenly, the lookout saw a light coming toward the ship. Though barely visible in the thick swirling fog, it was clear they were about to crash. The captain of the *U.S.S. Iowa* radioed, and with an urgent authoritative tone, said, "This is the *U.S.S. Iowa*. Move your vessel 20 degrees port."

A still calm voice came back and said, "Move *your* vessel 20 degrees starboard."

They kept getting closer, and the captain, angered at the impertinent response, said to himself, "They must not know who they are talking to." He barked back a second radio message, "This is Captain McPherson of the *U.S.S. Iowa*. I order you to move *your* vessel 20 degrees port immediately!"

The voice came back still and calm as ever and said, "Move *your* vessel 20 degrees starboard."

A crash being imminent, the captain, who wasn't about to alter his ship's course, decided to give it one last attempt. His voice, barely containing his rage, relayed one final message, "This is the twice decorated Captain Robert McPherson of the *U.S.S. Iowa*. I *order* you to move your vessel 20 degrees to port immediately and identify yourself!"

A still calm voice came back as firm as ever, "Move your vessel 20 degrees starboard. This is the Portland lighthouse."

We, of the pro-life movement, are that lighthouse. We have the heart-changing, direction-changing truth. The pro-abortion lobby can scream and shout, and even censor our message, but that won't change the facts: The being in the womb is a human being. It is so simple that even a child can see it.

This Is a Pretty Simple Issue

There is really only one question that must be answered in this debate: Is the being in the womb a human being? Everything rests on that answer. And for nearly 30 years this issue has been called complicated and so complex that the courts, the legislatures and the media can't figure it out.

The *Ohio State Lantern* documented this event by including this picture, Monday, April 26, 1993, with the caption, "Janet Folger, legislative director of Ohio Right to Life, asks a two-year old to identify a photograph of a child in vitro. The little girl said, 'baby.'" That little girl is Christine Mozzetti with her mother Dorothy. (Photo by Jim Douthitt/*The Lantern*)

One day when I was speaking at a rally in the Ohio State House rotunda, I decided to embark on a little experiment. I looked through the crowd for the smallest child I could find. Sitting in a stroller in the back of the audience was a little girl who was not even two years old.

In the middle of my speech I said to the girl's mother, "Excuse me ma'am, could you bring your stroller up here? I'd like to ask your little girl a question." The mother had this panicked look on her face, but complied. Before I could ask her daughter the question, she whispered, "Janet, (I don't know what you're trying to prove here) she's eighteen months old and she doesn't really *talk* much."

"That's O.K.," I assured her, "I think she can answer the question that has plagued us, that has divided our nation—the question that could settle this debate once and for all: Is the being in the womb a human being or is it not?

I held up a copy of a *Life Magazine* from 1965 that has the picture of the unborn "entity" that's been causing so much controversy on the cover and said, "Honey, settle this for us, *what* is this a picture of?"[1] I put the microphone to her little face and she said, "Baby." Isn't that amazing—an 18-month-old can recognize what so many of our elected officials in the State House and Supreme Court Justices could not—that this being in the womb is a baby! I was then accused of prepping her with what to say, to which I replied, "Yeah, and up until I told her to say "baby," she was referring to this as a "product of conception"—right?"

You see, we on the pro-life side have the heart-changing, direction-changing truth that even a child can recognize. Why do you think they try so hard to hide it?

Another time I was on a panel debate at Case Western Reserve University. One of the issues debated was our Woman's Right to Know bill that I lobbied for when I was the legislative director of Ohio Right to Life Society. Among other things, this bill would (and did) guarantee women access to the accurate scientific facts about fetal growth and development. The "pro-choice" side didn't want women to have accurate information to make a choice. They didn't even want the students at Case to see it and threatened to walk off the debate if we showed slides of fetal development. We steadfastly maintained that we would not be censored—particularly by individuals who wanted to keep information critical to this issue from reaching the students. They left. The students stayed. And we had the full hour and a half to make our case!

One of the things I often use is a biology book. I carry it with me to every debate—the pro-aborts hate it. I hold up my book with the unborn pictured on the front for the television cameras and they say, "Put that down!

That's emotional! That's controversial!" To which I reply, "This may make you *feel* emotional, but there is nothing controversial about human growth and development: it is a scientific fact."

In fact, there is not a biology book, an embryology, fetology, or a modern day science book *in existence* that says that life begins at any moment *other* than the moment of conception. Don't believe me? See for yourself— go to your library, find me *one* medical textbook, one fetology book that says that life begins at a moment other than the moment of conception. I've made that offer all over the country, but I've never had anyone accept that challenge. A unique, distinctive human life begins at the moment of conception: it is a scientific fact.

Even the Pro-Aborts Know It

What many people don't realize is not only do we agree with that fact, but the pro-abortion folks agree as well. Whether they admit that all the time or not is another matter.

Faye Wattleton, then the executive director of Planned Parenthood —the nation's largest abortion promoter and provider, appeared on the *Phil Donahue Show* with Randall Terry of Operation Rescue.[2] When Terry said, "It's not a frog or a ferret being killed, it's a baby," Wattleton responded, "I am fully aware of that, I am fully aware of that." You see, Planned Parenthood's position on abortion is "Yes, we know it's a baby, but we just don't care."

So even Faye Wattleton acknowledges the scientific fact that it is a baby in the mother's womb. The difference is, pro-lifers believe *that that baby's life matters.*

Get Government Out of the Issue

You see, the government's role is to protect that child. I once was sitting across the desk from an Ohio state senator who said to me, "Janet, I understand. You've made your point. I've seen the fetus sucking his thumb at eight weeks, and, of course, it's a human life—but we want to get government *out* of the issue." (Sound familiar?)

And I said to her, "Let me tell you, personally speaking, I believe the government *is* involved in too many areas of our lives. I think that it is too intrusive and overbearing—but I do recognize that there is a purpose for government—there is a legitimate reason for it." And then I pointed to a plaque on her desk with a quote from Thomas Jefferson. "Thomas Jefferson, a man *fairly* knowledgeable in American government, said it best with the quote on your table: 'The care of human life and not its destruction is the *first and only legitimate object of good government.*'" Get government out of this issue? Caring for human life is why we have government in the first place! That is the first and only legitimate reason for our government.

We could also look to the Declaration of Independence, where our forefathers said, "We hold these truths to be *self-evident.*" They're saying this is a no-brainer; it's self-evident, but just so nobody misses it, we'll write it down. ". . . we are endowed by our *Creator*"—not by the Clinton administration, not by the courts—but by "our *Creator* with the inalienable right to life." You see, the freedoms in the Bill of Rights are not given to us by the Founding Fathers. They are not even given to us by the Constitution. They are given to us by God. And guess which right is listed first? The right that makes all other rights possible: "the inalienable right to life." Without it, none of the other rights matter.

If you read a little further, it says ". . . to *secure* these rights, governments are instituted." Again, get government out of this issue? No. To protect human life—to secure our "inalienable right to life" is why government *exists.* We who are pro-life hold that truth to be self-evident. The problem is . . . not everyone does.

I've had reporters come up to me, stick a microphone in my face and say, "You're just trying to make women have babies, aren't you? Isn't that what you're all about?" No. What some people don't seem to understand is that once a woman is pregnant, she *already has* a child; the choice is whether the child is going to come out alive or dead. Rep. Henry Hyde has often said that birth is merely a change of address. It's the same child *before* and *after* he or she passes through the birth canal—it doesn't somehow magically become more human a minute after he's born as opposed to a minute before.[3]

A "Complicated Issue" Made Simple: Live Baby Good, Dead Baby Bad

So when you talk about the right to choose, here is what you're choosing: a live child or a dead child. For those who are easily confused by the pro-life/pro-choice labels, I sometimes clarify my position even more: We're the folks working to ensure a live child. *They're* the ones who are actually performing the procedures to make sure they'll end up dead. Still confused? A few times, when I was especially frustrated, I got a little carried away and said, "For those who still can't seem to get it (especially for members of the press), let me break this issue down into its simplest form: 'Live baby good, dead baby bad.'" I sometimes have groups repeat that with me to break this "complex, complicated" issue down to basics: "Live baby good, dead baby bad." See? It's really not so hard after all; it's not such a complicated issue if you just look at the facts.

A few years ago I was in Nashville for a National Right to Life Convention and took in some of the local sights—including a country line-dancing establishment. I ran into a friend of mine who was with a man from New Jersey. We talked for a few minutes and I asked him if he had ever gone to any New Jersey Right to Life conventions. I told him, "I spoke there a couple of times about two or three years ago."

He stared at me, and a look of amazement came over his face as he said, "Live baby good, dead baby bad!" It may be stupid, but he remembered it. So if you feel like you can't communicate on this issue, that it's so complex you just can't do it, remember, "Live baby good, dead baby bad." It's really not so hard after all. It would be comical if only the results weren't so tragic.

Another time I was at the University of Cincinnati when an angry woman came up to me after my debate insisting that I use the word "fetus" instead of "child." "It's not a baby—it's a fetus!" she shouted! I assured her that the two words were synonymous, but she would have nothing of it. "Quit calling it a baby!" she demanded. Right then, in the middle of our little "discussion," her young child, pointing to the fetal models on display, declared, "Mommy! Look at the babies!" The child was yanked by the arm and as they briskly walked away, I could hear the child's mother say, "*We* don't believe that."

The pro-abortion movement has a pretty tough job when you think about it. They have to overcome an obvious truth that even their own children can recognize. They can use dehumanizing terms like "fetus," or "products of conception," and pretend all they want, but it still doesn't change the truth.

Redefining human beings in dehumanizing terms is nothing new in history. In the very recent past, Native Americans, African Americans, Soviet Enemies, European Jews, Women, the Unwanted Unborn, and Dependent Discards have been referred to as everything from "diseases" to "parasites." It makes them easier to discard that way.[4] Take a look at the chart from *Dehumanizing the Vulnerable: When Word Games Take Lives,* by William Brennan, Ph.D. Language is critical. He who controls the language controls the debate, and he who controls the debate, wins.

That's why we in the pro-life movement cannot underestimate the power of words—they have been used to justify the taking of life throughout history. But *they* cannot underestimate the power of truth. And if a two-year-old can recognize that the being in the womb is a "baby," it's just a matter of time before the rest of the country does as well. For that to happen, however, we must continue to stand as the Portland lighthouse, with the heart-changing, direction-changing truth. Without it, the pro-abortion movement is headed for the rocks. The problem is, they are taking our country along with them.

The Semantics of Oppression

Dehumanizing Terminology

	DISEASE	INANIMATE OBJECT	WASTE PRODUCT	NONPERSON
Native American	"The Iroquois had proven more deadly ... than the pestilence." (Historian Francis Parkman, 1902)	"{Indians are} anthropological specimens." (American Press coverage, 1904)	"{Indians are} the very dregs, garbage ... of Earth." (Poet Christopher Brooke, 1622)	"An Indian is not a person within the meaning of the Constitution." (George Canfield, Am. Law Rev., 1881)
African American	"Free blacks in our country are ... a contagion." (American Colonization Soc., 1815-30)	"A negro of the African race was regarded ... as an article of property." (U.S. Supreme Court decision, 1857)	"The negro race is ... a heritage of organic and psychic debris." (Dr. William English, 1903)	"In the eyes of the law ... the slave is not a person." (Virginia Supreme Court Decision, 1858)
Soviet Enemies	"Every religious idea {is} ... 'contagion' of the most abominable kind." (Lenin, 1913)	"{Gulag slave laborers are} raw material." (Author Maxim Gorky, 1934)	"A foul-smelling heap of human garbage {Purge Trial Defendants}." (Prosecutor Andrei Vysbinsky, 1938)	"Unpersons who had never existed." (Designation for people purged by the Soviet government)
European Jews	"Some day Europe will perish of the Jewish disease." (Joseph Goebbels, Nazi Propaganda Minister, 1939)	"Transit material." (Portrayal of Jews dispatched to Nazi death camps, 1942-44)	"What shall we do with this garbage {Jews}?" (Christian Wirth, extermination expert, 1942)	"The Reichsgericht itself refused to recognize Jews ... as 'persons' in the legal sense." (1936 German Supreme Court decision)
Women	"The worst plague Zeus has made — women." (Ancient Greek poet Semonides)	"I consider my wife ... my property." (Former wife abuser, 1989)	"Emptying refuse into a sewer {the woman's body}." (Author Henry Miller, 1965)	"The statutory word 'person' did not in these circumstances include women." (British voting rights case, 1909)
Unwanted Unborn	"Pregnancy when not wanted is a disease ... in fact, a venereal disease." (Professor Joseph Fletcher, 1979)	"People's body parts {embryos} are their personal property." (Attorney Lori Andrews, 1986)	"An aborted baby is just garbage ... just refuse." (Dr.Marti Kekomaki, 1980)	"The word 'person' as used in the 14th Amendment, does not include the unborn." (U.S. Supreme Court decision, 1973)
Dependent Discards	"Those 'sicklers.'" (Doctors' portrayal of patients with sickle cell anemia, 1986)	"I came to see the patients as work objects." (Nursing home staff member, 1977)	"There's a lot of rubbish {patients} this morning." (ER doctor, 1979)	"New born humans are neither persons nor even quasi-persons." (Philosopher Michael Tooley, 1983)

The Semantics of Oppression

Dehumanizing Terminology

	DEFICIENT HUMAN	NONHUMAN	ANIMAL	PARASITE
Native American	"Indians {are} inferior to the Anglo-Saxon." (Henry Clay, Sec. of State, 1825	"The life of these {aborigines} is ... not human." (Author Hugh Brackenridge, 1779)	"The Indian ... is an untamable, carnivorous animal." (Dr. Joseph Nott, 1847)	"Clear the country of that vermin {Indians}." (Colonel Henry Bouquet, 1763)
African American	"A subordinate and inferior class of beings." (U.S. Supreme Court on the status of Black people, 1857)	"The negro is not a human being." Buckner Payne, Publisher, 1867)	"The negro is ... one of the lower animals." (Professor Charles Carrol, 1900)	"They {Negros} are parasites." (Dr. E. T. Brady, 1909)
Soviet Enemies	"The uncivilized, stupid, turgid people in the Russian villages." (Author Maxim Gorky, 1922)	"Kulaks are not human beings." (Lenin and Stalin, 1918-34)	"{Peasants are} beasts of burden." (George Plekbanov, founder of the Russian Marxism, 1823)	"The kulak, the parasite." (Lenin, 1918)
European Jews	"The inferior Jewish race." (Dr. Rudolph Ramm, Nazi medical educator, 1943)	"Jews are undoubtedly a race, but not human." (Adolf Hitler, 1923)	"The prisoners here are animals." (Nazi anatomy prof. Dr. August Hirt, 1942)	"The Jew is a parasite." (Nazi propaganda booklet, 1944)
Women	"They {women} form ... the second sex, inferior in every respect to the first." (Philosopher Arthur Schopenhauer, 1851)	"Women are not seen as human." (Report by women's group on pornographic images, 1980)	"Women are domestic animals." (19th-century poet Charles Baudelaire)	"Women's sexual parasitism is innate." (Philosopher Rene Guyon, 1950)
Unwanted Unborn	"The fetus, at most, represents only the potentiality of life." (U.S. Supreme Court decision, 1973)	"A fetus is not a human being." (Rabbi Wolfe Kelman, 1984)	"Like ... a primitive animal that's poked with a stick." (Dr. Hart Peterson on fetal movement, 1985)	"The fetus is a parasite." (Professor Rosalind Pollack Petchesky, 1984)
Dependent Discards	"A life ... devoid of those qualities which give it human dignity." (Assessment of child with disability, Dr. Harry Hartzell, 1978)	"No newborn infant should be declared human until it has passed certain tests." (Dr. Francis Clark, 1978)	"Until a living being can take conscious management of life ... it remains an animal." (Prof. George Ball, 1981)	"That's a real parasite." (Medical staff characterization of a debilitated patient, 1989)

Taken with permission from, *Dehumanizing the Vulnerable: When Word Games Take Lives*, by William Brennan, Ph.D (Loyola University Press, 1995, 3441 North Ashland Avenue, Chicago, Illinois 60657, 1-800-621-1008.

4

The Beginning

I was in the tenth grade when I found out the truth about abortion. It was Ron Ganim's health class where I heard speakers from both sides of the abortion issue. I can still remember how wonderful the woman from the local abortion facility made a "D & C" abortion sound: "The doctor inserts a 'curette'—which is a *spoon-shaped* instrument—into the cervical cavity and the 'products of conception' are gently scraped from the uterine wall." Sounds just fine.

Until you find out a 'curette' is *not* a spoon-shaped instrument, but rather, a loop-shaped steel knife. And yes, it is inserted into the cervical cavity, but what it does is cut the tiny child into pieces. It is then the nurses' job to put this baby back together—because if they leave an arm or a leg, or tissue inside the womb, the woman could develop an infection and perhaps become sterile—like several women I know who have had abortions. You see, this is a procedure that is performed blindly. When the abortionist sweeps that little knife around inside the woman, he may also swipe the opening to the fallopian tubes—causing scar tissue that prevents the egg from entering the uterus.

A pro-lifer named Tom Zabor came and gave the first pro-life presentation I ever heard. I don't know where I had been all that time, but I don't even remember hearing the word "abortion." What did it for me was one look at the pictures of the babies in the Hefty bag—the results of one day's work. When I saw that I knew there was absolutely no way you could talk yourself into making that acceptable. You couldn't talk about "products of conception," "women's rights," or the "right to choose," when you were staring directly at a perfectly formed baby who was never given a choice in the matter.

My mind made an immediate connection to the Holocaust. How could something as horrific as the Holocaust have ever happened? My great-grandparents were from Germany and yet never taught my grandmother the language. It was as if they were ashamed of it. We all have seen the pictures of the bodies stacked up outside the concentration camps. I couldn't imagine anyone being so evil as to participate in something so horrific. With German grandparents from *both* sides of my family, I remember wondering if maybe there was something intrinsically evil about the German people.

And then I learned the truth. There *is* something intrinsically evil about all of mankind. It is called sin, and if unchecked, we can even rationalize something as heinous as stacking the bodies of one day's killing at a concentration camp . . . or an abortion mill.

I just knew that had I been alive in pre-World War II Germany, I would *not* have sat idly by. I knew that I would have done something to stop it—even if it cost me my life. And then it hit me. I *am* living next door to *today's* Auschwitz, Treblinka, and Dachau—only now they're killing *babies*. They are stacking the bodies of innocent human beings in *my city*.

At the time I didn't know what I could do, so I began to talk to people, to research, and to write papers, but it never dawned on me to start a group—or that such a group would do any good.

Shortly after I graduated from high school I was looking for a job. My Aunt Sue was listening to her Christian radio station one day when she heard an ad for a sales position. She listened all day to get the number, and I, mostly as a favor to her, went and applied for a job. (Since she listened all day, it was the least I could do.) I got the job and was told to make cold calls to people whom I had never met and see if they would advertise on a station they had never heard of.

Here I was, a shy kid right out of high school with a new business card that said, "Account Executive" and not really sure what to do with it. My dad gave me what turned out to be some very good advice. He suggested that I tell people I was new and ask them to help me out by giving me just five minutes of their time. That technique worked so well, I think I used it for a year.

One call that stuck out in my mind was with Andy Sims Buick. They reluctantly gave me my five minutes, and somehow I got in to see Andy Sims himself. But he was not at all impressed. "Look, we just don't advertise on radio, and if we did advertise on radio, we certainly wouldn't advertise on *your* station." I pointed out that one of the churches that airs on that station *they* never heard of was the Cleveland Baptist Church. And if they drove by that church on any given Sunday, they would see about 2,000 cars in the parking lot—many of them Buicks. "They're getting Buicks from somebody. I just thought that maybe you would want them to get them from you." Andy Sims Buick turned out to be one of my best customers.

Without my dad's advice and my mother's encouraging pep talks that "I could do it," I know for certain I would have quit. I look back now and see that I needed and used that training to lobby for nine years. You don't always see why God has you go through everything He does. But many times you can look back and see that there's a reason for it all. He will work it all for our good.

I then wrote commercials for another client, Ernie Sanders, who is now a pastor. He was the guy standing in the rain, sleet, snow, and scorching sun in front of the abortion mills offering alternative help to the women going in. He has done this for as long as I've known him (and before) and has been instrumental in saving over 5,000 babies. He has actually closed down abortion clinics and was the driving force in stopping hospitals from doing abortions. I remember we spent about five minutes on business—(I wrote the commercials for his mattress store) and about 45 minutes talking about the issue. I mostly listened.

I continued to work at the station while going to school—but eventually switched to doing an on-air shift on evenings and weekends. While an undergrad student at Cleveland State University, I was sitting in a class on the 'mass media' when the professor asked, "what is the biggest problem in

America?" I remember wanting to shout "abortion!" *But I was too timid.* Someone else in the class said it, but the professor pretended not to hear as he wrote things like "crime" and "homelessness" on the blackboard.

I said something to the girl next to me about how the professor wrote down everyone's answer but that of the student who said "abortion." She then told me she was planning to start a "Students for Life" group on campus—and asked me if I wanted to help. I would love to be able to say that I was the one who started the group and had led the charge—but the truth is, I had to be asked. For those of you who have been waiting for an invitation to join, consider yourself asked.

Fear of Speaking

As an excuse for remaining on the sidelines, one woman came up to me at one of my seminars and told me, "You're bold. Speaking is easy for *you.*" What she didn't know is that public speaking was one of my greatest fears. Whenever this comes up while I am speaking, I ask for a show of hands from those who also share a fear of public speaking. Rooms are filled with them. In fact, that is the number one fear in America—death ranks sixth. It seems people would rather die than speak. I guess I was just a bit more pro-life than that.

I really didn't want to speak, yet I felt I should. In my mind I pictured a scale and had to decide which was more important. On one side was the fact that there were a million-and-a-half babies whose lives were going to be taken from them that year, and on the other side of the scale was the fact that I was afraid to tell anyone about it. My fear of public speaking lost that contest.

I was keynote speaker at the Memorial for the Unborn at Cleveland Music Hall one January 22nd—an event with about 3,000 people in attendance. I was used to working backstage lining up speakers like Henry Hyde and Dr. Jack Willke. One of the women I went through speaker's training with actually came up and told me, "I'm really surprised YOU ended up being our spokesperson." What, exactly, do you *say* to something like that? "*Thank you?*"

You see, she remembered the shaky, nervous college student who couldn't talk about abortion without getting teary-eyed. Humiliating. I'm surprised I even passed. One thing a priest friend of mine, Father Bill Witt, told me that I often pass along is, "The only ability you need to serve God is availability." I know that if God can use me, he can use anybody. That means *you*, too—you just have to make yourself available.

By the way, at that event, one woman reluctantly came to see her fiancé's child win a prize for the pro-life art and essay contest. Apparently, the father couldn't make it and she was filling in. She also happened to be pregnant at the time and scheduled for an abortion. But because she heard the truth that night, she cancelled her abortion appointment the next day, and her child is alive today. Make yourself available, and you never know what God will do.

People Magazine

In 1998, *People* magazine did a feature on me in their November 30 issue that said:

> Other little girls back in the 1960s in Columbus, Ohio, might have chosen to be a princess or a cheerleader for the local Fourth of July parade, but not 7-year-old, Janet Folger. "We started decorating her bicycle the night before," recalls her mother, Beth. "I attached a mop and a broom to it, and dressed her up like a cleaning lady. She had a banner reading: 'I'm going to clean up the world.'" Some might say that was Janet Folger's mission statement and has since become her life focus.[1]

What they didn't write was how I cried for about the first five blocks. I was seven years old and I felt stupid. When I read that article, however, I realized how symbolic that event was in my life. Not because that at seven I knew I wanted to "clean up the world" (I didn't even want to clean up my room), but because I wanted to quit the whole parade. You see my mom walked the entire parade route with me and encouraged me every step of the way, just like she has done my entire life. That's why I won the grand prize.

In fact, when the reporter from *People* magazine called my mom (at

Here I am at seven in the Fourth of July Parade. You would cry, too, if your mom made you dress like this. Yes, that's a globe in the back suspended with some kind of mop contraption. I had to "clean up the world," after all.

11:30 at night) she shared how she once gave me an Amplified Bible and wrote her favorite verses inside: Philippians 4:13 (AMP): "I have strength for all things in Christ who empowers me [I am ready for anything, equal to anything, through Him who infuses inner strength into me; I am self-sufficient in Christ's sufficiency], and Habakkuk 3:19 (AMP): "The Lord God is my strength, my personal bravery, and my invincible army; He makes my feet like hinds' feet and will make me to walk [not to stand still in terror, but to walk] and make [spiritual] progress upon my high places of [trouble, suffering, or responsibility.] My mother is an incredible encourager, and she loves a captive audience. But before she could get to the plan of salvation, the reporter hung up.

Necessary Boldness

I went from giving speeches to high school kids to confronting presidential candidates and crowds of their supporters—all alone. I could never have imagined doing it, but God gives you just what you need when you need it. It was 1988, and I had just moved into my new apartment in Columbus, Ohio. And of all the places to choose to film campaign commercials, Michael Dukakis picked my apartment complex. Of course I had to do something. But apparently my lobbying skills weren't refined enough, because I couldn't get anyone to help me. The only people I knew were from the office, and *none* of them would come. Some were concerned with the legalities of my apartment party-house (where the commercials were being filmed) being on semi-private land. Others didn't think it would do any good. I told them they could all come into my apartment and walk right back out. That way they were legitimately "my guests." No go.

I rushed back from work and hurriedly put up Bush/Quayle signs in both my apartment windows (with spotlights) and put some on my car. It looked like the campaign headquarters! And, as every good pro-lifer, I had blank poster board on hand—for such a time as this. I immediately started making signs saying, "Dukakis Supports Abortion with your Tax $," "Life, Yes! Dukakis, No!" I grabbed them and went out to a sea of Dukakis/Benson signs—all by myself. There was not a friendly face in the crowd—not a sign, not a smile. That's when I suggested to everyone that maybe it would be a good idea if we all started a cheer: "Bush, Yes! Dukakis, No!" Everyone laughed. People started screaming things out to me like, "What's Bush going to do for the poor?"

I yelled back, "Give them a job!"

They shouted, "Go Home!"

I replied, "I live here!" I then positioned myself right in front of the party-house door (where I later held the victory party)—about six feet from where the filming would be going on inside. There was a special police officer who I think was assigned just to me, so I yelled, "I'm really glad there's all this security here with Dukakis letting felons out of jail on furlough. You know, I'm afraid to walk home at night!" (That was a big campaign issue back in 1988—remember the Willie Horton commercial?) People started coming out of the woodwork wanting to hold my signs. I kept mine and got rid of all the rest.

Finally, Dukakis showed up and I was there to greet him. He was there to film commercials on "family values" with the wholesome mid-western families of Columbus, Ohio. About every other minute someone would open the door to go in, and when that door would open, I would shout something like, "What about the *unborn*, Mike? Aren't they part of your family?" Knowing that any filming would have to be redone, I even provided the "TAKE TWO" for them. I had to believe that by about "Take 27" or so, they were about to give up the whole thing. I'm happy to report that—to my knowledge—those commercials never aired.

When a reporter asked me why I was there, I told him I was a resident of the apartment complex who couldn't support someone so radically pro-abortion. I told him it was "just like *that guy's* sign says, 'Dukakis supports abortion with my tax dollars.'" That was the sign that I still had magic marker on my hands from making. When the paper came out the next day it said, "*Several* local residents turned out to protest Michael Dukakis' position on abortion and the use of tax-dollars to fund abortion." Even a quiet kid, too timid to make a public speech, can make a difference. From that day, people looked upon me as "bold."

God

For me this issue was a human rights issue—*the* human rights issue of our time. I was a Christian, but I wasn't in it because my church told me to be. It wasn't my family. I just saw the truth with one look and knew I had to do something, but the longer I worked in the pro-life movement, the more my faith in God grew. When you face the Goliath of the abortion industry, you soon realize you cannot win alone.

In addition to my experiences, two things helped me to grow closer to God more than anything else. One, I read the Bible all the way through. O.K., my "one-year Bible" took me *three* years to finish, but I read it! One of the things I think messes people up is when they view the Bible as some kind of smorgasbord—where you can pick and choose what you'd like. You'll find many people and many churches where all they say is "God is Love." He *is,* but He is *also* holy and just—a God who hates sin—particularly the shedding of innocent blood. You see, we can't just read what the Bible says, we must emphasize what the Bible emphasizes—we must look at the whole Word of God. Reading the Bible all the way through helps you understand the character of God more than sporadic readings over the course of your whole life ever will.

The second thing that really helped me is a Bible study called *Experiencing God: Knowing and Doing the Will of God,* by Henry T. Blackaby and Claude V. King, which was given to me by my friend Margie Moriarty. This study reveals how the results of a person working *for* God only bring the results of one person—and how much better it is to ask God to work *through* you and witness results that are *"God-sized."* Given a choice, I'd pick the latter.

Want to increase your faith in God? Focus on these three basic truths that this study spells out:

1. God is love: He pretty much settled that on the Cross—dying to provide a way to be with us. And because God is love, His way is *always best*—better than any plan you or I could ever come up with.

2. God is all knowing: He knows your circumstances; He knows the people involved along with their motivations; He knows the past and the future—so His directions are *always right.* That means you can trust Him. You can trust Him in everything.

3. And because God is all-powerful, He *will enable you* to do His will—regardless of the "impossible" hurdles that stand in the way. If we really believe this—don't you think that's going to change the way we think and act?

But Why This Issue?

One day I was meeting with Vern Riffe, who was the speaker of the Ohio House of Representatives back when they were under Democratic control. I can still hear him asking me, "Janet, there are a lot of issues—very important issues. There's health care, housing, education—why are you involved with *this* one?"

"Well, Mr. Speaker, life is a prerequisite to every single one of those issues. What good is health care or education if you're dead?" He never questioned my involvement again.

Just a "Single Issue"

I was doing a radio show in Youngstown, Ohio, one day before the 1992 elections and Richard Dreyfuss just happened to be on the program before me, promoting Bill Clinton. I got to the studio a little early that day, and so they let me on the show with him. He was singing Clinton's praises and pledging his allegiance to him when I spoke up and stated that Clinton was pro-abortion. Before I could finish, Dreyfuss snapped back, "That's just a *single* issue—you're just a single-issue fanatic. Who cares about that when Bill Clinton is good for the economy! You single-issue people drive me crazy!"

My reply went something like this, "You want to know what? There was another politician in history who was great in the economy—really great. He actually got rid of the soup lines, gave transportation to the common man, promoted all kinds of expansion, and really improved the morale of the people in the country. There was just *one* issue, one little issue, one *single issue* that I disagreed with Mr. Hitler on, that is genocide of a race of people. One issue, when we're talking about millions of human lives, is a *priority* issue— wouldn't you say?"

You don't have to be a bold, group-starting, public speaker to be used by God. The only ability you need is availability. If you just make yourself available to God, He *will* use you—and if you allow God to work *through you*, the results will be God-sized! He can take you from a timid pro-lifer, afraid to speak up in class, to one who walks out *alone* to confront a presidential candidate and all his supporters! All you have to do is take that first step and trust Him.

5

My Worldview

Your worldview affects everything you think, say, and do. One year, around Christmastime, I spent the night at Kinko's working on a project. It's amazing the people you meet at three in the morning. I met some folks who were working on some satanic artwork for their music, and they asked me if I had heard of their music. "Yeah," I said jokingly, "I think I have some of your CDs in my car— 'Bang Your Head,' 'Shoot Your Mom,' 'Kill Your Dog,' kind of stuff—Right?"

I joked around a little bit with these satanists (at three in the morning) and then said to them, "I have a question for you. If you want to follow Satan, the place you would turn to find out that Satan *even exists* would be the Bible—right? I mean, how else do you even know Satan *exists?* And if you turn to the Bible, you find out that Satan is not just out to kill, steal and destroy *your enemies,* he's out to steal, kill, and destroy *you.*"

They just stared and listened as I finished my thought, "And if you read the back of the Book, you find out that those who follow him . . . well, they don't turn out so good." I suggested that if they look in that same Book where they could find out about their hero, Satan, they would find out about a God who isn't out to destroy them, but a God who is *for* them who loves them enough to die for them.

BBC-TV Worldview

Producers from the British Broadcasting Company were traveling around the country last summer getting input from leaders about sex. For some reason, they wanted to talk to me. The interviewer asked me if I *actually believed* that people shouldn't have sex if they weren't married. I told him yes, I *really* did. His question, *"Why???"*

I told him, "It is all about your worldview. My worldview is that I believe there is a God, and I believe there is a place you can find out about Him. That place is the Bible. What it says in there is that this God is *for* us, that He's on *our* side." The God we serve came to give us life more abundantly (John 10:10). He is a God who plans to prosper us and not to harm us—to give us a hope and a future (Jeremiah 29:11). A God who satisfies our desires with *good* things (Psalm 103: 1–22) and richly provides us with everything for our *enjoyment* (1 Timothy 6:17).

God thought up the whole idea of sex, so I think He's free to set the boundaries. Because God created us, His rules are for *our benefit*. There are certain things you may feel like doing. You may feel like committing adultery, for example. But God says "Don't do it." Why? Is it because He wants us to miss out on a good time? No. He says don't commit adultery because He knows adultery destroys lives, destroys marriages, and destroys families. The BBC reporter was astounded. I think, frankly, he was blown away by this truth—he just kept saying, "Wow!" So I kept going:

> What has sex outside of marriage given us? Nearly 40 million dead children—and an effort to cover up the truth! The incidence of sexually transmitted diseases has gone through the roof. Out of wedlock births have also skyrocketed. A friend of mine from Washington just told me to pray for his friend Eric. Eric is in a home for troubled teens and just found out he has genital herpes—something he'll have for the rest of his life. He is also afraid he may have AIDS. I think my friend summarized it best when he said what Eric was just finding out, "What do you know? The devil is a liar after all."

"There is a way that seems right to a man, but its end is the way of death" (Proverbs 16:25).

We have some options in this world. We can follow the ways that seem right to us and reap these kind of results, or we can recognize that maybe we've been doing something wrong—and give God's way a try.

I think a lot of people are afraid God is out to steal from us, and if we follow God's plan, we will miss out on a lot of fun and be denied dessert forever. Some even fear that if they follow God's plan for their lives they'll get sent to a foreign mission field in some far away country where they don't want to go. No. God is *for* us. Not that He won't call those He has suited for it to foreign missions. But Psalm 37:4-5 says, (this was my computer screensaver for a long time) "Delight yourself also in the Lord, and He shall give you *the desires of your heart.*" What an awesome thing to know. He's not the one that came to steal, kill, and destroy—He came that we might have life and have it *abundantly* (John 10:10).

The issue of whether God is for us and loves us was forever settled when He took the form of man in the person of Jesus Christ. He paid the penalty for our sins, and it cost Him His life. You either accept this or reject it (Isaiah 53:6).

I know this is real—that every word God spoke is true because everything around us proves it.

Abortion

Back in 1973 we were told by the pro-abortion crowd that thanks to *Roe v. Wade*, there would be fewer unwanted children, and a whole myriad of society's problems would be solved. Teen pregnancy, child neglect, the high school dropout rate, teenage suicide, poverty among women, spousal abuse, child abuse, divorce, and poverty among children were all going to cease to be problems as a result of legalized abortion. But as we can see, the *exact opposite* has happened. Just as the rate of abortions went up during the '70s, '80s and early '90s, so did all of these problems.[1]

We bought the big lie and we are reaping the consequences. You see, the words "choose life" didn't come from a pro-life bumper sticker; they came from the Bible. Deuteronomy 30:19 says,

> "I call heaven and earth as witnesses today against you, that
> I have set before you life and death, blessing and cursing; there-
> fore choose life, that both you and your descendants may live."

We are now reaping the curses that come with the choice of death. You see, God says to follow His commands so we will live and prosper, and so He can bless us! And because we're not always the best judges of what's right, God spells it out for us.

> "See, I have set before you today life and good, and death and evil, in that I command you today to love the Lord your God, to walk in His ways, and to keep His commandments, His statutes, and His judgments, that you may live and multiply; and the Lord your God will bless you in the land which you go to possess"
> —Deuteronomy 30:15, 16

God says to keep His commandments and statutes on other issues as well—but it's not to keep us from a good time.

Pornography

Take a look at the porn industry, for example. It went from a multi-million dollar business in the eighties to a multi-*billion* dollar business today. With the expansion of the Internet, the porn industry is booming. Compare, for a moment, God's plan versus the world's cheap imitation. God's plan is that you have someone beautiful whom you love and who will love you for the rest of your life. Satan's plan is for you to go and *look* at people who could care less about you and whom you can *never have*. What a rip-off!

Gambling

I've seen bumper stickers that say, "The lottery is a tax on people who are bad in math." Pretty accurate. I'm not a financial advisor, but I'm pretty sure that the slot machine is not the wisest investment you can make. You see, the odds are stacked very highly in favor of the folks building and operating the casinos. That's how they can pay for people's drinks, travel, and lodging. If you play long enough, you *will lose*. And yet, as a nation we throw away more money gambling every year than we spend on groceries.[2] What a rip-off! Just like drugs—short time "fun" leading to addiction, pain, and death.

Homosexuality

What about homosexuality? God calls it sin, like other sins for which you can repent and find forgiveness, but the world says you're born that way.

Well, if that were true, there wouldn't be any *former* homosexuals—but there are—thousands of them. What about the studies that suggest a "gay gene?" They have been disproved, although you probably didn't hear about it.[3] Even our own bodies tell us otherwise, as we each are born with reproductive organs—regardless of our "lifestyle."

And whether it's "politically correct" to say it or not, homosexuality is a very dangerous practice. By engaging in behavior the body was not created for, there are increased health risks. According to the Centers for Disease Control, two-thirds of the cases of AIDS in this country are men engaging in homosexual sex.[4] Homosexuals also account for an overwhelmingly disproportionate number of cases of Gonorrhea, Hepatitis A, and Hepatitis B.[5] God's way really is best, and because He is all-powerful, He can set anyone free even from this (1 Corinthians 6:9-11).

Pick an issue—any issue—and you will see even by *the world's evidence* that God's way is best.

Evolution

How about evolution? I recently visited South Dakota where there's a mountain that proves what evolutionists have been saying all along: that if you just have enough time, wind, rain, erosion, and *pure chance,* anything is possible. It's a truly amazing thing to witness how millions and millions of years of evolution have left us a mountain with the faces of four U.S. presidents on it! It's as if someone actually *carved* the faces of Washington, Jefferson, Lincoln and Roosevelt on this mountain on purpose!

Obviously, I'm talking about Mt. Rushmore, and the idea that the faces "just happened to appear" is laughable. *Of course* they were not the result of an accident—they had a creator—just like *the people* those carvings represent. They didn't "just happen" any more than Mt. Rushmore did. Just how difficult is this to see?

God said He created the heavens and the earth. Satan says you're the result of one big accident. If you think about it, it takes a bigger leap of faith to believe *that* than believing in an "accidental" Mt. Rushmore—we are *a bit more complex* than stone images, all things considered!

And when one's worldview is not grounded in Truth, it's frightening to see how far off course we can drift. When you live in a world without absolutes, where we're the result of one big accident, how are humans any better than rats or gnats? We're not, according to Pentti Linkola of the Finnish Green Party. He said, without apology, that he has more sympathy for a threatened insect species than for children dying of hunger in Africa.[6] Nice guy. And *we're* the extremists? You have to be kidding!

Or listen to what Ingrid Newkirk, president of People for the Ethical Treatment of Animals has to say, *"A rat is a pig is a dog is a boy."* You would think, then that they would join us in protecting children if, after all, they *are* as valuable as those lab rats they care so much about.

This, in essence, is what our government schools are teaching: "Well kids, you're all just a mass of cells that happened by accident; you were formed out of the primordial slime, and you're really nothing more then a complex food processor. But hurry up, because you're going to be late for your self-esteem class."

Your worldview affects everything you think, say, and do. One worldview leads to life and blessings, and another leads to death and curses. Everything God said is *really true*—and everything around us backs it up. We can, just by looking at the real world evidence, see the consequences (including our own statistics) of deviating from God's plan.

"There is a way that seems right to a man, but its end is the way of death" (Proverbs 16:25). Just as adultery may sound like a fun thing to do, there are reasons we're told not to do it—and they're for our own good: Because the God we serve is *for us*—He's our strongest advocate. That's why He's spelled things out so very clearly—so there wouldn't be any mistaking which way was best to choose—even when our feelings, emotions, and desires tell us differently.

Life and blessing, or death and curses—we all have a choice. I know which one I'd rather have.

6

God Intervenes

W hen you read the paper it's very easy to get discouraged. There are a lot of bad things going on. As a result, it is so easy to forget that the God of the universe hears us when we pray and is intricately involved in our lives. And if He is going to concern Himself with such petty information as the number of hairs on my head, I'm pretty sure He cares about what I'm going through.

Last year I went to Israel and *saw* where Christ was born, the Sea of Galilee, where He fed the 5,000, where He rose from the dead, and the empty tomb. This wasn't just some story. This *really* happened. The God of the universe intersected human history, became man, and underwent torture and death to pay the penalty for my sins. There's a song by the Christian group *Third Day* that I think puts it into perspective:

> I've heard it said that a man would climb a mountain
> Just to be with the one he loves.
> How many times has he broken that promise.
> It has never been done.
> I've never climbed the highest mountain,
> But I've walked the hill of Calvary.
>
> Just to be with you, I'd do anything.
> There's no price I would not pay.
> Just to be with you, I'd give anything.
> I would give my life away.
>
> I know that you don't understand
> The fullness of My love,

How I died upon the Cross for your sins.
And I know that you don't realize how much that I gave you
But I promise, I would do it all again.

Just to be with you, I've done everything.
There's no price I did not pay.
Just to be with you, I gave everything.
Yes, I gave my life away.

It is appropriately called "Love Song."[1]

God is *for* us. I don't fully understand why, but I know that if I'm going to place my complete trust in anyone, there is no One better.

Remember

Jesus had just fed the 5,000 (Matthew 14:1–17). And just *one chapter later* the disciples are faced with feeding 4,000 and all they have is a *few loaves of bread and a couple of fish* (Matthew 15:32–38). Sound familiar?

Jesus said, "I have compassion on the multitude, because they have now continued with Me three days and have nothing to eat. And I do not want to send them away hungry, lest they faint on the way."

What was the disciples' reply? "Where could we get enough bread in the wilderness to fill such a great multitude?" (Matthew 15:32–33).

Kind of makes you want to say, "Duh! Where were you a chapter ago? Did you forget Whom you are dealing with? You just saw Jesus feed 5,000 right in front of you. Now you only have 4,000. This should be a cakewalk." It kind of makes you wonder, "Are the disciples just not too bright?"

And yet, when you think about it, that is exactly how *we* are. We forget. God gets us through something, and we forget it.

Incidentally, I have really worked to take that word "Duh" out of my vocabulary ever since my *Los Angeles Times* interview where they asked me, "You know, the other side says you're against *more* than just partial-birth abortion—they accuse you of being against *all* abortions." And I said the first thing that came to mind, "Duh!" It didn't look very good in print. "'Duh!' said Janet Folger of Ohio Right to Life." That's what a Master's degree in communication will get you. Mom and Dad were so proud.

God worked through those disciples to change the world. But was it because *they* were so extraordinary? Peter constantly made a fool of himself in the Gospels, always jumping to conclusions. Matthew was a former tax collector (they didn't trust them back then, either). John was very young, as perhaps many of the other disciples were. In fact, if you were to look at these twelve men through human eyes, Judas was probably the most likely to succeed. After all, they all trusted him enough to be their treasurer.

No. While God worked through them in incredible ways, the disciples weren't "super heroes for God"—they were men—human beings who forget—just like us. God gets us through something and we forget it.

To help remember, I customized (yes, at Kinko's) a notebook with a picture of the CENTER FOR RECLAIMING AMERICA with Bible verses like: 1 Samuel 17:37, which says, "The LORD, who delivered me from the paw of the lion and from the paw of the bear, He will deliver me from the hand of this Philistine."

If you want to be like the great men and women of faith in the Bible, do what they did. We're facing the Goliath of the abortion industry, the courts and the media. We're facing a lot of Goliaths. But what did David do when *he* faced Goliath? David had courage because he *remembered* what God had done for him in the past.

The Los Angeles Times Interview

In March of 1997, while I was still at Ohio Right to Life, a *Los Angeles Times* reporter decided he wanted to do a feature story on me—this was the same article where my stellar quote, "Duh!" appeared. I had met the reporter, Bob Sipchen, a few years earlier at a convention in Nashville when our Ohio Partial-Birth Abortion Ban was on it's way to the Governor for his signature. He said he wanted to do a story on me because "everything I had told him was going to happen, happened."

Mark Lally, the former Ohio Right to Life president, and I were working on passing the Amstutz Amendment to keep state family planning funds from being used to refer women for abortion. And although we had a pro-life governor, and a somewhat workable state health director, we had some folks from *within* the health department working against us. (That is why it is so imperative that those at the top, whether governor or president, place people who are like-minded in positions all the way down—from the department heads to record keepers and file clerks.) They can make your life miserable. That is what was happening to us when Bob Sipchen, from the *Los Angeles Times*, showed up to spend the week finding out "who Janet Folger really is."

I had to spend the first day lobbying and really couldn't do my job with a reporter following me around. I had a short time to get the votes in line because of faulty information that was released from the Health Department; we lost the vote in committee, and we lost big. I had to go to the Governor to get the misinformation retracted.

Mark Lally is an unspoken hero in every legislative battle—especially this one. The many victories we saw were due largely to his expert strategy and incredible legal expertise. On this day he had come to help me lobby and get to as many of our people as possible before the issue was brought to the floor for a full-House vote. It seemed *everyone* had gotten the faulty Health Department memo negating our facts and statistics. It was wrong, but we couldn't reach the Governor to get it reversed. It looked like we were going down in flames.

To top if off, I had to leave that afternoon to fly to New York to do the *Rolanda* show. It was on the topic of open adoption records, which I hadn't worked on in over a year-and-a-half. We had fought open records in the legislature, and Rolanda's producers found my name in various newspaper articles. To clarify, we fought the effort to make "open adoption records" the women's only choice. We didn't want those women who felt they *needed confidentiality* and wanted their records to remain closed to be driven to abort their child. And so we fought the very strong "open-records" adoption lobby and won. Women were given an option to choose—something my opponent from NARAL fought against!

I talked to Mr. Sipchen and told him I really didn't know when I would be able to see him, since I was leaving the Statehouse and going directly to the airport to fly to New York to do the show that night. He suggested that he ride with me to the airport, and I consented. One of my problems is that I don't put a lot of margins in my life. I lobbied until the absolute last minute I could before leaving, which meant that, as usual, I was running late in getting to the airport.

So to recap my day, we were going down in flames in the Statehouse, and I had to leave in the middle of it to do a show on a subject I hadn't even looked at for a year and a half. That was when Bob told me that he made good use of *his* day by talking to all my enemies. "Oh, great," I thought. One, in particular, was Joan Lawrence, a pro-abortion Republican. He said, "She doesn't like you very much."

"*Really?* What did Joan have to say?" I had debated her on television and radio a number of times, and I knew the woman couldn't stand the sight of me.

"Well, for starters," she said, "you're 35 and not married—what does *that* mean?"

I answered, "Well for starters, I'm 34. And what exactly *does* that mean?"

He said he thought she was trying to imply that maybe I might be a lesbian or something. (Kind of ironic, considering I would end up coordinating the national Truth in Love campaign with 17 other organizations—running television commercials and full-page ads in every major newspaper paper in the country expressing hope for change for those struggling with homosexuality.)

Joan knew full well that what she was implying was a lie. I just did not know if Bob Sipchen knew that. Then he said to me, "I've been reading your clips and found that you don't believe in pre-marital sex. Is that true?"

"Well, actually, Bob, we have some pretty strong evidence that pre-marital sex is going on—and I happen to believe it is."

"But what about for you?" he pressed.

"That's a pretty personal question for someone I've just met—don't you think? I really don't want to read an article about my sex life if you don't mind."

He kept pushing, insisting that it was a fair question, until he finally said, "Well, do you have sex or don't you?"

I responded, "No."

But before I could expound on my reasoning, he gave me a follow-up, "Isn't that neurotic?"

As we were talking, I missed my exit for the airport. I now had to drive around the outer-belt to get there, and it didn't look as if I was going to make it. We were losing in the legislature, I was going to do a national show I was completely unprepared for, a state representative just told a reporter I was lesbian, that reporter thinks I'm neurotic, and I just missed my exit. Think it couldn't get worse? That's what I thought.

I pulled up to the gate, grabbed my bag and told the reporter from *The Los Angeles Times*—who had flown in to do a story on me—that if I was going to make my plane, he would have to park my car for me. He appeared to be in shock, I guess most people he interviews don't ask him to do things like that. Given no choice, he simply said, "Where?"

My answer? "Red lot, Blue lot, I don't care." With that I sprinted to the door, and it started to rain.

So imagine you're on a plane to New York after all of this, sitting next to a screaming baby and trying to brief yourself on the subject of adoption for a show you will be doing in a few hours. How well do you think that would go? That's about where *I* was.

I called my friend Cyndy Rees in a panic. She reminded me— "Janet, he still has a week to find out you're not neurotic."

"If it's a week full of days like today, I probably will be," I said.

Cyndy, along with her friend Julie Mercer, helped me out from the beginning of this *LA Times* ordeal. They helped put together a gift basket that was waiting for him when he arrived and, apparently, it made quite an impression. In the article he wrote:

> Even before meeting with Folger, a visiting reporter
> glimpses the odd incongruity of her style in the cheerful welcome

basket she has delivered to his hotel room. Nestled in the shavings are a big Ohio coffee mug—and a bumper sticker ("Abortion? Pick on someone your own size"); muffin mix—and fuzzy teddy bear stickers reading "Choose Life"; chocolates—and a gold pin of two tiny footprints on a pin saying "These feet are the exact size and shape of an unborn baby's feet at 10 weeks after conception."[2]

He continues, "Then there's the fact sheet, complete with photographs of developing fetuses, a motif that carries over to Ohio Right to Life headquarters across the street from the Statehouse." Not bad for a welcome basket.

I came back from New York to find my car keys waiting for me in an envelope at the ticket counter. From there I went straight to the Statehouse to try to put out the fires. They were still burning strong. However, I had to speak at Capital University that night. I remember thinking, "There is absolutely no way I am ever going to get through this."

But I did—and I was shocked at just how well it went.

The article? With the exception of "Duh!"—a very big exception, I know—turned out very well:

> Here in Ohio's capital people discuss Folger in tones that range from mere respect to awe, exasperation, and thinly veiled loathing. What most agree on is that the energetic—some might even say hip—young lobbyist does not fit the stereotype.[3]

When I got back to the Statehouse we were able to get Governor Voinovich to have the health director issue a retraction of their misinformation. We then got that into the hands of the legislators *as they made their way to the floor for the vote*, and successfully kept state family planning funds from going to refer for abortion—we won!

After the vote, Joan Lawrence came up to me and shouted, "BOO! HISS!" I guess you can't please everybody.

A Prayer Journal That "Didn't Work"

I bought a prayer journal when I was a counselor at a Billy Graham

Crusade several years ago. I wanted to keep track of the prayers that God answered. I made only one entry in it. It was an entry about an appointment to the Ohio State Senate.

There was a vacancy left by a great pro-life friend who had become a judge, and I knew the most likely candidate to fill it was a pro-abortion *activist* who served on the governor's cabinet. This woman, I was told, tried to orchestrate a "walk out" on the 1992 Republican Convention floor in Houston to protest the pro-life plank in the Platform—she had told a friend of mine who worked under her to remove his pro-life "precious feet" pin because it "offended" her. This wasn't just going to be a vote against us, this was going to be an abortion activist fighting us in everything we did.

We didn't have votes to spare in the Senate, and the thought of replacing one of our pro-life heroes with someone like that was simply unacceptable. So I prayed. The only strategy I could see that would beat her was if we could get someone who had greater name recognition and a greater likelihood of holding onto the seat in a re-election. Ultimately, that would be what the Senate caucus would be looking for when they made their appointment. I had the perfect candidate: Clarence Miller, a former congressman who got redistricted out of office.

My first (and only) entry in that prayer journal was the prayer for God to help us get Clarence Miller appointed to the state Senate. The journal had a place for you to record when God answered each prayer, and I had it ready to check off.

We didn't know where Clarence Miller was, but we set out on a mission to find him. We couldn't reach him by phone, so my friends Susie Gualtieri, Brian Kirk, and I went searching for him in his district (about an hour away). He wasn't home when we knocked on his door so we started asking around town. One of the people we asked just happened to be his son-in-law. I won't give you all the details of that little adventure, but we finally found him. He wasn't interested. He was retired and not at all excited about a step down to the state Senate—even though he would have liked to help.

We searched for others who could run and came up empty. Nancy

Dix was appointed to the Senate and there was nothing we could do about it. I put the prayer journal aside and never put another entry in it. After all, it didn't work.

Senator Dix's office called and wanted to meet with me. A room full of people, including friends from the governor's office, all tried to pressure me into somehow supporting this abortion activist. Of course, that was not going to happen. I was cordial, but no matter what face she tried to put on it, she was in favor of legal abortion.

But the Senate leaders were concerned. Their selection was facing some problems running against a Democrat in that conservative district, and they were frightened that they would lose a substantial voting block. They were right. So they called me in again. This time they were ready to listen. My friend, Susie G., went with me. We explained how abortion was legal for *all nine months*—something Senator Dix, as well as the rest of the country, had a hard time believing. Limitations on abortion are "allowed" after the first trimester (three months) according to the 1973 Supreme Court decision, *Roe v. Wade*, and it's companion decision, *Doe v. Bolton*, unless they interfere with the "health" of the mother. That may sound "reasonable" to some, until you find out the court interprets "health" to include everything under the sun, including "emotional health."

The *Doe v. Bolton* decision defined "health":

> . . . in light of all factors—physical, emotional, psycho-
> logical, familial, and the woman's age—relevant to the well-being
> of the patient. All these factors may relate to health.[4]

That means that two 27-year-olds could each state that they were "too old" and "too young" to have a child, and abortion would be perfectly legal under *Doe. v. Bolton* since "age" is a factor of health.

But most people have never heard of this decision, let alone that *Roe v. Wade* cannot be interpreted by the courts without it. But because Senator Dix needed to prevent us from actively opposing her in her election, she listened. She was shocked by what she heard. We told her more—she listened, and became pro-life.

I know what you are thinking. The same thing we were. She'll sign the questionnaire to get our help and then vote pro-abortion. She didn't want to announce to the world that she had become pro-life lest anyone call her a flip-flopper. She wanted to "ease into it." Sounded suspect.

That friend of mine who had been told to remove his pro-life pin called me a fool to think she might be sincere. He told me that if she ever actually *voted* pro-life, he would buy me lunch. Turns out she not only voted pro-life on every bill to come before her, she actually helped me lobby the senators to our position who were *supposed to be* pro-life!

Still waiting on that lunch.

And, yeah, that prayer journal? Well if I had gotten what I prayed for, none of that would have happened. If Mr. Miller would have taken the seat, he never would have run for re-election. He died shortly thereafter. God knew what would help the pro-life cause better than I did—scribbling in my little journal. If God ever wants to do better than what you pray for, by all means, cancel your original request.

Moving On

A few months later I interviewed with the Christian Coalition for the executive director position vacated by Ralph Reed—somewhat of an intimidating endeavor. When I was checking into my hotel, I met Evan Parker, my bellhop, now one of my best friends, who asked what brought me to Virginia Beach. Not satisfied with my replies of "a meeting," and "business," he began a conversation that started our friendship. He gave me one of his famous "mustard seed" pens with the words: "If you have faith as small as a mustard seed, you can move mountains. Nothing will be impossible for you." The timing was perfect.

I opened up my suitcase, and in it was a flyer. Not just *any* flyer. My neighbor, Jeff Froling, had written me a note on the back of a very special flyer. It was what promoted my speech at Capital University—the one written about in the *Los Angeles Times*. It said, "Remember. Remember when you didn't think you could get through that speech? God saw you through . . . and it turned out better than you could have hoped or imagined. The same

God that did *that* is going to see you through *this.*" That little reminder made me cry.

When I told my friend Kathleen that I didn't get the job "because they had selected a former Reagan cabinet member and a former congressman," her response was, "What were they *thinking*?" Pretty funny.

But I was still disappointed. I thought that was the perfect job—I could still make an impact on the right to life issues, but take on others, like religious liberty that were of growing concern to me. I wanted to spend my life making a difference on issues that mattered most to me and to do it from a beach—well, that was about as good as it could get for me. I didn't know of any other job in the country where I could do that. I remember saying, "I'm never going to find a job more perfect for me."

Now think of David for a minute. Not King David, just David. He killed Goliath, and the thanks he gets is a jealous king pursuing him in order to kill him. David is in a dark, damp cave—tired and hungry—while his disgruntled men question his moves and his judgment. Now *we* see this as David's "pre-king" days and matter-of-factly view it as just something David had to go through to get there. That's because we can see the whole picture. David's character was being built through those trials so that he could lead the nation. David couldn't see around the corner to what was coming; he could *see* only darkness.

Kind of like Joseph. He was thrown into a pit, sold into slavery, and thrown into jail on false charges. The guy who promised to remember him when he was freed forgot about him. And there he sits. And sits. Now, God knew that all of that had to happen so he could be brought to the king at the right time, interpret his dream, become second in command, and save his people from starvation. Joseph didn't know that was coming—he just sat in prison waiting on God.

A lot of times we feel the same way. Like David and Joseph, we don't see what's around the corner. But, like them, we must trust God. God is in control and promises to *work all things* to our good if we love Him and are called according to His purpose—even a lunatic king, evil brothers, or an unjust sentence. So if you are in that cave, thank God. First, because you are assured that He is working your current situation for your good. Second, because He says to thank him in *all* things. And third, because no plan of God's will be thwarted (Job 42:1–2). He is still in control—and nothing is impossible for Him.

I sat in "the cave" and had given up on what I hoped to do. I had forgotten who I was dealing with—the God of the Universe who knows a whole bunch of stuff I don't. He knew He had something even better for me than what I thought was "perfect."

Several weeks later I got a call from the CENTER FOR RECLAIMING AMERICA. I didn't return it because I was working to try and pass three bills at the Statehouse. Besides, I had never heard of it. I knew of Dr. D. James Kennedy of Coral Ridge Ministries, but didn't know of the CENTER because it was brand new.

The first director, Pat Gartland, was leaving, and a mutual friend of ours, Michael Swartz, had recommended me to him for the job. I had been on Michael's National Empowerment Television show years earlier and would run into him at various state Right to Life conventions. Apparently he did quite a sales job. Pat called back and said, "Janet, you are perfect for this job." He told me all about this CENTER FOR RECLAIMING AMERICA, when finally I asked, "Don't you want to know anything about me?"

He simply said, "I already do. When can you come?"

Dr. D. James Kennedy, senior pastor of Coral Ridge Presbyterian Church for over 40 years, founder of Evangelism Explosion, and host of the *Coral Ridge Hour*, founded the CENTER FOR RECLAIMING AMERICA in July, 1996. The CENTER'S mission is to equip Christians to make an impact in their communities on whatever biblical issue God has called them to, from protecting life and the family to the biblical values that hold them intact. So I would be dealing with the "non-controversial" stuff that began with abortion but reached to issues like religious liberty, homosexuality, pornography, gambling, and evolution—or, more the case—equipping others to deal with it where they live. A challenge is what I wanted, and that's exactly what this was.

I flew down and realized then that the Christian Coalition wasn't the perfect job for me. *This* was. A chance to affect all the issues I cared about the most in an organization founded by one of the most respected Christian leaders in the nation—all about two miles from the beach in Ft. Lauderdale! The potential to impact the nation was without limit. A reporter once asked me to describe my job, and I jokingly told him, "think stuff up and do it." It wasn't too far off, but I didn't expect to see it in print. Never joke with a reporter.

Look for God at Work in the Hurdles and Road Blocks

Just like God was at work in bringing me to the CENTER FOR RECLAIMING AMERICA, He continued to work once I got there—even in the small things. For example, shortly after I started working at my new job, I was working on a handout for a presentation at Coral Ridge Ministries' chapel service. I wasn't quite done with it, but I left the office to go to an aerobics class. When I got back from working out, I finished and tried to print out my handouts. It was now eight o'clock at night. I'm in my "sweats," and when I went to make copies . . . the copy machine was broken down. A woman from across the hall, who was also working late, suggested I should use the copier at the church.

We went to use the church copy machine and found it out of toner—with none in sight. But on this day, I was so focused on how God takes an active role in our lives—the subject of my handout—that I remember thinking, "I'll bet *somebody* at Kinko's needs to see this sheet." So I went to Kinko's to get the handouts printed, and the man behind the counter said, "Where did you get this?"

I said, "I wrote it."

"You???" (He was used to me printing party flyers and the like.)

He said, "Would you mind if I *kept* one of these?"

"Not at all." We started talking, and a few weeks later I saw him in church.

When your focus is on God, it is amazing how much you see Him take an active role in your life. Look for it. Look for it in the roadblocks.

Gretta

Once I got settled into my new job, I signed up for Evangelism Explosion (EE) training. I could talk to anyone about most issues, but I needed help in learning how to share the Gospel. The one day in the whole year I was home sick was the first day of class. It was something I really felt I should do, and so I dragged my body out of bed and went to where I thought it was held. Wrong building. So I dragged myself over to the church and found out I had the wrong night—classes didn't start for another week. It really wasn't at all like me to be early.

Thinking I could at least have some guilt-free sleep out of the trip, I drove home—longing for my bed. I got to the door and realized, after emptying everything out of my purse, that I had locked my key in my apartment. I asked around until I found the building of the manager who could help. He wasn't in, so I wrote him a note. This was not a very good day.

I didn't remember that God was at work in all things and that He could use even this blunder for my good, and I wasn't particularly thankful this time. As I was knocking on the manager's door one last time, a lady at the other end of the hallway opened her door and asked, "Were you knocking on *my* door?"

I explained what happened and she let me use the phone to find someone to help. She told me that she had no family in the area and had been very lonely since her husband had died years before. I thanked her, and the next day I sent her tulips. Turned out they were her favorite flower. We became friends. Her niece from New Jersey found out about the flowers given to her beloved aunt and was so happy that she cried. Wow. All I did was send her some flowers.

One day I told her I was bringing lunch by and asked her what she had a taste for. After some prompting, she admitted that she has had a taste for fish and chips for "more than a year." I can't imagine having a taste for anything for a year (with the exception of chocolate—which is pretty much ongoing). While I was there she showed me some photos of her family, and I took a few when she looked away to make into a calendar (at Kinko's, of course). I asked her if I could bring some friends from my EE team by the following week, and she readily agreed and offered to make some dessert.

I found out some pretty cool things about Gretta. She is 90 years old and *knew* Thomas Edison; her father used to be his butler. She can tell stories about how he came up from the basement with news of his latest invention to tell his wife, "Deary!" She knew Henry Ford, Calvin Coolidge, and the Colgates, but didn't think it significant enough to tell me until much later.

The next week my EE trainer was meeting with the governor, then candidate Jeb Bush, and wasn't going to be there. I called Gretta to cancel and she sounded disappointed. I asked her, "You made dessert—didn't you Gretta?"

A hesitant, "Yeeees," was her response.

I told her, "I'll be over Gretta, even if I come by myself." Dr. Kennedy wasn't able to come, as he was going out on "EE calls" with another group, but his daughter Jennifer, also a trainer, could.

That night I gave Gretta her personalized calendar. She was so moved she said later she got up in the middle of the night just to look at it. That night she accepted Christ's free gift of eternal life—all because I locked my keys in my apartment. We need to remember to give thanks in all things— because God has a plan we can't see that is far greater than we can think or imagine.

Prayer is the key. When you think about it, prayer is nothing short of communicating with the Creator of the Universe—the God who is for us and the God who has the power to intervene. God is a personal God who hears us when we call to Him—and acts. Imagine if we lived our lives like we really believed that. Rich Nathan, my former pastor, once said, "Use the waiting times to pray." That is, make use of the times we're in traffic and standing in lines to speak to God. Then look for the results—and write them down.

God Intervenes

When I first moved to Florida, I knew no one. I was in Washington, D.C., where I knew a lot of people, and was dreading going back to Florida, where I hadn't made friends yet. My state representative back in Ohio had

been looking for years to leave his House seat to become a judge. I was waiting to run for his seat when I decided to move. Once I moved to Florida, he
was appointed a judge. My Ohio home had not sold yet, and I was wondering if I had made the right move.

I woke up at four in the morning and read from Psalm 139, verse 9:

> If I take the wings of the morning [like at 4:00 a.m.], and
> dwell in the uttermost parts of the sea [like the Atlantic Ocean,
> for example], *even there* Your hand shall lead me, and your right
> hand shall hold me.

Wow. Personal. That's how God is—even when we don't always see
it. And if you read a little further in that same chapter, in verses 13-15, it
speaks of His plan for us and has something to say about the abortion issue:

> For You formed my inward parts; You covered me in my
> mother's womb. I will praise You, for I am fearfully and wonder-
> fully made; Marvelous are Your works, And that my soul knows
> very well. My frame was not hidden from You, when I was made
> in secret.

God gives you just what you need just when you need it—like when
I was speaking in Oregon directly after they legalized assisted suicide. I was
their morning keynote speaker and had no idea what I was going to tell these
distraught people who had just suffered a devastating defeat. So I prayed the
prayer of desperation and asked God to please help me, since I was going on
in twenty minutes. Normally, I'd spend that time working on my notes, but
I was drawing a blank. I turned to the Bible and immediately found this: "I
will help you speak and I will teach you what to say" (Exodus 4:12 NIV).
That just happened to be the reassurance I was looking for. And He did. One
of the main things I stressed that morning is that God is in control, no matter what happens. Many of these people, who were so downtrodden after losing such a major statewide battle, thanked me for reminding them, saying,
"That's exactly what I needed to hear."

It is easy to forget with whom we are dealing—the God of the universe who hears us when we pray and who is intricately involved in our lives.

He works even through the roadblocks and hurdles—and turns them for our good. We need to write down when He does so, like the disciples, so we won't forget it by the next chapter. And when our prayers aren't answered in the way we asked, we have to remember that God's way is best. He is all knowing, and because He is all knowing, we can trust that His way is right—even when we don't see it. And finally, God is for us. We can put our trust completely in Him because He has earned that trust.

7

Creativity for the Cause

Here are some ingredients for a successful event in an ideal world: time, money, people, influence and exposure. It would be great to have months to plan, money for staging and promotion, people—in droves—making an impact at the perfect opportunity to multiply your message with something so newsworthy that the media can't help but flock to it. In actual practice, these are five ingredients that seldom come together.

Here's the real world: Hillary Clinton is coming to town in two days with her "Healthcare Express" to push her program for socialized medicine—complete with tax-funded abortions and healthcare rationing. There's no time to get a mailing out, and no money to buy ads in opposition. What do you do?

Healthcare Funeral

We wanted to greet her (and all the media that would follow) with something that most closely symbolized her plan—a funeral.

In addition to paying for abortions, her plan would have placed limitations on what kind of care you could get, regardless of whether or not you needed it to save your life. The Canadian system is much like this and has experienced long waiting lists for life-saving care—causing many to come to the U.S. for treatment. The sound-bite that best sums up their system originated with former State Rep. Ed Kasputis' statement that "when they get sick in Canada, they don't call a doctor, they call a travel agent." Needless to say, that was not the kind of healthcare we wanted to see here in the United States, and I couldn't think of anything better than a funeral to demonstrate that point.

I spent six hours on the phone looking for a hearse that weekend, but came up empty, so I went and bought a cardboard coffin—yes, they really sell them! I also made huge banners held up with retractable paint-poles, and folded-over bed sheets—which, by the way, can be re-used by making your letters out of colored contact paper instead of paint. There were about twenty kids from the Ohio State University pro-life group who played various roles in our little funeral procession: a priest, complete with white cardboard (from a paper plate) in the collar of his black shirt, pallbearers, mourners, and an undertaker! The undertaker was a guy who showed up for the rally with a white shirt and tie—he was *perfect* for the part. His sign read: "Undertakers for Clinton Care."

On the casket was another sign that read something like: "Here Lies Ray Sine, Needed an Aspirin, Died Standing in Line." My boyfriend at the time came, expecting that maybe he would come and discreetly stand in a crowd with me for an hour before we did something he wanted to do. We made him the Grim Reaper—complete with white face paint. I can still remember his face as he was putting on the white make-up—the face I've seen quite a bit from people I've dated: "I can't believe I'm doing this!"

By the end of our little funeral procession, complete with funeral music, of course, I think he actually got into the role. He started hamming it up, and would point his long, rubbery Grim-Reaper fingers (you can buy those, too) at people indicating that it was "their time." Mark Pecot, my former intern, was dressed as Bill Clinton. Not too hard to do, I already had the mask (don't ask), and he just stuffed a towel in the back of his sweat-pants and jogged up and down the protest rally with a McDonalds bag in one hand hitting on every woman there. He also did a jig in the middle of the street with my Grim-Reaper boyfriend. The image of Clinton arm in arm with the Grim Reaper was what ended up on the news. The message was sent and delivered—for the price of a cardboard coffin and some props.

The challenge was to take a small window of opportunity to make an impact when we had neither time nor money to work with. What we *did* have was one of the most under-utilized and effective tools to overcome these obstacles—creativity. It has gotten us people, votes, headlines, and results on more than one occasion. Not to mention it can be a lot of fun.

Boats

Deborah Pryce, a local judge, decided she wanted to be a U.S. Congresswoman. Trouble is, no one knew where she stood on the important issues. The night of the Republican Party endorsement, everyone was scrambling to find out. She said she was pro-life, which put her in the running. In fact, that's why she was nominated. The field started to narrow and people asked me for advice. "I told them to see what kind of commitments they could get."

It was down to two candidates, and Pryce wanted the vote so badly she apparently was willing to lie to get it. She told the committee members and me that if elected, she would support a Human Life Amendment to the Constitution. That was the pinnacle of the pro-life movement—the ultimate goal in child protection.

If I hadn't heard it myself, I might not have believed it. But she said it, and it got her the endorsement of the Republican Party by a whopping one vote. (Don't ever think that one person can't make a difference.) Once she got it, she waited until it was too late for anybody else to file against her in the primary, and then announced that she was really pro-abortion after all.

The Democratic candidate was also pro-abortion. That meant it was time to strategize. At a meeting in my apartment, Linda Reidelbach, a true pro-lifer, decided to run against Pryce as an Independent. Maybe we weren't going to win, but people were going to be offered an alternative—and hopefully think twice about lying to pro-lifers in the future.

Meanwhile, Debbie Pryce was having a little fundraiser . . . uh, make that a *big* fundraiser.

It turned out that Marilyn Quayle was coming to town to help a fellow Republican. So was the pro-life Governor's wife. Not good. I spent a lot of time on the phone with Bill Kristol, Dan Quayle's then Chief of Staff, saying, "Marilyn does not want to be at *this* event. By standing for a pro-abortion candidate who lied to the pro-life community to get the nomination, it could cost the [Bush/Quayle] ticket critical pro-life votes. She'll be in the middle of an abortion controversy—precisely where you don't want her."

They wouldn't listen and there was nothing more we could do. This event—and whatever we were going to do about it—just went national.

The breakfast fundraiser was being held at the River Club in Columbus, Ohio—where two rivers come together. Windows overlooking the beautiful river view are the central focus of every room. Perfect conditions for a "picket by boat." (Who said doing the right thing couldn't be fun?)

The Republican Party called me in a panic. They got wind of the warning calls I had made to the White House. They called again to talk me out of whatever I might be dreaming up. They loved our little antics when we were fighting pro-abortion Democrats, but didn't think much of our free speech rights when pro-abortion *Republicans* were the target.

The state director of the Bush campaign, Doug Preisse, knowing my disdain for flip-floppers, called to "reason" with me: "Janet, you've got to call off the troops. Don't make your point at *this* event. If you show up, it will hurt the Bush campaign."

"Then tell them not to come," I said. "Tell them the kind of candidate they'd be supporting—how she lied to pro-lifers to get where she is. They need to back away from this one."

But they wouldn't hear of it. "Janet, Janet, we can't do that," he chided. "You know they're coming, and I need your word that you won't have your people there in opposition."

I said, "Look Doug, *I* can't control these people. I can't speak for them. I can't tell them what to do. If *they* want to do something, I can't stop them."

No sooner did I say that than I got paged over the intercom, "Janet, U-Haul Boat Rental, line two! Janet, U-Haul Boat Rental, line two!"

"Gotta go." Perhaps that wasn't the best timing in the world.

The next morning a power boat pulled three row boats with huge sails made of bed sheets carrying the messages like: "Pryce has no integrity."

"Integrity has no Pryce." "The Pryce is wrong." Lovely slogans—I thought. The Secret Service boat looked like it was part of *our* little demonstration. Upstairs in the River Club the curtains were purposely drawn so nobody would see our flotilla parading around their whole event.

Word got back to me that the chairman of the county party looked out the curtained windows and said, "Well, you know, I've got to hand it to them. This one was good." (Shutting off the view only made people want to look more.)

This was one of the most successful demonstrations I have ever seen, with news coverage on every channel—not to mention the national media. It was a break in on the morning news, and at noon, six, and eleven. It even made the morning *traffic reports.* "We don't know what's going on, but there's a tie-up over by the River Club. People are looking at *something;* we're just not sure *what.*"

Don't let excuses stop you from acting: "Oh gosh, they're coming tomorrow." "There's not enough time to organize anything," "We don't have any money," and "People will get mad at us."

While our Independent didn't pull off a win, Reidelbach got more than three times the vote of any independent in the history of Ohio. The campaign was written up in the Congressional Directories.

When the odds are against you, and you feel like there is nothing you can do, just remember Ohio's official motto: "With God all things are possible."

That was the last flip-flopper I can recall who ran for a major public office in the state. No, I take that back. In subsequent elections, candidates for Congress flipped to become *pro-life . . .* and won.

What you do matters!

Celebrezze

That reminds me of the time we had a candidate back in 1990 who was running for governor: Attorney General Tony Celebrezze. He was very pro-life—even spoke at our pro-life conventions. But when he began thinking about running for governor, the Democratic Party began pressuring him to become pro-abortion. And days after vowing, "I've been right to life my entire career, I'm not going to change now," he flip-flopped in favor of killing babies for political expediency.

Ohio Right to Life was prepared to stay out of the race, with both candidates for governor being pro-life, but now we were forced to enter in— in a big way. On one occasion, our former pro-life candidate gave a luncheon with none other than NARAL Director Kate Michelman. Of course, we had to be there. I didn't just want *any* protest; we needed something catchy— something that would follow him wherever he went. So I went to one of my favorite stores in Columbus and bought a few hundred pinwheels—you know, the kind that blow in the wind? Everyone who was lined up around the building had one. Remember—the media loves visuals; they like to have something to film, and the more unique, the better. I utilized paint-poles/banners again with the words: "Which Way Does the Celebrezze Blow?"

Every television news station started their news story with a close-up of a little kid holding a pinwheel blowing in the wind, while the reporter voiced the words of my banner: "'Which way does the Celebrezze blow?' That was the question being asked today. . . ." They should have planned their entrance a bit better, because Celebrezze had to walk under my banner to get in the door!

The good news is that when Celebrezze flip-flopped on abortion, he took a double-digit nose-dive in the polls from which he never recovered. I think it helped that pro-lifers followed him wherever he went on the campaign trail.

One day at an outdoor rally, I had posters that highlighted his survey response where he said he would not oppose abortions even if they were being done for sex-selection. It pictured a baby with a red circle and a line drawn through him—with the words "**SORRY,** <u>TONY SAYS</u> YOU'RE THE **WRONG SEX.**" That one cost me more, but it was worth it.

By the way, after the election the media claimed that abortion had nothing to do with Celebrezze's defeat. One day after the election my dad read these words in the Cleveland morning paper:

> Hey Janet Folger, you are wrong , wrong, wrong. . . . She says abortion played a significant role in Voinovich's defeat of Democrat Anthony J . Celebrezze, Jr. Well, Folger is sadly, sorely, and surely mistaken.
>
> That, ladies and gentlemen, is the kind of pro-LIFE distortion that continues to taint the credibility of Ohio Right To Life and the entire Right To Life movement.[1]

My response included:

> "The number one issue was abortion," said Paul Mifsud, who probably will become Voinovich's chief of staff.
> —*The Cincinnati Enquirer,* November 8, 1990

If Tony Celebrezze had won the election, there would have been no question in the eyes of the liberal media that it was because he had forsaken his pro-life position and was now pro-abortion. But because Voinovich was the victor (by a landslide), abortion suddenly had nothing to do with the outcome of the race. Color me surprised. That, ladies and gentlemen, *is the kind of pro-abortion distortion that continues to taint the credibility of reporters and the entire newspaper industry.*

The *Plain Dealer's* Jim Underwood was sitting right next to Voinovich's campaign director, Paul Mifsud, on November 7 when Mifsud clearly stated that the abortion issue cost Celebrezze the race. Maybe Underwood was dozing off.

Underwood, in his November 18 article, went so far as to say, "One of the factors that came to play in Celebrezze's defeat was that he was not clearly defined on the abortion issue." I responded, "Maybe he slept through the entire campaign."[2]

Clinton = Abortion

One really neat idea, that I had nothing to do with, was aimed at the presidential race. When Bill Clinton came to town, there were some college kids that were somewhat bolder than I've been in the past. They were bolder than anyone I knew. They had big letters that spelled out the word Clinton. C-L-I-N-T-O-N. They took those letters with them to the big rally and went up to the organizers and said, "Hey, we'd like to do a Clinton cheer—would that be OK?" And the rally organizers, eager to show the face of the young Americans up on stage, said, "Sure."

All seven students got up there and stretched out across the stage—right before Clinton came on—and said, "Give me a C!" "C!" "Give me an L!" "L!" and all the way through, and then they said what does it spell?" They then turned their letters over and they spelled out the word "A-B-O-R-T-I-O-N" This really happened. Not once, but twice during the Clinton campaign! I'm not sure how something like this ever happens—*twice*—but it did. You must have all heard about it on the national news. Neither did I.

Mother's Day Flowers

Creativity has made up for both money and time deficiencies. Creative ways to get your message out don't always have to be extravagant. For example, when I was public relations director on the board of Greater Cleveland Right to Life, every Mother's Day, we would send red silk roses to all the new mothers in the area hospitals. The cameras would follow me as I handed each new mother a silk rose with the message (also attached), "On behalf of Greater Cleveland Right to Life, thank you for choosing life." You have to remember that the television stations are almost compelled to run some sappy Mother's Day story that weekend—why not provide it for them? They loved the close-up of a happy young mother holding her baby and getting a flower from us. And, for once, we weren't protesting anything.

The Numbers

I think we'll go farther if we think visually. We can say nearly a million and a half kids are killed every year in our country by abortion, but that number is so large that nobody can picture a million of anything. At Cleveland State we decided to depict the abortion numbers visually. Our Student's for Life group made a huge banner in the middle of the University Center with the words, "AMERICAN WAR CASUALTIES." What you may have seen depicted with crosses, we did with a bar graph. One inch equaled

AMERICAN WAR CASUALTIES: You can't see it by the photo, but the "War on the Unborn went two and a half stories high. By today's figures it would be more than twice as high. I'm wearing the "Choose Life" shirt, and one of my very best friends, Kathleen McGervey, is to my right.

50,000 lives and we had all our wars represented. Most of the wars were only a few inches high with this scale, with the Civil War being the tallest—ten inches. Vietnam was a fraction of an inch, as I recall, and stood in stark contrast to the "War on the Unborn" which was a bar graph that went *two and a half stories* high. We held this huge thing up with dozens of helium balloons. This was done when there were about 17 million American abortions—more than all the casualties of all of our nation's wars—combined. It has more than doubled that now. There is simply no issue that affects so many human lives. That poster put it all into perspective.

Another effective visual is the "Cemetery of the Innocents," which usually only depicts a few hundred crosses and Stars of David, or over

4,000—one day's worth of American abortions. Some put pink and blue ribbons on them. There are several of these that travel from city to city around the country for use by universities and churches. I have never seen any place hosting this display remain unaffected. Frequently, women who have had abortions will sit at the crosses to mourn their loss. The pro-abortion groups hate this. I think that means it's effective.

Cincinnati Right to Life came up with a great visual by depicting one day's abortion rate with 4,000 baby shoes. It tends to make this horrific statistic more personal. That's what we need to do—take the facts and statistics and bring it closer to people's hearts. I was speaking at a banquet in Kansas City a year ago and started talking to a Pregnancy Help Center that had a booth there. Thinking I was passing along some great pro-life insight to them, I told them that some pro-life groups are giving women contemplating abortion little baby sleepers. I told them they "might want to think about that" as it gets women to start thinking about their baby as a baby and not a problem.

They then *showed me* a basket filled with every little baby thing you can think of: a pacifier, baby bottle, baby spoon, stuffed animal, baby lotion, tiny diaper, baby toy, bib, baby sleeper, and a pastel-colored New Testament—complete with the salvation plan. They told me of a woman they had given the basket to just a few weeks prior. Although she was married, her positive pregnancy test was "bad news." She didn't want an abortion but said she knew her husband would insist on one. They told her to take the basket anyway.

She woke up that night and her husband was not in the bed. She found him sitting at the dining room table going through each item in the baby basket, sobbing. He looked up, saw her, and said, "There is no way we can have this abortion." The baby had become real to him.

Former abortionist Eric Harrah speaks of the women who stood outside his abortion clinics handing out baby booties—white, pink, and blue—to the women going inside for abortions. "These girls would come into the procedure room, get on the table, and all of a sudden look at these booties and change their minds," he recalls. The booties, a fuzzy symbol of the unborn son or daughter they were carrying, would jolt them out of denial. That tells me this is very much worth doing. We must show the baby and the numbers of abortions in a real and tangible way.

Pro-Life Numbers

One of the most successful events we had was Ohio's Congressional Breakfast, held every year in Washington, D.C., prior to the January 22 Pro-life March. This breakfast is always sold out with well over 2,000 Ohioans in attendance, along with members of Congress and their staffers, who sit at the tables with people from their districts. I believe it was Congressman Steve Chabot, from Cincinnati, who arrived for the first time and asked if someone could guide him to the "Ohio Table." The reply, "No Congressman, they're *all* Ohio tables!" January 22 is Steve's birthday and we now sing to him every year and assure him that we are very glad he was born.

Even though the breakfast was sold out, and additional busses of Ohioans were at the march, I wanted to show everyone that there are many, many more pro-lifers standing with them that weren't in Washington. We had petitions of about 75,000 names of others back in Ohio who also wanted to see children protected again. I could have stood up at the podium and said that, but it wouldn't have meant anything, since people can't visualize 75,000 of anything. Instead, I had the names printed on attached computer paper and had two huge boxes of it in the front of the ballroom.

While the president of Ohio Right to Life looked at me in horror— afraid of whatever it was that I was going *to do now*—I called for all the teenagers to come to the front of the room. I then told the audience that, while they were unable to make it, there were several people who wanted to send their regards and let everyone at the breakfast know they were standing for life right beside them. And while the teens took the sheets of names and encircled the room from both sides, I let people know that these were 75,000 of their friends and neighbors who had signed our Petition for Life. As the paper kept coming, more teens kept marching it around the room as "The Loco-motion" played on the speaker system. People started clapping and the congressmen and senators looked on in awe.

I then acted like I was going to read them all: "Abigail Aaronson, Adam Abelmyer, Ann Andrews. . . ." You get the idea. It was a visual that I hoped would stay with them when they were stuffing envelopes at their kitchen table and feeling like they were all alone. Visuals work! Creativity works! Make the numbers count!

Unfortunately, in the real world we don't always have months to plan and money to promote events that make a lasting impression. And for some reason the media doesn't get all that excited about covering our same old candlelight vigils, rallies, and events every year. We can increase our exposure and our impact if we just use some creativity. "Think outside the box" to what has never been done before. Coming up with a unique idea is a great draw for people who will want to be a part of it—especially if it's fun.

Not creative? Don't be afraid to ask around and brainstorm with others who are. Pick who you go to carefully though—nay-sayers can spoil even an ideal event. Check out what others have done (even in other movements) and put a new twist on it. Call other states that have gone through what you are facing. We shouldn't have to re-invent the wheel in all 50 states—yet we do it every day.

And finally, if you are not creative, go to the Creator. He's not called the Creator for nothing!

Partial-Birth Abortion

Here's what partial-birth abortion is, based on a highly reliable source: the abortionist performing them. He spelled out the procedure in grizzly detail in the written report he submitted to the National Abortion Federation in 1992. "Once the child is delivered to the neck," he said, "the surgeon then forces the scissors into the base of the skull. Having safely entered the skull, he spreads the scissors to enlarge the opening. The surgeon . . . introduces a suction catheter into this hole and evacuates the skull contents."

As I read this quote on the air during a debate on public radio, my NARAL counterpart tried her usual tactic: rather than defend what she stands for, she chose to attack the messenger who described it—me.

She explained how this was simply "not true" and went on to berate my "dramatic reading" of such a "necessary procedure" that "helps women."

I replied, "You may not like my voice inflections, and for that I'm sorry, but the words I read are the words of *the abortionist himself*, as he described exactly *how he performs a partial-birth abortion* in his written report to the National Abortion Federation. If *I* have that report and I work at *Right to Life*, how is it that you work for the National *Abortion* and Reproductive Rights Action League, *and you don't*? Here—let me give you mine so you'll have a copy."

She wasn't at all appreciative of my kind gesture.

Getting the Ban Passed in Ohio

Ohio was the first state in the nation to pass a law against what is now known as "partial-birth abortion." No one had ever heard of it before, but we knew about it, unfortunately, because one of the main proponents of partial-birth abortion had already killed at least 1,000 children this way (by his own admission) in Ohio.

Our legislation was referred to as the "Brain-Suction Abortion Bill" (also an accurate description of the procedure), and while I was in the midst of gathering co-sponsors for it, I made a call to the Humane Society. "What if I told you some fraternity brothers at Ohio State were pulling puppies out as they were being born and sticking scissors in their heads and sucking their brains out? Would the Humane Society have a problem with that?"

They responded, "They would be jailed for cruelty." They were hoping I would give them names.

It seems to me that we should treat a living, kicking, half-born baby at least as well as we treat a dog. A rather appropriate analogy I think. I voiced this analogy, along with a few others, at the press conference announcing our bill. The city counsel had just passed an ordinance prohibiting "bear wrestling" because it was considered "cruel." And several pro-abortion legislators had just voted to pass a bill to outlaw the hunting of mourning doves. They didn't want to hurt a *bird* but had no problem with sucking the brains out of a viable child. They didn't much care for the comparisons, which made them appear as obvious hypocrites, but it seemed to me that a human child during delivery deserved at least as much protection as a dog, or a bear, or a bird.

I was sitting in my office looking at a model of an unborn child at six months. I held my fingers up to the baby's head and asked my friend Don, "How big would you say this is? Three inches? Four inches?" He said, "About three."

That's where the sound-bite, "The difference between abortion and homicide in *this* procedure is about three inches," was conceived. Those were the same words used by Congressman Charles Canady (R-FL), the main sponsor of the first Partial-Birth Abortion Ban Act of 1995, on the floor of the U.S. House of Representatives.

When we introduced the bill in Ohio, we had well over half of the

Statehouse as co-sponsors. When legislators put their name on a bill, it's usually a pretty good indication that we would have their vote, but not always. When I approached Representative John Garcia to see if he wanted to sign on to the bill, I already had 55 out of 99 legislators as co-sponsors. I thought he might sign on—after all, he had answered his Ohio Right to Life candidate's survey 100 percent pro-life. But he had also answered the NARAL survey 100 percent pro-abortion—a real statesman.

He welcomed me into his office touting his pro-life beliefs—grabbing the pen from my hand, he anxiously added his name to the list. I remember thinking, "I wish they all were this easy." I was glad I had stopped by, because our bill was sent to a committee where *he* was our swing vote, which was not a position I was at all comfortable with.

Then I heard him speak against the bill in committee. Chad Bresson, a local reporter from the Christian radio station, stopped me after the hearing and said, "I noticed that your face went pale—what just happened in there?" I informed him that we had just lost our majority on the committee, but even at that point in time I had no idea of the battle we were in for.

With the pro-life chairman, Ed Kasputis, and the other pro-life members gone, the pro-abortion members of the committee held a secret meeting of their own and "voted" to kill our bill. The pro-abortion speaker let "the committee vote" stand due to a "parliamentary" loophole—the previous meeting was not properly adjourned because no quorum was present. Practically speaking, it was over. Our bill was dead!

But you have to remember our state motto: "With God all things are possible." That meant even this. Years prior, State Representative (now senator) Lou Blessing, told me about something he had just read in the House rules that allowed a bill to be pulled from a hostile committee and brought to the floor for a vote. While parliamentary procedure was never really my specialty, for some reason, I thought this might be useful someday and remembered the name: "discharge petition." I brought it up to our emergency meeting of pro-life legislative leaders.

I told them, "If we can get half the House to sign one of these things, we can bring it to the floor for a vote!" Their reply was somewhat less than enthusiastic. "Janet, this has never been done." Someone else added, "I remember they tried that once in the 1970s but couldn't get enough signatures."

But after much deliberation, we could find no better way—this "discharge petition" that had never been done before was our "only hope." Our strategy was a two-prong approach: my assistant, Lorraine, started making calls to get pro-lifers all over the state praying, while I went to work at the Statehouse to reach 50 legislators and ask them to sign something they had never heard of: *a discharge petition.*

Just because something has never been done before doesn't mean it can't be done *now*: in less than 24 hours, we had *more* than enough signatures to do it! Chairman Ed Kasputis wanted to be the last signature, at number 50, but Rep. Mike Fox (who wasn't even a pro-lifer) insisted on being number 51—even though there weren't enough lines. Thanks be to God and the pro-lifers praying all over the state!

Pro-abortion legislators were referring to me as "Representative Folger," and in the next session the House leadership passed a rule that "only *members* can circulate discharge petitions." I wonder who that one was written for?

Their "perfect plan" to kill our bill didn't work and the pro-aborts weren't particularly happy with me. To try and explain his actions (of co-sponsoring a bill he voted against), Representative John Garcia said he felt that I had "held a gun to his head." Poor legislator up against a 5' 3" lobbyist—I can see where he would feel intimidated.

Frankly, I think spreading the rumor that I lobby fully armed actually gave me a bit more influence. One afternoon, after the "gun to the head" quote appeared in every Ohio newspaper, a group of pro-life legislators were walking back from a reception when I crossed their path. They all yelled and "ran for cover" for "fear I might shoot." Yeah, really funny guys. And no, I can't testify for the "concealed carry bill."

Sometimes there are pitfalls in lobbying you can't anticipate. For example, there was one liberal senior Democrat from the Black Caucus by the name of Troy Lee James who was pro-life. But getting to him was next to impossible. His staffers were incredibly hostile—they never gave him my messages and did everything possible to keep me from getting in. But I knew if I could get to him, I would get his vote.

One day, before session, I saw him standing in the lobby and headed over to him, but a pro-abortion state representative from his caucus ran interference. She was a pro-abortion activist and I had never met with her (since I concentrated on people with whom I had a chance). She wasn't really sure who I was, but I knew she suspected. If her suspicions were verified, all she had to do was take Troy with her to the House floor (where I couldn't follow) and my chance to reach him would be gone.

She came up to me and demanded, "What's your name?"

I said, "My name's Janet, nice to meet you."

She snapped back, "Janet *what?*"

"Folger," as I extended a hand of greeting.

Ignoring my hand, she barked, "Where do you work?"

I replied, "I work for a child-protection, women-helping agency." It was true, after all.

She demanded, "Which *iss???*"

My response: "Non-profit. Gotta run!" As I turned to leave, I said, "Great hat!"

I looped around the back to talk to Troy, and I got more than his vote. The day the partial-birth ban was brought to the floor, he gave an unexpected speech. He was motioning to be recognized for several minutes. I can still hear the pro-abortion Democrats yelling in unison for their pal: "Let Troy speak! Let Troy speak!"

I guess they didn't spend a lot of time discussing the subject together because they were counting on their buddy to side with *them*. He wasn't one to give a lot of floor speeches, and having just been through the John Garcia ordeal, Mark looked over to me with a somewhat worried, questioning look.

When the Speaker recognized Troy Lee James, he said, "I'm *really glad* that my parents aren't alive to see this. They *wouldn't believe* what they are hearing today." He exclaimed, "*Sucking out babies' brains? Is this what we're really discussing?*" He talked about how very poor he was growing up and how his parents worked and "sacrificed just to provide the next meal." He then announced something I was waiting for: "I am the youngest of *eighteen*—and I am *so very glad* that *my* parents didn't shut the door on me!"

As he sat down the crowd that was calling for him to be recognized was silent—dumb-founded. Pro-life Democrats like Ron Suster, and Jerry Luebbers rallied to his support. Mark looked over at me with a surprised look of relief and exhilaration. I was thankful I was able to get to Troy that day to explain what was coming, but I don't think it would have made any difference if I hadn't.

We still had the Senate to go . . . and that was about the time I heard about a woman who had signed out a pro-life video from Dayton Right to Life a year or two prior. Looking at the line drawings of partial-birth abortion in the office, this woman had commented that she had witnessed "one of *those* abortions." I was informed of this and said, "We MUST find her."

Looking through the records, the folks in Dayton found her name: Brenda Shafer. As I dialed her number from my kitchen table, I paused to pray, knowing how important this call could be. Whatever I said had to be right. She got her husband on the other line and I told her what we were doing in the legislature. We spent hours on the phone over the next several days.

She told me how she was very "pro-choice," and when the temporary agency asked her if she wanted to take a job with an abortion clinic, she didn't hesitate. Her daughter, however, was pro-life. She told me how the two of them would get into arguments. "I told [my daughter] that if she ever got pregnant, she was *going* to have an abortion—no doubt about it," Brenda recalled. She admitted that wasn't very "pro-choice."

She told me she had no idea what she was getting herself into. "I remember looking at the ultra-sound monitor," she said, "asking the doctor if 'this' was the heart." He confirmed it. She said, "Here I was, a trained nurse, with no real understanding about fetal development." She said all she could think of was that bumper-sticker, "Abortion stops a beating heart."

She told me what she saw:

> I stood at the doctor's side and watched him perform this "brain-suction abortion" (it wasn't called a partial-birth abortion yet) on a woman who was six-months pregnant. The doctor delivered the baby's body and arms, everything but his little head. The baby's body was moving. His little fingers were clasping together. He was kicking his feet. The doctor took a pair of scissors and inserted them into the back of the baby's head, and the baby's arms jerked out in a flinch, a "startle" reaction, like a baby does when he thinks that he might fall. Then the doctor opened the scissors up. He then stuck the high-powered suction tube into the hole and sucked the baby's brains out. Now the baby was completely limp. I never went back to the clinic. But I am still haunted by the face of that little boy. It was the most perfect, angelic face I have ever seen.

She then told me something that, frankly, made me question her credibility. She told me how one woman who had a partial-birth abortion on her Down's Syndrome child regretted it the moment it happened—and the abortion facility wrapped up the dead child in a blanket (covering the back of the head) and allowed her to hold him. Brenda told me how she could hear her sobbing uncontrollably for hours repeating the same thing—"I am so sorry! I am so *very sorry!*"

That didn't seem to me like something an abortion facility would do. After selling the abortion on the false premise that "it's really not a child yet," why would they let the mother actually *see* that it was? I then found out that this is precisely what an abortionist in Los Angeles was doing at the time. In fact, based on the congressional testimony, they went a bit further in their twisted compassion. After they performed their partial-birth abortions, they took "family pictures" with the dead child.

One woman appeared before Congress and gave some of the most twisted testimony I have ever heard since the Nuremberg trials. She had her disabled (and perhaps terminal) daughter "MacKenzie" aborted by a partial-birth abortion and then testified against the ban with these words:

> I still have my baby's room and her memory cards from her memorial service, her foot and her hand prints. Those are good things and good memories, but she's gone. The best thing I can do for her is continue this fight. I know she would want me to. So for her, for MacKenzie, I respectfully ask you [to] reject this legislation (the Ban on Partial Birth Abortion).[1]

MacKenzie "would have wanted" Congress to pass a bill to have her aborted? I guess we'll never know for sure—she won't have an opportunity to testify—MacKenzie had her brains sucked out.

This confirmed Brenda's story—there could be no way she would have known this if she hadn't been there. And even though Brenda had proof she worked there, I warned her that she would be called a liar, and prepared her for the character assassination attempt that was sure to follow. But in the end she decided that a chance at stopping this horrific procedure was well worth the risk.

Our bill passed the Senate on June 28, and was signed into law on August 16, 1995.

Our victory in Ohio had a steamroller effect on the rest of the country. I got calls from as far away as England asking us how they could do what we did. I spent hours on the phone with Doug Johnston from National Right to Life, telling them what we did wrong and what we did right so they could learn from our experience. Congress introduced the bill next, and then 26 other states followed suit, although the courts have since struck down all but 10 of them.

As it turned out, we didn't need Brenda's testimony for our bill in the Ohio Senate and thought it a good idea to save her as a surprise witness for the congressional battle that was gearing up for a launch. The Ohio abortionist, Dr. Martin Haskell, had just written to Congress stating, "Representations that fetuses are living, conscious, feeling pain, wiggling,

Governor George Voinovich is signing the first ban on Partial-Birth Abortions in the nation. From left to right are, Rep. Jerry Luebbers (D), me (R), Dr. Jack Willke (R), Senator Merle Kearns (R), and Mark Lally (D).

kicking or trying to escape are totally fictitious." He further alleged that death occurred early in the procedure, if not before. He presumes in his letter that people who have spoken out against partial-birth abortion "have never seen the procedure."[2]

That's what *he* thought.

So Brenda went to Washington, where the battles—and the lies—got more intense.

I summarized what happened in an editorial that ran in the *Columbus Dispatch* on September 25, 1996, under their headline: "Partial-birth abortion too common, never necessary to protect women." Here's what they ran:

> A partial-birth abortion involves delivering a living, late-term
> baby, feet first, except for the head, and then puncturing the skull

with scissors and suctioning out the brain. If the child were to be pulled out three more inches and then stabbed in the skull with scissors, the person responsible would be charged with homicide. But this child is only four-fifths of the way born, so it's called an abortion: a partial-birth abortion.

If you did this "procedure" to a dog in Ohio, you'd be jailed for cruelty. So how can President Clinton support it? Even the most hardened pro-abortion groups lobby for it? With a campaign of misinformation, of course.

First, the National Abortion Federation claimed the procedure didn't exist. Oops. The federation must have forgotten that this was featured at its own convention in 1992 by an Ohio abortionist, Dr. Martin Haskell, who presented a written report. Once the child is delivered to the neck, he said, "the surgeon then forces the scissors into the base of the skull. Having safely entered the skull, he spreads the scissors to enlarge the opening. The surgeon . . . introduces a suction catheter into this hole and evacuates the skull contents. *Darned NAF report.*

Then the NAF, the National Abortion and Reproductive Rights Action League, and Planned Parenthood claimed that such procedures were "so rare, they were almost never done."

Oops. The Ohio abortionist himself admitted to performing more than 1,000 of them in this state alone. And then *The Record* of Hackensack, New Jersey, reported that a single clinic in that state performed 1,500 partial-birth abortions in one year alone— three times as many as the NAF had said occur annually nationwide.

Then the infamous Ohio abortionist said, "They're done for medical necessity." He must have forgotten about his interview with the *American Medical News* in July 1993, in which he said, "80 percent are purely elective."

He denied saying it, insisting he'd been misquoted—until the *American Medical News* informed him that the interview had been taped. *Darned tape recorders.*

What of those who keep screaming about "partial-birth

abortions to save the life of the mother"? That exception is already in the bill, and they know it.

What about the "health of the mother" argument? Health, as the courts define it in the context of abortion, means virtually anything that has to do with a woman's overall "well-being." This includes such reasons as a woman is "too young," "emotionally upset by pregnancy" or "unmarried." More than 300 doctors, including former Surgeon General C. Everett Koop, have joined to state the medical fact that "partial-birth abortion is never medically necessary to protect the health of a woman or her future fertility." The pro-abortion gang even tried to claim that the child was killed by the anesthesia, until the American Society of Anesthesiologists called them on that one, too. *Darned experts.*

Then, the defenders of partial-birth abortion tried to discredit Shafer, a nurse who assisted with the procedure and told Congress what she witnessed. They said Shafer never worked for the Ohio abortionist—until she delivered proof. Oops. (See a trend?)

If people are so extreme as to lobby for a procedure that most closely resembles infanticide—a procedure appropriately referred to as a crime against humanity—what makes us think they are not going to lie?

Shafer testified to lawmakers: "The baby's body was moving—his little fingers clasping together. He was kicking his feet. The doctor took a pair of scissors and inserted them into the back of the baby's head, and the baby's arms jerked out in flinch, a "startle" reaction, as a baby does when he thinks he might fall. Then the doctor opened the scissors . . . and sucked the baby's brains out."

As Rep. Henry Hyde, R-Ill., put it on the House floor, "People who say, 'I feel your pain,' can't be referring to that little infant."[3] Please remember that little infant and thousands like him on November 5.[4]

Congressional Roll Call put it this way: "One of the most basic rules of lobbying is 'never lie to a member of Congress, particularly one of your friends.' Another is, 'never ask a member to do something that will later jeopardize his seat.' The pro-choice movement did both and will pay a price for it."[5]

A few months later, then executive director of the National Coalition of Abortion Providers, Ron Fitzsimmons, admitted to *The New York Times* (Feb. 26, 1997) that *he* lied too. He said, " [I] lied through my teeth," to a *Nightline* camera when he "said the procedure was used rarely and only on women whose lives were in danger or whose fetuses were damaged." According to *The New York Times*, "[Fitzsimmons] now says the procedure is performed far more often than his colleagues have acknowledged, and on healthy women bearing healthy fetuses."[6]

Even after this admission, the pro-aborts kept repeating the lie—apparently hoping no one had read the *New York Times* article. You have to remember that the *only* way the pro-abortion side can win is if it keeps the truth from reaching the people. Expect it.

The pro-aborts

Partial-Birth Abortion

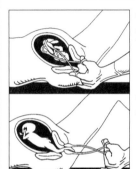

Guided by ultrasound, the abortionist grabs the baby's leg with forceps.

The baby's leg is pulled out into the birth canal.

The abortionist delivers the baby's entire body, except for the head.

The abortionist jams scissors into the baby's skull. The scissors are then opened to enlarge the hole.

The scissors are removed and a suction catheter is inserted. The child's brains are sucked out, causing the skull to collapse. The dead baby is then removed.

were so used to getting away with lying that they couldn't believe it when their lies were actually being exposed. Then something happened they didn't expect. Unlike every other abortion procedure in which the baby is hidden in the womb, this one revealed a living, kicking baby—more *born* than unborn. If people could see that child, the dehumanizing words would have no effect.

And nothing explained this better than the partial-birth abortion line drawings—drawings that the Ohio abortionist himself admitted accurately depicted what he did. They were so powerful, that I didn't even need to elaborate with one legislator, Mike Fox, who was on a phone call when he motioned me into his office. He put his hand over the mouthpiece and asked me what he could do for me. I laid the line drawings on his desk and said, "They're doing this in Ohio, and we'd like to stop it."

He looked at the pictures and said, "Put me on." That was all it took.

A partial-birth abortion really isn't any crueler than ripping the same child apart limb by limb *inside* the womb, as is done in a "dilation and evacuation" abortion. What was different is that this was a child they could see. After seeing legislators who had previously been unmoved on the abortion debate break down and cry at the site of these drawings, I knew what a powerful tool we had—something the pro-aborts had yet to find out.

That's why we put the posters behind us in the press conference—so the entire state (and then the nation) could see for themselves just what we were talking about. And that was why (former) Congresswoman Patricia Schroeder fought so hard to keep the line drawings from being shown in the congressional debate in Washington.

We couldn't possibly "*show* these drawings on the floor of the House of Representatives!" she exclaimed! "The pages (young staffers) might *see* them!"

Brenda Shafer looked Congresswoman Schroeder in the eye and said, "If you think the drawings are bad, you ought to see the *real thing.*"

Santorum v. Feingold and Boxer

Senator Rick Santorum (R-PA), who has sponsored the Senate versions of the ban, has gone to great lengths to expose how extreme his pro-abortion colleagues in the Senate really are. For example, when the debate first got started in 1995 he had an exchange with Senator Russell Feingold (D-WI) that was very telling:

Senator Santorum: Let's assume that this procedure is being performed . . . and the head is accidentally delivered. Would you allow the doctor to kill the baby?

Senator Feingold: I am not the person to be answering that question. That is a question that should be answered by a doctor and by the woman who receives the advice from the doctor.

So according to Senator Feingold—who later tried to get this remark removed from the official Congressional Record—it doesn't matter that the baby was "accidentally" born and is now a fully protected citizen of this country. The mother and doctor could decide that the baby should be killed anyway!

Then in October 1999, Santorum had this exchange of dialogue with Senator Barbara Boxer (D-CA):

Senator Santorum: So you would accept the fact that once the baby is separated from the mother, that baby cannot be killed?

Senator Boxer: I support the right—and I will repeat this, again, because I saw you ask the same question to another Senator.

Senator Santorum: All the Senator has to do is give me a straight answer.

Senator Boxer: Define "separation." You answer that question.

Senator Santorum: Let's define that. Let's say the baby is completely separated; in other words, no part of the baby is inside the mother.

Senator Boxer: You mean the baby has been birthed and is now in the mother's arms? It is a human being?

Senator Santorum: Say it is in the obstetrician's hands.

Senator Boxer: I had two babies, and within seconds of them being born—

Senator Santorum: We had six.

Senator Boxer: You didn't have any.

Senator Santorum: My wife and I did. WE do things together in my family.

Senator Boxer: Your wife gave birth. I gave birth. I can tell you that I know when the baby was born.

Senator Santorum: Good. All I am asking you is that once the baby leaves the mother's birth canal and is through the vaginal orifice and in the hands of the obstetrician, you would agree that you cannot then abort the baby?

Senator Boxer: I would say when the baby is born, the baby is born and would then have every right of every other human being living in this country, and I don't know why this would even be a question.

Senator Santorum: Because we are talking about a situation here where the baby is *almost* born. So if the baby was born, except for the baby's foot, and if the baby's foot was inside the mother but the rest of the baby was outside, could that baby be killed?

Senator Boxer: The baby is born when the baby is born.

Senator Santorum: I am asking for you to define for me what that is.

Senator Boxer: I can't believe the Senator from Pennsylvania has a question with it. I have never been troubled by this question. You gave birth to a baby. The baby is there, and it is born, and that is my answer to the question.

Senator Santorum: What we are talking about here with partial-birth, as the Senator from California knows, is the baby is in the process of being born—

Senator Boxer: In the process of being born. This is why this conversation makes no sense, because to me it is obvious when a baby is born; to you, it isn't obvious.

Senator Santorum: I am asking you again. Can you answer that?

Senator Boxer: I will answer the question when the baby is born. The baby is born when the baby is outside the mother's body. The baby is born.

Senator Santorum: But, again, what you are suggesting is that if the baby's toe is inside the mother, you can, in fact, kill the baby.

Senator Boxer: Absolutely not.

Senator Santorum: OK. So if the baby's toe is in, you can't kill the baby. How about if the baby's foot is in?

Senator Boxer: You are the one who is making these statements.

Senator Santorum: We are trying to draw a line here.

Senator Boxer: I am not answering these questions.

Senator Boxer: What the Senator was trying to do was bait me on his terms of how he sees this issue . . . but I never got into the issue of when is someone born. I said to you that I am very clear on that, and I understand that completely. But it was my friend who kept on asking these questions, which to me do not make any sense, because the issue here is an emergency procedure that my friend from Pennsylvania wants to make illegal, and it will hurt the women, and it will hurt the families of this country.

Senator Santorum: . . . first off, the Senator from California said this was an "emergency procedure." Name me an emergency procedure that takes three days. That is what the procedure takes . . . in no emergency do you present yourself in an emergency condition and get sent [home] with pills for three days to present yourself back.

That says it all.

"We've Lost the Battle"

Eric Harrah (the former abortionist who cancelled our debate), now tells his story to audiences in both the U.S. and Europe, and believes the campaign to ban partial-birth abortion is critical to restoring legal protection to unborn human beings. He tells how he and three other abortionists watched an airport television monitor as the partial-birth abortion drawings were shown from the floor of the U.S. House of Representatives. "Here we were, four of the biggest abortionists in the country. We stopped dead in our tracks and were shocked, because the right-to-lifers had finally accomplished something . . . Here for the first time on national television was a diagram of what a partial-birth abortion really was."

One of those watching, Eric recalls, said, "We've lost the battle. It may not be today, it may not be next year, it may not be twenty years, but we've lost the battle. Since they were able to do that—get that up on that screen—we're done."

When you feel like giving up, I want you to remember that. Now on the other side of the debate, Eric urges Christians not to give up the fight to ban partial-birth abortion. "Christians on the local, statewide, and national level cannot let this opportunity pass them by."

What It Did to the Debate

A recent *New York Times* poll found that since 1989, public support for legal abortion has dropped from 40 percent to 32 percent. That support drops even further during the second trimester, when only 15 percent of Americans support abortion for any reason. A May 1999 CNN/*USA Today*/Gallup poll found that 58 percent of the public believed that abortion should be "illegal in all circumstances" or "legal only in a few circumstances."

And finally, a July 1998 survey of American *women*, conducted by the Princeton Survey Research Associates for the pro-abortion Center for Gender Equality, found that 70 percent of American women favor "more restrictions" on abortion and 53 percent believe that abortion should be legal (at most) in cases of rape, incest, or to save the mother's life.

Former Planned Parenthood director, Faye Wattleton, found these statistics "disturbing."

She should.

More Legislative Lessons

Congressman Chris Smith, a pro-life hero from New Jersey, once told me about a conversation he had with leaders from other nations who were meeting at the UN conference in Cairo. They were sick of how the Clinton Administration officials had pushed their pro-abortion agenda on them and the rest of the world. They were sick of having money for aid tied to birth control and abortion. And they told him, "We don't want what you have to offer: We don't want your abortion, we don't want your pregnancy rate, and we don't want your morals."

Congressman Smith explained to them that not everyone in America believes as the Clinton-Gore administration does and assured them that there were people like himself, and Congressman Henry Hyde who were doing everything they could to fight for life. Their answer was very profound. Their answer was, "That means there is hope for your country."

Because people are fighting for life, there is hope for our country.

Rally of Hope

In 1989, the Supreme Court handed down the *Webster* decision— which dealt with viability testing to see if late-term babies slated for abortion could survive. If the baby could survive outside the womb, the state of Missouri would be required to protect the child. But you would never know this by the pro-abortion reaction to the decision. They screamed and shouted about how terrible this decision was and, doggone it, they weren't going to take it. NARAL's Kate Michelman appeared on stations nationwide with her pre-planned sound-bite, "Take our rights? Lose your jobs!" A more accurate threat would have been: "Protect viable children? Lose your jobs!" That just didn't quite have the spin they were looking for.

I hated to admit it, but their threat, as ridiculous as it was, was starting to have an impact. Legislators became frightened. Some actually hid behind their doors when they saw me coming down the hall. They were afraid I would ask them to do something that might put them in jeopardy, come election time. I remember one pro-life senator whom I had asked to co-sponsor the Woman's Right to Know bill, which gave women access to all the pertinent information regarding their unborn child and the help available to them. Even though I had shown him evidence that more than eight out of ten people in the state wanted such a law, he was hesitant. By the way, commissioning a poll with a local university or firm trusted by the legislature is a good first step toward passing such a law. But all of this didn't seem to matter to him. He saw the news and feared for his job.

I need to vent for just a minute. Some people in office are such incredible wimps! They say they're pro-life, yet when you ask them to do what you elected them to do, they're afraid. I have often wanted to ask them, "If you're afraid to vote to pass the kind of laws you said you wanted when you ran for office, just exactly *why* did you run? For a fancy office in the Capitol or in Washington? That may be one of your personal goals, but you'll excuse me if that doesn't quite motivate me to go out and knock on doors for you." I feel a little better finally being able to say that. Thanks.

With this atmosphere of fear and trepidation, we needed to do something. We decided to show our strength in a giant rally. We had a "Rally of Hope" in downtown Columbus and formed a coalition with every pro-family/pro-life group in the state to help. On Saturday, October 28, 1989 people from all over Ohio came by the busload and backed up traffic on the freeway for miles. Each person brought a letter (more effectively called "a note"—it doesn't seem as overwhelming that way) for their representative and state senator. Many wrote their notes on the busses with the stationery we provided for them. When they got to the rally, they eagerly bought up pro-life buttons to commemorate the event. We had a lot to sell because the pro-aborts went to *a pro-life printer* for their buttons, who turned around and used the proceeds from that transaction to print us twice as many pro-life buttons for FREE. I thought that worked out nicely.

The pro-abortion crowd held a rally of its own the following day. Now, imagine you are in our shoes—you know what you need to accomplish, and you know what the media is likely to do (see chapter 10 on the media). What do you do? We rented a plane to take pictures of the two rallies. We gave these aerial photos to every state legislator and member of Congress, along with the press—because our rally totally blew their rally away! When an ABC affiliate says we had 30,000 people . . . well you have to know we had *at least* that much! (I think to determine pro-life crowd size, the media usually divides by a factor of ten!) One of the legislators, pro-life Democrat Jerry Luebbers, overwhelmed with the crowd said, "This is about the most moving experience I have ever had in my life. We have a pro-life majority in the General Assembly, but we must keep it."[1]

We had a room completely filled with pro-life letters that volunteers sorted, boxed, and helped deliver to the legislators. I still remember one Senator who said, "I pride myself on answering every letter I get. If you'd just give me my letters from that box of yours, I'd be happy to answer them."

To which I responded, "No, Senator, this *whole box* is for you, as well as the two in the hallway." Our message was sent so loudly that the very next year, after we proved ourselves in the elections, that same "pro-life" senator who was afraid to sign on our Woman's Right to Know Law the previous year had a change of heart. He eagerly grabbed his pen saying, "I don't know why *anyone* wouldn't sign onto a bill like this!" I just said, "Me either, Senator, me either."

Breakfast

I then met with a state representative (who wasn't pro-life) on that same bill. I asked him to co-sponsor the bill to insure that women received accurate scientific information on the medical complications associated with abortion and childbirth, along with information on the developing child and available help. The bill also contained a 24-hour waiting period for women to consider the information they've received. His response was one of disgust, "You people just want women to feel guilty for having an abortion! If I wanted to be like you I could tell my daughter not to have breakfast every day—and the only thing that would accomplish is that every time she had breakfast, she would feel guilty."

I asked, "Wouldn't a better way be to tell your daughter all of the medical advantages of eating breakfast, and give her that information in enough time to make up her mind about whether or not to have breakfast?" (just like our bill would do on abortion). He told me he had to think about it.

I responded, "I understand your need to think about it—a decision as important as whether or not to co-sponsor a significant piece of legislation I think deserves at least . . . 24 hours. How about I check back with you at this time tomorrow?" He ended up co-sponsoring the bill—and then voted against it. I hope he doesn't do that with his breakfast.

We should make more use of their inconsistencies. The good news is that they are always there. Representative Jim Buchy, one of our good pro-life friends in the House, made a point of this during the floor debate. I passed it onto him, but originally stole it from an attorney friend of mine, Pat Perotti, who said, "If your wife purchases ten dollars worth of Tupperware, the state of Ohio is so concerned about her purchase that they give her, not 24 hours, but *three days* in which to change her mind. Isn't the decision about whether or not to abort your child at least as important as whether or not to buy a lettuce keeper?"

Tattoos: Making Hay of Hypocrisy

After serving as the chief lobbyist for Ohio Right to Life for nine years, I saw a lot of legislation pass—but none quite like our Parental Consent Law. On Tuesday, September 9, 1997, my last day at Ohio Right to Life, I was given an incredible going-away present: the passage of three pro-life bills—including a surprise floor amendment that turned our Parental Notification law into Parental Consent (before a minor could get an abortion).

It all started with a bit of research down in the bill room. As it turns out, just a few months prior, *every single* pro-abortion legislator in the Ohio

General Assembly had voted for a parent's permission (or consent) to be obtained before a minor could get a *tattoo or body piercing*. What a bunch of hypocrites—these legislators, including the sponsor of the Tattoo bill, wanted parents to have to give permission before their daughter could get a *tattoo*—but not before she could have an *abortion!*

Now legislators think, and are very often correct in doing so, that no one will remember their votes or hold them accountable for them. I know there were many who said to themselves, "I cast that vote four months ago—so no one's going to remember it, right?"

Well, *I* remembered.

So I went to my favorite novelty store and purchased some temporary tattoos—one for each legislator and for members of the esteemed press. I printed up a flyer that read: "Parental Consent for Tattoos and *Not Abortion?*" And I listed the name of every representative who voted for parental consent for tattoos. I stapled the tattoos on the corner of each of the flyers, along with instructions for application, and gave them to Representative Ron Hood who sat on the floor of the House waiting for the right moment to unveil them.

On that day we passed our first pro-life bill to take abortion out of state employees' health insurance (we wanted to get the government out of abortion, after all), and introduced a bill to close up the loopholes in our Woman's Right to Know bill (informed consent). After a few minutes of debate on this bill, Representative Jim Jordan surprised them with his Parental Consent floor amendment. *This was just not done. A major bill of this kind certainly had to be referred to committee for weeks and weeks of lengthy hearings!* It was unheard of. "Sooo?" I really liked Jim's way of looking at things.

We waited for the floor debate to get going: pro-abortion legislators were saying, "This is terrible! Parents shouldn't interfere with their daughter's right to choose what to do with their own body!" "How dare we give parents a right to do such a thing?"

In the middle of this outrage and indignation, Ron Hood looked up

at me in the balcony and mouthed, "Now?" I nodded, "Yeah, now." The flyers were passed out throughout the entire House . . . and the atmosphere of
the State House quickly transformed. As the legislators began getting their
colored flyers, they began laughing. Some turned around to others who had
not gotten theirs yet, while others began comparing tattoos! Some of them
started putting the tattoos on—but all scanned the list to look for their name.

In the midst of the uproar, Representative June Lucas, a pro-abortion woman from Youngstown and the sponsor of the Tattoo bill, was standing—microphone in hand—ready to speak out fervently against *our* Parental
Consent abortion bill. She then saw what was coming around and suddenly
lost her desire to speak to the amendment, and immediately sat back down.

The pro-lifers were in their glory. One of our legislators stood up
and said, "Look at the hypocrisy. You mean to tell me that you think a tattoo
is more significant, more important for parents to be informed of, than a sur-
gery that could take her life, that could leave her sterile, that takes her unborn
child? It seems to me your vote is purely political." One pro-abortion legislator later confided that when she got the flyer with the tattoo on it, she said,
"Oh, [expletive], now we have to vote for it." Without this little stunt she
would have gotten away with her hypocrisy. The headlines *would have* talked
about the poor state employees losing their right to abort their children. But
that is not what happened. Temporary tattoos helped to change the outcome.
They also made my last day at Ohio Right to Life a very enjoyable one.

Fetal Homicide

A show of strength and creativity are important for success in the
legislature, but the most important factor for victory is persistence. Even
when you do everything right, you can expect a crisis that puts it all in jeopardy at every turn. That is where we were with a bill against "fetal homicide."

A man by the name of Joe Daly, from Cincinnati, had just lost his
wife and nine-month unborn child in a car accident when someone in a stolen
car, driving the wrong way on the highway, hit them head-on. The legislature
was ready to act, but the bill only would protect unborn children who were
viable (old enough to survive outside the womb).

We felt it was critical that in an area where we *could* constitutionally protect unborn children against outside attackers who were *not* abortionists that we do it right. If we didn't, not only would those younger children not be protected, but it also would have sent a signal to the courts that Ohio didn't really care about them. We didn't want them thinking that when we *could* legally protect them, we chose not to.

After doing some research I found out about a woman in the northern part of the state who had just lost her unborn daughter in a similar tragedy—only her little girl was between 20 and 23 weeks along. She testified compellingly before the committee, while making the point that her loss was no less tragic because the baby she lost was younger and not yet able to survive outside the womb.

In addition to compelling testimony, we also had an incredible committee chairman, Representative (now Senator) Lynn Watchman. He told the press about laws on the books against vandalism that protect against such things as someone spray-painting your property. "My *garage door* has more protection than my unborn child," he said.

But the folks from NARAL, didn't want women and their unborn children protected under *any* circumstances—even against an intentional assault. They announced that if the legislature voted on this, "THERE WILL BE A BLOODBATH."[2] An idle threat they couldn't deliver on, but legislators aren't often known for their courage.

I was called in by a few of the *pro-life* legislators from the committee for a "frank discussion" on the "reality" of the situation. I was told that, while they may agree with the concept, a bill that protected the unborn from conception was for "another time."

When I disagreed, I was asked, "Well, *who* are you going to get to *introduce* your amendment?"

"Ron Hood." As best as my non-verbal communication skills could interpret, their reaction most closely resembled, "[expletive] we forgot about *him!*" What they *said* was, "That's right, he's on that committee—isn't he?" And with the support of our chairman, that amendment was going to get a vote! Those pro-life members were going to *have* to vote for it, or be on record against it—not something they would have wanted to face at re-election, I'm sure.

We had called their bluff and had won. And a "bloodbath?" Not even a scratch. They didn't have the votes. It wasn't even close.

The Winning Team

Re-election is usually the most important thing on a legislator's mind. With that in mind, I had some T-shirts and buttons printed for the day of the brain-suction abortion vote (now called partial-birth abortion—are you catching on to this yet?). It was the line drawing of a four-fifths delivered baby being given a partial-birth abortion with the words: "Does Your Legislator Support *This?*" I know for a fact that legislators looked at those T-shirts and buttons and saw what the campaign literature would look like if they didn't vote our way. And they were right. The Ohio House vote was 82-15. It did the job.

It's a good idea to fill the gallery and committee hearings with your people—and an easy way to show they're with you is to have them wear the same button. Legislators need to feel that they are with the winning team. We just have to make sure that's the case come election time as well.

Focus

When you're lobbying it's important to keep your focus. Legislators will want to talk about everything else under the sun except the way they are going to vote on your bill. As Zig Ziglar has often said in sales seminars: If you don't *close* the sale, you're really nothing more than a "professional visitor." Whether you win or lose really depends on how well you "close the sale" and count the votes.

One thing I learned early on is that "positive talk about your bill" doesn't count when the votes are cast. You must have a firm commitment from a majority—and often votes to spare for unexpected surprises that come up so often, that, well, they're not really unexpected.

As a vote draws near, time becomes more valuable and distractions more plentiful, but you must maintain focus. The media will often try to get you on camera right before a vote is taken because of their (often-contrived) "deadline." But no matter how far ahead you are in votes, spend every minute you have making sure of that outcome. I would much rather win the vote and not be on the news, than be on the news about a loss.

This focus and persistence also takes away all regret. You never have that plaguing "if I just would have done a little more, we could have won." Do everything you can *before the vote,* and you can sleep at night knowing you did your best no matter what the outcome.

On one particularly busy day one legislator just wanted to "shoot the breeze"—something I didn't have time for until after I lined up my votes. He asked, "Why would we want to reverse *Wade v. Roe* anyway?" Rather than taking the rest of the afternoon to tell him about a decision he obviously didn't know much about, I simply said, "You *just did,* sir." He heard my full line of reasoning later that day. Distractions can kill you.

This brings to mind a barely related story of when my friend Susie G. and I were working the pro-life booth at the Ohio State Fair. We were late getting there and were hurrying to find it when a man from the *Encyclopedia Britannica* booth called out to us to show us his books. We explained to him that we couldn't stop by right then because we were in a hurry. He told us it "would only take a minute," and when we told him we didn't really have a minute, he got angry. He looked at Susie's "BUSH/QUAYLE" T-shirt and shouted "CLINTON!" She, without a second thought, looked at the man with his *Encyclopedia Britannica* collection, and said, "WORLD BOOK!" I guess you can use whatever works.

Where It Begins

Finally, pro-life state representatives, governors, U.S. congressmen and senators don't just come out of nowhere. Where do they get started? The same place pro-abortion officeholders begin their careers: city and county-wide elected offices, as well as local school and hospital boards. Many begin by running for a seat on their party's county and state central committee—the group that endorses candidates and, as a result, decide many elections before the public ever votes. This is where candidates earn their credentials and name recognition—and make critical decisions that affect life and the family!

While people consider them unimportant, it's in these positions where the decisions are made that affect policy and how laws are implemented. For example, if the state passes a law that says we should teach abstinence in the schools, it's the school board that can undermine the whole thing by putting pro-abortion groups like Planned Parenthood in charge of carrying it out. You see? This is where we need pro-lifers the most! And because this is the launching pad for higher office, by filling these positions with pro-life majorities, we are doing the very best thing to assure pro-life majorities in our statehouses and in Congress!

And because the fewest people vote for local offices, they are the easiest to win. Some pro-lifers have formed committees of their own for the purpose of finding pro-lifers to run for the central committees and local offices. I strongly recommend this. This is how we will win.

It all begins by activating your pro-life groups, your church, and neighborhood to make the difference where you live. Don't overlook pro-life teens—they want to make a difference, and this is one of the very best ways they can. If you're interested in getting started, contact your board of elections to see what offices are available. Contact your county party central committee, talk to those already in office, and give us a call at the CENTER FOR RECLAIMING AMERICA; we're here to help you.

Strength begins at the local level with those so-called "unimportant" offices. In order to gain legislative victory, that strength must be demonstrated at the ballot box and then reinforced in the legislature. Creativity adds to your effectiveness (and your fun), but the most important factor for victory is persistence.

Don't forget that you are in a spiritual battle—and you should expect to be attacked. Satan doesn't have to worry about the people who aren't making a difference. So even when you do everything right, expect a crisis that puts it all in jeopardy. But focus, and never give up until the vote has been taken. Remember, win or lose, votes in the legislature and at the ballot box can always be reversed.

10
The Media

Y ou hear a lot about the violence supposedly perpetrated by "pro-lifers," but do you ever hear about the attacks *on pro-lifers*? On Friday, May 13, 1994, the banner headline on the front page of *The Cleveland Plain Dealer* read: "Right to Life leader's car sabotaged. Odds are, [the fire] is connected to abortion issue, police say." That was my car.

The Columbus Dispatch, incidentally, ran *their* seven-sentence story about it on page 5-C. Why would they bury a story on violence against a pro-lifer so far back? It must have been a busy news day—right? Well, page 3-A on the same day carried a story with the headline: "Jury ponders rights to glow-in-the-dark lingerie." I'm sure that if a jury was pondering such an important issue on the same day as an attack on an abortion clinic, they'd push the abortion-related attack to page 5-C too—right?

I had paid only $8,000 for my white 1987 Porsche—lest you think your donations to the pro-life cause are going for big salaries. But I loved that car. I was planning on driving to speak at a fundraiser in Cincinnati for a pro-life Democrat leader in the Ohio House. I pulled out of my driveway and saw a trail of fire behind me. Then smoke and flames started billowing from under the hood so I jumped out of my car. By the time I called the fire department, they were already on their way. I can still see the men taking a hatchet to open the hood of my beloved car while I stood there in shock saying, "You know, it *has* a latch." Needless to say, the car was totaled.

The bumper sticker on the back said, "Abortion? Pick on someone your own size." One that apparently somebody took seriously. I had files full

This is what was left of my beloved car. The photo ran in newspapers, including the *Cleveland Plain Dealer* **and** *Los Angeles Times.* **(Photo by Chris Kasson)**

of hate mail, death threats, and a stalker, but I never really took too much of it seriously . . . until then. I remember being awakened by noises near my garage the night before it happened—the only time I had ever actually gotten out of bed to check on a noise since moving into my Columbus home—something I did every night for the next two months. I went unlisted as the security system, motion lights, and caller ID were installed.

A local Associated Press photographer called me to go with him for a photo shoot of the burned-out car, which was now sitting in a junk yard about 30 minutes away. Afterwards he told me how much he had dreaded his assignment. He had whined to his editor, "What? I have to ride with some pro-lifer for 30 minutes? Aggghhh!" Of course he had a pre-conceived image from the media of what pro-lifers were like and was certain he would hate me. He said, "I have to tell you: you are nothing like I'd thought you'd be. I never expected you to be . . . cool." We became friends—something he never in his wildest dreams imagined possible.

The reason for telling this story is to reiterate the point that the media doesn't know us. With few exceptions, they have no pro-life friends, and chances are very good they don't even *know* anyone who is pro-life. And in order for them to like us, they need to get to know us. We need to go to lunch with them and get to know each other. We need to communicate with them and let them know when they do things fairly—as well as when they don't.

Having said that, in working with the media it's important to know some of the basics. For those of you who have been living in a cave, the first is: *The media is biased.*

The Media Elite

Who are the people that control the media? The *Lichter-Rothman* report on the "media elite" provides us with a definitive profile. S. Robert Lichter is a research professor in political science at George Washington University. Stanley Rothman is a professor of government at Smith College. Linda Lichter is co-director (along with Robert Lichter) of the Center for Media and Public Affairs in Washington, D.C. They did an important survey of 104 of the "most influential television writers, producers, and executives," which found—as could be expected—that these were very liberal people.[1]

- Ninety-three percent "say they seldom or never attend religious services."
- Seventy-five percent "describe themselves as left of center politically, compared to only 14 percent who place themselves to the right of center."
- **Ninety-seven percent "believe that 'a woman has the right to decide for herself' whether to have an abortion."**
- Eighty percent "do not regard homosexual feelings as wrong."
- Only 5 percent "agree strongly that homosexuality is wrong, compared to 49 percent who disagree strongly."
- Eighty-six percent "support the rights of homosexuals to teach in public schools."

- Fifty-one percent "do not regard adultery as wrong."
- Only 15 percent "strongly agree that extra-marital affairs are wrong."[2] (Something you might want to keep in mind when deciding who to date).

But unless you have a lot of money to buy media time and space, we must figure out the best way to work effectively *with* them. Being aware of their very real bias can help you make some important decisions. Suppose Channel Six News is coming out to interview you, and they give you a choice of going live or having the interview taped. Which do you choose?

Well, if channel six is the network affiliate, and you don't know the reporter, you want to go live. It's pretty simple, really. The media is biased (see above or watch the news tonight). If I do a twenty-minute interview, I'm pretty sure that some of what I say isn't going to be perfect. Some of what I say may actually be irrelevant or downright stupid. Now imagine you're an editor with a bit of a bias. You could search through twenty minutes of tape and find the worst things said if you really wanted to. Paranoid? I've had it done to me more times than I care to recall.

If you go live, you may say something less than stellar, but it's better than having a biased editor searching through everything you've said to find the worst of it. **Going live means never having to be edited.** Some of my best interviews have been live hook-ups from the newsroom.

If you are doing an interview with your local Christian radio station or with someone you know to be fair, then a taped interview may be preferable. In a twenty-minute interview, they will most often pick out the *best* of what you had to say for their story.

Lessons Learned From the "Truth In Love" Campaign

In the summer of 1998, I coordinated the nationwide "Truth In Love" campaign where we, along with 17 other pro-family organizations, communicated to homosexuals that there is hope for change through Jesus Christ—as thousands have already discovered and left that lifestyle. I thought I had seen bias before, but it was only the tip of the iceberg. To give you an idea of what it was like, *Newsweek's* first question to me was, "How long have you known that you were a heterosexual?" It went down hill from there.

As you might have guessed by the book, the right-to-life issue has always been closest to my heart. Imagine you are doing the very first television show you have ever done on the subject . . . on *Nightline*. That's where I was . . . on the subject of homosexuality. Like I said before, I get all the *easy* jobs at the CENTER FOR RECLAIMING AMERICA.

I had recommended several *other* people to do the show instead of me when they called. I felt, and still feel that there's no one better to discuss this issue than a *former* homosexual—they are living proof that change is possible. But *Nightline* insisted that they had to have *me*—because I was coordinating the campaign.

While there are several things I would have changed about my July, 1998 *Nightline* appearance, there were *some* things that couldn't be changed. First, counting the host it was two against one. Nothing new there. But what was *most distressing* was that when I watched *Nightline* that evening, I couldn't believe it—they actually *edited out* the good things I *did* say.

For example, when I made the statement that homosexuality is dangerous behavior, my opponent said I was wrong, I then responded by citing the U.S. Centers for Disease Control, which reported that 65 percent of all AIDS cases in this country come as a direct result of homosexual sex. But guess what *Nightline* did? They left in my opponent's charge and *selectively* edited *just MY RESPONSE to it*—making it look like I was stating an opinion, rather than a fact![3]

At another time in the program I was accused of working with a man that supposedly "wants the death penalty for homosexuals." I responded, "Not only is that NOT what I believe," and "NOT what the campaign is about" but "I have NEVER even HEARD of this guy you say I'm working with!" *Just my RESPONSE WAS EDITED OUT*—making it appear that I was trying to dodge the question.

If that's the kind of thing they do to *everybody* they disagree with— it's a wonder we're still in this debate at all!

I had experienced being edited before—like the time I went up against some lovely ladies on *Jerry Springer* with an at-home abortion kit (that was before they started throwing chairs in the show). Honestly, I wasn't all that surprised when Jerry Springer edited out the best thing I said. After all— it was *Jerry Springer.* (I was just relieved that I didn't have any surprises, like my boyfriend admitting he was a cross-dresser). I had just made the point that for every abortion clinic in my state (Ohio at the time) there were FOUR 'Pregnancy Help Centers' where women could turn to for *free* help. A woman from the audience commented that she had "heard about those deceptive pregnancy centers" that tried to "trick" women into not having an abortion.

My response was this: "If you're looking through the yellow pages and you're not sure if you're looking at an abortion facility or a pregnancy help center, here's a quick rule of thumb: If there's any reference to VISA or Mastercard—or if money changes hands, that's abortion. Our services are *free.* And I think that speaks very clearly as to who it is that cares about women." It never made it on the air. Color me surprised.

But even Jerry Springer edited *both* of these comments out instead of just *my* response. Had they left her accusation stand while taking out my reply, it would have appeared that I had agreed with what she was saying. That's what *Nightline* did. Good thing I'm not bitter about it. Suffice it to say, after that *Nightline* interview I wasn't anxious to do another one any time soon.

My friend Evan called me the morning after the show and I told him I wanted to give up. "What's the use?" I asked him, "Forget about the two-against one scenario—just *how* do you go up against an edit machine?"

That's when he told me about "the Coach." Evan said, "Janet, when a runner is on first base—how does the runner know when to go to second? What the first base runner does is *look at the coach*. It's the coach who tells you when to run, when to stay, and when to steal a base. The coach is where your focus must be. You can't be standing on first base thinking about how biased the umpires are. You can't be looking at the scoreboard seeing how badly you're losing. You can't think about the time you struck out or look at the people jeering at you in the stands. *You have to focus on the coach.*"

"The coach," he said, "is God."

"God is going to tell you when to stay. God is going to tell you when to run. He's going to tell you when to steal." Well, O.K. Maybe God won't tell you when to *steal*—but you get the idea!

Our focus must be on Him. If we seek God first, the rest will be added unto us. Focus on the Coach, and do your best—we're not responsible for the umpires.

A few weeks later, the *Cleveland Plain Dealer* called and asked if they could run a feature on me for their magazine section. I was a bit on the hesitant side—especially after *Nightline*—but after weeks of coaxing by the reporter and looking at some of his previous articles, and after multiple assurances of his fairness, I agreed.

I can still remember sitting across from reporter Michael Heaton at a Fort Lauderdale beach restaurant as he told me a little more about himself. That's where he informed me that he had been kicked out of Kent State School of Journalism—for "being too *liberal.*"

I couldn't believe what I had just heard, "You have to be kidding."

"Nope."

I said, "You know, that might have been something you could have mentioned *before* flying down for an interview." Somehow, he didn't think it was relevant.

He actually turned out to be fair. I let him sit in on some commercials we were filming, and he talked to everyone I worked with. I told him I was tempted to have various people come up to me during the day thanking me *for helping to talk them off the ledge*, get them off the bottle, as well as for all my efforts at the soup kitchen and homeless shelters. I think he would have seen through that anyway.

We had lunch the next week in Cleveland at my favorite restaurant of all, the Courtyard—best ribs you will ever have. Hey, if the reporter's buying, you may as well go where you want. I felt comfortable that, despite that initial frightening disclosure, he was going to be fair. So when he stepped away from the table, I grabbed his notebook and wrote, "I have come to realize that Janet Folger is right on all the issues and we should all join her in her efforts to reclaim America." He found it later and was pretty sure he didn't write that. He wrote:

> Folger is smart. She has a quick, self-deprecating sense of humor and is media-savvy to the point of wariness. She gives seminars to fellow religious right members on how to handle reporters and asks interviewers to submit examples of their work to her before agreeing to talk with them.[4]

He also included some pretty good stuff from my friends, including a quote by State Rep. Ed Kasputis: "Out of 600 lobbyists in Columbus, she was by far the hardest working and most effective," he said . . . "When Janet Folger goes to work, God smiles."[5] I didn't have much of a reason to put that in this book, but if someone said that about you—wouldn't you put it in your book?

What to Watch For

I've been told that one of Barbara Walters' favorite interview techniques is to wait before asking another question. If she isn't satisfied with a person's answer, she will wait up to one full minute before asking another question. The person will answer the question in a different way or continue talking, just to avoid silence—and that's when they mess up. Another frequently used technique is to re-ask the same question in different ways in hopes that you will say something different—even just for variety's sake. ABC's Jackie Judd once asked me the same question six times. She was looking for her pre-determined sound-bite. I knew it and wasn't going to give it to her.

These are two techniques used by the pros to make you slip up and say something stupid. From there, you've got about a 98 percent chance of watching that particular quote on the news that night. I have had that happen to me a couple of hundred times. On one particular day I decided this was not going to happen again. I told myself, "No matter what happens, I'm going to say only what I want to air." This particular interview was on the Woman's Right to Know Bill.

It is critical that you know your sound-bites—usually two or three main points of the issue you are discussing said in a short, poignant way. The message I wanted out in the media was that we were trying to "give women access to accurate scientific information." That's what we wanted to do. The other side was trying to block them from getting that information. I was determined there would be no way they would deter me from getting that word out. Forget about what they ask you. Say what you want to say. I did not care if they asked me, "What kind of car do you drive?" I was going to give them my answer: "It's not really what kind of car I drive that's important as much as it is that I get into that car and drive down to the Statehouse to ensure women access to accurate scientific information."

The *Athens News* ran a story about that interview (April 2, 1992) which said, "The Statehouse lobbyist for Ohio's Right to Life Society has perfected the art of being interviewed by news reporters. She's taken to new heights the tactic some newsmakers have used for years—no matter what questions reporters ask, answer as if they've posed the only question you WANT to be asked. And keep giving the same response over and over again. Even when the questions change . . . when asked to respond, Folger said that criticism of the booklet is off-base because the photos and facts about fetal development are 'scientifically accurate.' Then, during a nine-minute interview she repeated the phrase 25 more times. She got her point across. Reporters had to use it—it was the only point she made."

Sometimes a written statement is the only way to go. A reporter who worked for the *Dayton Daily News* (who has since moved on to the *Cleveland Plain Dealer*) is someone I affectionately refer to as the "Misquote Queen." After our Rally of Hope, we took aerial shots of both our rally as well as the pro-abortion rally the following day and sent the photos to the press. After all, a picture is worth a thousand protesters—sometimes even more.

Her approach was rather unique, considering it was coming from someone who is at least supposed to be operating under the *guise* of objectivity: "So what are you saying Janet? You're lording the notion that your little rally beat them in some *contest?*"

Here I'm speaking to 30,000 people in our Rally of Hope in October of 1989. "Na Na Na-Na Na."

Let me preface my response by saying that some things are better spoken than they appear in print. Now think of that little sing-songy phrase you used to use when you were a kid making fun of your sister. Got it? In print it looks like this: "Na Na Na-Na Na." Like the word, "Duh," this is not something you ever want attributed to your name. She asked her question, and I responded with the first thing that came to mind, "No, we're not saying, Na Na Na-Na Na, our rally beat theirs, we are just looking for accuracy." So another winning quote from Janet Folger made the front page. By now you have to be wondering just how I kept my job.

That part was not supposed to be for print. But if you say it, it's fair game. Remember that.

Another day I was watching the outcome of hearings on the "constitutionality" of our legislation in state court. We lost at the initial level. The press were there to get my reaction, but this day I was ready for them. I had prepared two releases—one for each outcome—and handed out the version for a defeat. I finished talking to several reporters when I was approached by the Misquote Queen. Having just experienced the little "Na Na Na" incident, I wasn't very anxious to see her. Friends of mine were still asking me, "Hey Folger, what's with the Na Na Na? Shouldn't there be a Doo-wop in there?"

There was no way I was going to give her anything beyond what was already in writing. If it's in writing, it's a bit tougher to distort. I gave her a copy of my written statement and told her that everything was there. She asked a question and I told her *again* that everything was right there in writing. That wasn't good enough for her; she was not going to leave without my saying something about the case (which she could then distort). So whatever question she asked me, I responded by pointing to the exact words on the printed page as I spoke them. "But how do you feel about the judge's ruling? Are you going to give up or start all over from scratch?" Then I would point to the words as I read them, "We are very optimistic that the judge's ruling will be reversed by the Court of Appeals. . . ." Like I said, it was all there. Sometimes a written statement is the only way to go. And, by the way, the decision *was* reversed by the Court of Appeals.

Tips for Dealing With the Media

Are you involved in a pro-life organization? Well, if you're not, what are you waiting for? You were invited to join one in chapter four. Here are some tips I've picked up along the way that just might be of use to you.

Draw them in: <u>Give Exclusives Occasionally</u>. If you want to get your message across, you have to give them a reason to listen to you. I had just received the candidates survey from our flip-flopper gubernatorial candidate, who went from being pro-life to advocating sex-selection abortions at taxpayer expense. I called a friend at the *Columbus Dispatch* and offered him the exclusive. Rather than have it faxed, he came to get it from me personally. The next day the front page of the paper had a graphic that could not have been better if we had made it ourselves. In comparison to our pro-life candidate, it outlined how the pro-abortion candidate was against parental consent, informed consent, and testing to see if the child could survive, as well as being *for* abortion, *for* sex-selection, and tax-payer funding.

Be Persistent. Send your press releases often and early. Make follow-up calls—make sure you call the morning of the event to give the press time to respond.

Be Credible. Make sure you have source material and proof to back up every statement you make. Use your opponent's evidence against them and look for flaws in their logic.

You Say Where and When. If you know they need the story, and you're the only one they can get it from, don't let them dictate—you say where and when. After the *Webster* Supreme Court decision, which was a major victory for the pro-life movement, we knew they would be coming to us for a comment. The only way they were going to get it was under our terms. We wanted to focus on the help going to women—so our news conference was held at the Pregnancy Distress Center to put the focus on how we "love them both—the mother and the child." When reporters called saying they "needed" their sound-bite before 10:00, we told them we would be issuing our statement at 10:00—and there was nothing we could do before that. It worked. Reporters saw a loving, helpful, hopeful image of women who had been helped and babies who had been saved—something they never would have seen otherwise.

Don't Let Them Bully You. After a different Supreme Court decision, another television crew wanted our comment. The reporter set up an appointment with me in an hour from the time she called. About four minutes later I got a call from her cell-phone, *"We're right outside your office; we need a comment and we'll be up in two minutes."*

If you're not ready, make them wait. I had been pressured to go on before I was ready—and regretted it. I wasn't about to do it again. I have also learned that the early wire releases (and many times, the later ones) are often far from accurate. It is ill-advised to give a comment before talking to someone on your side (preferably an attorney) who has actually read the case—if you can't get to it yourself, and not just rely on the wire reports. On this day I said, *"You're about forty-five minutes early; here's something for you to watch while you wait.*" I then popped in a tape that showed a late-term abortion called *Eclipse of Reason.* They never came early again.

Take Control. Given the first basic premise (the media is biased), it's a good idea to tape-record your encounters. I remember an interview I had reluctantly agreed to do with a very pro-abortion reporter—who actually became a friend. I had done several radio shows with him as a guest on his program that aired on the news/talk station in town. I had been on the show so many times that on one particular show I suggested on the air that *I* should be given a turn as host one night—to which he agreed! I decided what calls to take and when to let them go. It was a good time. My conditions for the news magazine article were that he would *print* every word I said in response to every question. When he came in with his tape-recorder, I pulled out mine. When my tape ran out, I stopped talking—mid sentence—so that every word would be documented. We laughed about it—but it did the trick. While you rarely can get one, an unedited article is like "going live."

You Pick the Background. Make them film you where you want— they don't like the fetal models behind you? Too bad! Let them know that you aren't inclined to rearrange your office.

Think of the Message You Want to Convey. Again, make the media film you where you want to be filmed. One press conference in Dayton, Ohio, was held in front of the dumpster in an alley behind an abortion clinic. It was where pro-lifers had found the body of what the coroner described as a 16-week-old unborn child. The press conference was to announce the release of lie detector tests of the woman who found the child to expose the truth about what they were doing—and what they were doing with the bodies. The pro-aborts like to talk about "illegal back-alley abortions." A press conference held in the back alley of an abortion mill showed the world how *legal* abortion is every bit as bad.

The best way I can summarize the media is with the 1992 election. I remember watching the morning talk show hosts gloating about Clinton's win, unable to mask their sheer glee as they celebrated the success of their campaign of misinformation. In fact, it wasn't until after Clinton was elected that the media began reporting that the economy was recovering. For example, on November 30, *The New York Times* ran a story that credited Clinton with the recent economic upswing—and he hadn't even taken office yet!"[6] Two years later we saw the most pro-life victories I had ever witnessed. There weren't as many reporters scurrying for my comments *that* election night. On their way to visit Senator DeWine's campaign office in my building, the Misquote Queen, along with several other reporters who couldn't wait to talk to me after the *last* election, stopped on our floor by mistake. The elevator doors opened and they realized they were on the wrong floor. Before the doors could close I remarked: "Not interested in our comments *this election*—huh?"

One reporter took the bait and came back. He said, "O.K. What's *your spin* on the elections?"

I remember the conversation well, "We don't need any spin; the numbers speak for themselves: Thirty pro-abortion incumbents were taken out by pro-life challengers in Congress and governors seats nationwide."

The reporter looked at me with pure skepticism, with sarcasm dripping from every syllable, he asked, "Oh yeah? How many pro-life incumbents were taken out by pro-*choice* challengers?"

I simply responded, "That's easy. ZERO. And that is no coincidence. By the way," I added, "in the most Republican year in memory, did you know that not a SINGLE Ohio Right to Life endorsed *Democrat* incumbent was replaced by a pro-abortion challenger? That included pro-life Democrat Rep. Jerry Luebbers who lives in a 54 percent REPUBLICAN district where nearly $300,000 was spent in the race to take him out."

A Final Comment

Working with the media isn't always a lot of fun, but until we have our own network for news dissemination (if anyone wants to contribute to this effort, please let me know), we have to work with them if we are going to reach people with our message. They buy their ink by the barrel and they reach a whole lot more people than typically come to hear a pro-life speech. They are biased—but that doesn't mean we should give up. We need to insist on fairness up front—but you're not always going to get it. And when we don't, keep focused on the "Coach." He'll show us what to do next.

As many times as we've been burned, it's easy to treat the media with disdain—but they have to know that we're not always against them. We need to call them and tell them when they do something right (even if you have to wait a while to do that!) Just like in the legislature, persistence and credibility are a must. Creativity. It goes without saying—if you can pick a background that fits your message, you're half-way there. And, to the extent possible, exercise as much control as you can.

And remember, as the Ohio motto says, "With God all things are possible." And that includes overcoming the hurdle of a biased media to stop the horror of abortion.

11

The Debate

One of the first rules of debate is to keep your focus. We have the truth and all the facts that back it up—that's why the other side's strongest and most used tactic is to try to get you off the subject of killing babies. They will talk about rape, birth control, violence—they would rather talk about *the weather* than defend their position of legal child dismemberment.

When they hit you with all the reasons a woman "shouldn't have a child," the thing to remember is that if she is pregnant, she already *does have* a child! When they try to pile on the reasons, I try to see if any of those reasons would be valid if the child were already born. After all, there is no magical formula that suddenly makes the child "more human" the moment after he's born than the moment before. Again, it's just a "change of address."

A woman called me on a radio show one time with this beauty: "Do you mean to tell me that if a woman *with six children*, whose *husband leaves her* for a younger woman, who finds out that she's pregnant—and can barely make ends meet—shouldn't have the choice to have an abortion??? Is that what you're telling us?"

My answer? "Let me ask *you* something. If this woman has not six, but *seven* children, *ages two to twenty-two*, and she can barely make ends meet, and her husband leaves her for a younger woman, should she have the choice to kill one of those children ages two to twenty-two? I hate to say it, especially for our younger audience, but it would probably be the *teens* who'd go." Whenever you're not sure how to answer—think of the child as if he were born.

The Trial

I took this—transference from unborn to born—into high school assemblies and workshops and successfully used a mock "trial"—an idea that first originated with Mark Crutcher of Life Dynamics. I get the audience to give me every reason they've ever heard for why we "need" abortion, and I write it on the board, leaving rape, incest, and life of the mother to discuss at another time. I then establish first and foremost that the being in the womb is a human being and that even Planned Parenthood has admitted that fact. With biology book in hand, I ask, "How many in this room, regardless of where you stand on abortion, at *least* agree with science and those in favor of legal abortion, as well as the pro-life community, that the 'being' in the womb is a human being?" While the hands go up, I clarify, "How many of you know it's not a rabbit or a carrot we're talking about—rather it is a member of the human family?" Looking at all the hands, I conclude, "OK. It's a human being."

Another quick show of hands, "How many in the room say we should not discriminate on . . . race?" While they're deciding, "Any racists in the room?" This one's a gimme.

I quickly jump to the next question, "How many think we should not discriminate on . . . age?" Same thing.

So what you've done is you've gotten them to agree that the being in the womb is a human being, and that we shouldn't discriminate based on age. That means that a three-month-old unborn child is no different than a three-year-old child or a thirty-year-old—since we just said that all are human beings, and we don't discriminate on the basis of age.

At this point I pull a guy out of the audience who looks to be a bit on the rowdy side (the kind that points to friends when I'm looking for volunteers). This type is generally more fun. I inform him that he has just killed his three-year-old daughter and ask him to give me his daughter's name. I inform part of the audience (perhaps the first two rows) that they were eyewitnesses to the killing, and the rest of the audience is now going to play the part of the jury. I try to alleviate the alleged killer's fear by informing him that

I am going to be his defense attorney. I swear him in and sit him down.

Addressing the jury, I say, "Yes, my client Mike took the life of his three-year-old daughter Michelle. Yes, it was a killing by dismemberment, but that is not the issue! The issue is that my client had some *very good* reasons for doing what he did." I then proceed down the list they gave me to legitimize abortion: "too young, birth control failed, money, career, parents, world over-population, and the child was handicapped"—reasons that if we're talking about a *born* child just don't cut it.

I then ask the audience if they believe these reasons (even all of them combined) are enough to legitimize my client's dismembering of his three-year-old daughter, Michelle. With "thumbs up for innocent" and "thumbs down for guilty," I ask them to vote. No matter how many reasons are given, they are never quite enough to legitimatize killing a three-year-old. I then ask for a hand for my client and tell him I have some "nice parting gifts."

I then go back to the original point that "if the being in the womb is indeed a human being, as we all agreed, and we don't discriminate against age, as we all agreed, then there is no difference between three-year-old Michelle and a three-month-old *unborn* Michelle."

I can't think of any other exercises that have proven as effective. I once spoke to a youth group in Michigan where one girl who was very vocally pro-abortion protested my even coming. I was told that this "trial" changed her mind. I like using it because you can have fun with the kids while you make your point.

Incidentally, I can't let this section go without giving you a summary of Mark Crutcher's answer to the question, "How are we going to feed these children when millions are already starving?" His answer makes the transfer to a "born" person:

"I will agree with you that when you kill someone, he's no longer hungry. And when you think about it, *if we are* going to use death as a way to address the problem of hunger, why kill *babies?* Adults eat a lot more! In fact, we could solve many other problems with this very same approach—prison overpopulation, unemployment. . . ."

My memory may not have done it justice, but his was the most effective answer I have ever heard to this question.

Losing the Debate Before It Begins

Kent State was bringing in a pro-abortion speaker and called me and said, "Janet, we would like you to sit on a panel following a speaker from the ACLU who will be doing a forty-minute presentation."

I responded, "Well, let me ask you . . . who else is on the panel?"

"There'll be someone there from Planned Parenthood and the speaker, of course, and a representative from Students for Choice as well"—it was 3 to 1.

We're so anxious to get our message out that I think we too often jump at every little crumb we're thrown, whether it's a level playing field or not. I told her, "No, I'm not interested. Now, if you want to put on a *fair* program, *that's* something I might be interested in."

She knew she had to get someone from our side to give the appearance of objectivity—otherwise, she might not get to bring her speaker in with university money. Not at all pleased with the prospect of giving me more than the bare minimum to get me to agree to participate, she relented, "Well, what would you *need* to come?"

Then I rattled off exactly what I wanted, "I'd like 20 minutes of the ACLU's 40-minute presentation, and I'd like two pro-lifers to join me—someone from Lawyers for Life and someone from Students for Life."

She agreed.

But I was feeling a little cocky just then, and I said, "Oh, yes, and I'd like an honorarium."

Disgusted, she asked, "How much?"

I knew they were bringing in their speaker from Washington (she's been on *Crossfire* and CNN) and I knew they were paying her big bucks. The normal pro-life response is: "Well, if you could cover my gas money and maybe the cost of making some copies, that would be really great." Instead, I said, "I'll just have what she's having; that would be fine." That was a $2,000 honorarium that went to Ohio Right to Life.

When we're asked to speak on terms that put us at a disadvantage, we should just say no. Another thing I've learned, unfortunately by experience, is that there is no such thing as an "objective third party"—or "objective legal scholar." If the news channel or debate committee wants someone like that to sit in on the show or be on the panel, fight it at all costs. Remember the first point from the last chapter: the media is biased. That holds for most universities, too. If one of them is putting on your event, it would be the same as what KSU's offer was: three against one, in which the moderator, the pro-abort, and the "objective third party" are all teamed up against you. I've been there and it's not all that much fun.

Alone versus together? My experience is that <u>two separate presentations</u> always beat a battle where you can't get a word in.

I have found that the debate format is not the best way to get our message out. Your opponents can tell more lies in their allotted time slot than you can refute in yours. If you have a say at all, I would strongly recommend that you do separate presentations. The only advantage of a debate is that you can often draw more of an audience from the curious middle-of-the-road folks. But I would far rather take every question from the audience—hecklers included—and have adequate time to respond than I would to debate. In fact, I often tell pro-life university groups to design their flyers with things like: "Bring your toughest questions!" That seems to draw them in—without giving up the control. You see, when you have the truth *and the time to tell it*, it doesn't matter what you are asked.

I think perhaps the best show I ever did was when I was on alone and took the hostile calls, one after the other, on the News/Talk station in Columbus, Ohio. I remember that day very well—it was a lot of fun. A woman phoned in and called me a liar—insisting that there were no abortions performed in Columbus after 18 weeks, to which I responded with the yellow pages. "If you'll look at page 37 of the yellow pages you will find advertisements for abortions at 20 weeks; on page 38, there's one for abortions at 22 weeks, 24 weeks." You get the idea.

On that same show an abortionist called to inform the listeners that

I was lying to everyone. We didn't need the "Woman's-Right-to-Know law" (informed-consent legislation I was advocating), because women in her clinic were "very well informed" by a nifty brochure they handed out called "Point/Counterpoint."

For some reason I had that little piece of propaganda with me that day and began to read from it on the air. It listed the fetal ages by weeks and the descriptions were in *inches and grams,* which meant that a woman who was 12 weeks pregnant would know nothing about the fact that her developing child had a beating heart (18 days), measurable brainwaves (40 Days), and that every part and every organ of that child was complete and functioning (8 weeks). Even the lungs are working by breathing in fluid (11-12 weeks).[1]

To say "we don't think you can handle this, so we're going to keep you in the dark" is completely anti-women. How insulting it is to say, "women are so frail and so fragile that we can't give them the facts!" Women can't be hurt by accurate information, but the abortion industry can. To oppose "informed consent" legislation isn't "pro-choice" either. One needs *information* to make a choice. You see, when you're standing on the truth, as long as you keep your focus, it doesn't matter what they ask. What this format gives you is adequate time to respond.

Ask and Expect to Get It

Ask for questions ahead of time. I think your attitude has a lot to do with the outcome. I have found that the "assumptive close" works very well. I was to debate the issue of assisted suicide on a Fox affiliate station and wanted to know what the questions were going to be. Many times we do not have because we do not ask. I merely said, "Can you just fax them over?"

They did! That gave me adequate time to prepare an answer to this little ditty: "Janet, let me read a quote I read from a local paper: 'We are talking about bodies that may just become like animals because the mind is gone. Those who help a sick pet or a terminally ill person die are committing an act of love.' What's your response to that?"

I wasn't sure of the best response to that, so I called Rita Marker from the International Anti-Euthanasia Task Force, an excellent group in Steubenville, Ohio. Rita gave me this answer which made me look brilliant and spontaneous: "People do not become animals when they become ill. Sometimes people act like animals the way they *treat* sick people." All because I had the questions ahead of time—and friends I could get counsel from.

By the way, this has also worked with those journalistic television standard-bearers, *Hard Copy* and *Extra*. They were interviewing me on another subject, but I remembered this principle. We befriended the camera crew that was sympathetic to us, and they said, "Sure! Go ahead and take a look (at the questions)!" That meant we were ready. I don't know why they don't do this anyway; it only helps them to have a better sound-bite and a better show! When we got a call to appear on *Extra*, we asked for the questions ahead of time, but were told, "We don't do that." My response? "Well, *Hard Copy* was just here, and *they* did." I acted like I might not do the interview otherwise, and a few minutes later, they were coming through the fax.

Ask to respond. Call when you see a biased story . . . in enough time for them to correct it. This one is pretty basic, yet few people actually do it. I woke up one morning and heard Kevorkian quoted in the news. There was no response from our side given . . . until I called them up, that is. We often do not have because we do not ask.

The same thing applies to print. Very often when we see a full spread editorial against us, we timidly ask, "Would it be OK if I responded with a letter to the editor?" Ask for a full article in the opinions/editorial section. I have found the ass*umptive close* works best: *"How many words are you looking for in an op-ed* piece?" It works—and even if it doesn't, what have you lost by asking? You have probably increased your chances of at least getting your letter printed.

Respond to Your Audience

Find out what their hot buttons are. I was speaking at a university where the student group had just put up the "cemetery of innocents"—hundreds of white crosses to represent a portion of one day's killings by abortion. The pro-abort group was livid! They put all of their slogans in chalk along the sidewalk where the crosses were displayed. I wrote them down on the way to my speech and that became my speech. As well as being very "current," it answered the objections the pro-life students were faced with and equipped them to carry the message to their campus.

Hecklers Are Your Friends

Don't be afraid of opposition. They make your speeches and events newsworthy—and increase your chances of being covered by the press and heard by curious bystanders. While we may not reach those clearly in opposition to us, they are not really our audience. We must tailor our message to those in the middle who are not wholly committed to one side or the other.

At Florida Atlantic University last year I had a roving microphone so hecklers could be heard better. As long as you don't hand it to them—this can work. I remember one student: "You keep talking about the law. Well, the Supreme Court of the United States declared abortion to be legal—so why don't you just shut up about it and obey the law!"

I pointed out, "The Supreme Court also declared slavery legal—does that mean we shouldn't have spoken out against that injustice, too?"

He replied, "Well, then you had human lives involved!"

"Same thing here. With 46 human chromosomes, we're pretty sure we're not talking about a frog. There is no question it's a human life. That's the only reason I'm standing here. Why should we protect human lives against the Supreme Court then, but not now?"

His answer: "Well, that was a long time ago." Beautiful.

By the way, that was a day we prayed fervently before I went on. We prayed that people would be drawn to hear the truth and, specifically, that there would be a life saved. I guess I wasn't much of a crowd draw because there wasn't anyone around, and Jonathan, a student and former intern, sheepishly asked, "Should we go ahead?"

We took the step of faith and I started talking to four or five students, in addition to those from Intervarsity who had put on the event. We were outside in a congregated area, and within minutes we had nearly a hundred kids listening. After the talk a woman came up to me and told me she was eight weeks pregnant and scheduled for an abortion—which she was canceling because she heard the truth. The late singer Rich Mullins said it best, "Our God Is an Awesome God!"

Have fun. When I was debating ACLU representatives at Cleveland State University, they made the accusation that the only reason for a particular clause in one of our bills was so Right to Life could file frivolous lawsuits. I simply responded, "I can't believe my ears. Did I just *hear the ACLU* accusing someone *else* of filing frivolous lawsuits? They *have got to be kidding!*" Everyone laughed, and the point was made—that's what they're famous for.

Diverse Views Not Welcome

On another day I was greeted at the University of Cincinnati with an incredible display of tolerance and respect for pluralism and my diverse views: Signs put together by the student abortion, communist, and homosexual groups included my favorite: "Janet Go Home." It made me feel all warm inside.

This talk was outside in the common area called "the bridge," where all the students were congregated. I used a tactic I recommend to you. I've done it many times and always with good responses. If you promise to answer the opposition's questions after your opening talk, you'll get them all to stay and listen. When I opened it up to questions, I got them all, including: "Are you married?" To which I responded, "No." And the follow-up in front of a few hundred students, "DO YOU HAVE SEX?" To which I replied, "If you're asking me out, that's something we can discuss in private."

Another yell: "Are you a VEGETARIAN???" And I answered that there were those in the pro-life movement, even in my office, who were, and other's who were not, but all were in agreement that we wanted to return protection to the unborn child. He then screamed, "But are YOU a vegetarian???"

I said, "No," but immediately asked him if he was.

He gave an enthusiastic, "Yes, I am!"

My follow-up, "Are you in favor of legal abortion?"

"Yes, I am!" I then addressed the audience and asked them if it seemed a little strange to *them* that this gentleman doesn't want to kill a cow, but has no problem in killing a child—if that child has not passed through the birth canal yet?

The point I made throughout the talk is that there is no difference between a born child and an unborn child—as Congressman Henry Hyde says, "It's merely a change of address!"

Opening Eyes

At Kent State [again] I was greeted by gagged and blindfolded protesters holding corresponding signs: "Right to Life refuses to speak the truth," "Right to Life refuses to see the truth." I invited them into the auditorium—they couldn't make too much of a fuss because half of them had gags on, after all! My first line: "The signs read, 'Right to Life refuses to SEE the truth,' but I ask you tonight, WHO are they that are sitting here with the blindfolds???"

At the end of that evening, with protesters sitting quietly through over an hour-long talk and another hour of questions, the reporter from the Kent State newspaper came up to me. "I have to tell you," she said, "I came here to cover this event pro-choice and I am leaving pro-life." The headline read, "Opposition sits blindfolded as speaker tries to open eyes." That was a good day. Even the pro-aborts had to admit it.

The next week a pro-abortion student wrote a letter to the editor of the *Daily Kent Stater*:

> I, however, do respect the views of the right to life movement, thanks to the golden tongue of one Janet Folger, member of Ohio Right to Life. She had the dubious task of facing such pig-headed people—people who I thought were on my side . . . Janet can turn pro-choice arguments into soup if pro-choicers let their guard down. So, those of you who chose to be blind Wednesday night—watch Janet next time."[2]

Every now and then you feel like you've made a dent.
Sometimes you can even reach those who are there to protest you.

Another time, several rows of a university audience were filled by people wearing big yellow "pro-choice" buttons. I decided to ask them a few questions.

"How do you feel about abortions because the child is the wrong sex. Are you *for* the ultimate in sex discrimination?" No. They all said they weren't.

"How about abortions once the child could survive outside the womb?" No way.

Then I asked, "How about as a means of birth control—are you for the 'choice of abortion' *then?*" No, they said they didn't favor that either. (Although, if they were opposite me in a formal debate, I would have asked them *why*. . .if the being that was aborted wasn't a human being . . .why not abort as a means of birth control?)

I continued my line of questioning to these protesters, "What about an abortion to advance your career?" No again.

By the time I was done I was able to make my point that those there to protest me actually *agreed with me* far more than they agreed with the people whose buttons they wore.

In fact, if you know people who call themselves "pro-choice" because of the issues of rape and incest, they actually agree with us about 99 percent of the time! That's right, according to Alan Guttmacher, the research arm of Planned Parenthood (they're doing the killing; they should know), 99 percent of all abortions are done for reasons other than rape and incest."[3] Are you aware of any *other* issue where people who agree with 99 percent of one side, sign up to join the opposite side? It's completely absurd. There are a lot of mislabeled people walking around—we just have to fill them in on what the two sides actually believe.

Rape/Incest

In every single debate I've been in, the issues of rape and incest come up. They talk about it 99 percent of the time, so that people often believe that that's why 99 percent of abortions are being done. I very often ask them if they would support legislation if we took care of their main concern—if we added a rape and incest exception to the bill. If they represent Planned

Parenthood, NARAL, or NOW, after avoiding the question as much as they can, they will have to say no. We must press this point to show how extreme they are so we can make the next point—why then do you keep talking about rape and incest when what you really want is abortion on demand for *any reason* whatsoever?

Any time there is a bill to return protection to children in this country, the pro-aborts start screaming "rape and incest!" In Louisiana, for example, a few years back, when the legislature was considering a bill to reinstate full protection to children not yet born, the NARAL and Planned Parent- hood crowd brought in every rape and incest victim they could find. They made them tell their stories before the legislature, the media, and the world. And when the Louisiana legislature added an assault rape exception (tightly worded with reporting to a law enforcement agency required), they opposed it. You see, that's all they had talked about, but when they got what they said they wanted, they had absolutely no interest in supporting the bill. A more honest reply to the Louisiana legislators might have been, "No thanks. We were just *using* these women to get what we really wanted all along—abortion on demand for any reason whatsoever." All the rest is a smokescreen.

Incidentally, I would fully support a bill of this kind in the same way I would support most any bill that would limit *any* abortions. Right now no unborn child is fully protected. If we could protect 99 percent of them, I would do it in a fetal heartbeat (which is pretty fast)! That is not to say that I wouldn't then go back and work to protect the rest of the children, who, through no fault of their own, were being punished for the crime of their father.

A few months ago I had a teary-eyed woman come up to me and tell me that she was the product of rape. I know others as well, and I am so very glad their lives were spared. One woman I know, who played with Cleveland's Musicians for Life, would often ask the audience, "If a 12-year-old was raped by her father and became pregnant, how many think she should have the abortion?" Nearly every hand goes up. She then says, "You have just killed me. I am that baby." As tragic as the instance of her conception was, she deserved a chance to live. She announced that *her* daughter had just given birth. Abortion kills not just an innocent child; it kills generations.

Abortion is a second act of violence that does not erase the first act of violence—the rape. And while the woman has no choice in the first violent act that is done to her, the violence of abortion is performed with her consent. When she gets on that table to have an abortion, she is consenting to kill what is biologically her child—because of the crime of that baby's father. That is why every independent study I have ever seen shows that it is more psychologically harmful for the woman to have an abortion following a rape than to place her child for adoption.

One final point on this. Consider what would happen if we took a child who, through no fault of her own, was conceived through rape, and placed her next to a baby who was the result of a loving marriage, and experts from around the world took X-rays, drew blood, and examined each child fully. They would find no difference. Why? Because there is none.

Yet, I believe in the burning building approach. If I see a day-care center building on fire, I don't stand there and say, "Since I can't save them all at once, I had better not try to get any." I believe what you do is you go in and carry out as many kids as you can, and then go back and carry out more until you have as many as you can possibly get. I believe the same idea applies in legislation.

It pains me to see well-meaning pro-lifers take the approach that if a bill has any exception whatsoever, they'll oppose it. I have heard of pro-life groups actually opposing legislation to ban partial-birth abortions because they don't protect *all* the children. I've asked representatives from this group, "Let me get this straight. When you go to testify in the legislature, you sign in on the same side with Planned Parenthood, NARAL and the ACLU in opposition to a bill that would protect children from infanticide?" Sometimes all a wimpy, fence-sitting legislator uses as justification to vote against a protective bill is: "Well, even the pro-life groups can't seem to agree on it." We are sometimes our own worst enemies.

Our Audience

Mark Crutcher, in his seminars, talks about our audience in a debate. It is not the groups on either side of the spectrum; their minds are already made up. We need to tailor our message to the folks in the "middle." Crutcher teaches that regardless of the product, selling is a battle of *images and personalities*—not products. The average person, he says, tends to favor the position of the person they *like most*, and they determine who they like and don't like by the images they have of each. That's where we're at a disadvantage.

Guess which side has the following images: "religious fanatics," "insensitive to women," "unintelligent," "outside mainstream America"— one might even say "right wing," "intolerant," "judgmental," and "inflexible." If you've watched television at any time in the last 27 years, it's not too hard a guess. All the other side has to do is reinforce these stereotypes, and it won't matter what we say. We must create our own image that is both rational and credible—and it wouldn't hurt for them to see us smile! I used to come to debates with half the Willke book (now called *Why Can't We Love Them Both?*) memorized and with more facts and figures than anyone needs in a lifetime. We need to focus less on statistics and more on getting out the truth in a more human way.

Questions

In the debate itself, Crutcher points out that our opponents never ask us a question to gain information. They are asked to make you say something they want the folks in the middle—the real audience—to hear. Every assumption placed within a question is assumed true if it is not challenged. Just like the question: "When did you stop beating your wife?" We must first deal with all false assumptions before we answer. "First, let me say that I NEVER beat my wife, and secondly, I'm NOT married." Of course, if you were on *Nightline*, they would probably *edit out* your reply! (OK, OK, I'll let it go.)

Remember, our "audience" is mainly made up of the folks who haven't made up their minds yet. So when you're speaking, you're not really talking to your opponent—you are using them to make points you want your audience to hear.

I used this once on a radio debate with a state senator's aide. I asked the question, "Does it bother you that abortion is legal beyond the point where medical science has proven that the unborn child *feels pain?*"

I can still hear her answer in my head: "It *doesn't matter* if the fetus feels pain; that's not the issue—the issue is the right to abort that fetus. If we had the interest and technology to prevent pain to the fetus, we could, but that is not the issue." Think about just how cold and callused that must have sounded to the average listener who is in our audience.

Here are a couple more questions Crutcher suggests asking in a debate—keeping in mind that we cannot let them get away without answering the question (or with answering a different question):

"Pro-abortionists say that the unborn child is part of the mother's body. If that is so, why does it have a completely different genetic code and often a different blood type? How do you explain the fact that it has its own immune system? Why is the child male half of the time?" (They will most likely try to get you off track by talking about viability. This issue is not about age—it is about a completely separate human being—complete with his or her own separate genetic code.)

"We are now seeing the unborn being treated for disease, given blood transfusions, and even operated on. When a doctor does one of these procedures, who is the patient?" (Don't let them off the hook with an analogy to operations repairing diseased organs or tissue. There is a separate and distinct patient—the baby.)

If we use the absence of brain waves to determine that a person's life has ended, why shouldn't we use the presence of brain waves to determine when someone's life has begun?"

One more thing I learned in this movement is to never get caught with the same question twice. If you get something that stumps you, I guarantee you will hear it again—probably at your next debate. There are only so many ways to come at this, so you will be hearing many of the same questions in each debate. Every once and a while you'll get a new one, like the time I was on a public radio show and the caller asked, "If there were aliens that landed and their rights were being violated—would you start an 'Aliens for Life' group?" I assured the caller if that was something he was interested in, I wouldn't stand in his way.

I was caught off guard once when debating abortion activist Bill Baird, whose name appears on several pro-abortion Supreme Court Cases. He loves to talk about how "an acorn is not an oak tree," and an "egg is not a chicken"; therefore, he assumes, a "fetus is not a person."

Think of what he's really saying: that picking an acorn out of the dirt is morally similar to pulling the arms, legs, and head off an unborn child. We need to call them on their ridiculous assertions.

I wish I had had Crutcher's answer to this one at the time. Here's my summary of it: "Your comparison between an unborn child and an acorn suggests that when we hear of a woman who is suffering the emotional trauma of a miscarriage, we should just tell her to stop her whining. After all, what she lost was no more valuable than an acorn. If that's what you believe, I would like you to address the women in the audience—some of whom have had a miscarriage—and tell them to quit their crying. . . ."

Love Conquers All

In the first chapter, I told you about the debate that was canceled— when former abortionist Eric Harrah became a Christian. Since that time I have wondered, would *I* have been loving enough? While our main audience in any debate is folks in the middle on the issue—not the opponent—we can sometimes forget that our opponents are human beings made in the image of God, *even* if they kill children for a living.

When I was speaking in Wisconsin several months ago a woman came up to me and said, "I was an abortionist in Washington, D.C., and I have to tell you, I have a lot of friends who are still abortionists—and they want out." She belonged to a group of former abortionists called the Centurions—named after the Roman soldiers who killed Christ. She told me that these abortionists desperately want out of what they're doing, but in order to do that, they must first admit to what they've been doing—taking the lives of innocent human beings. They somehow have to live with the fact that this is what they've spent years doing. If we want them to get out, we have to let them know that they have a place to come—that they are welcome among our ranks.

Madeline Murray O'Hare, who successfully took prayer out of the schools (whose son, the plaintiff in the case, is now a Christian), disappeared without a trace. Her belongings were auctioned off to pay her delinquent back taxes, and among her items were a Bible and a diary. In the diary several times were the words, "Somebody, somewhere, love me." God really loves these people—even if we view them as villains. I wonder if Mrs. O'Hare would have devoted her life to working against God if she had felt that love. We must make ourselves available to be used as an instrument of God's love—to our opponents in the debate and even to those in the abortion industry.

Eric Harrah has said, "It makes the biggest impact" when people seek to befriend an abortionist. "People are not going to listen to someone unless they have a relationship with him." Having come out of the abortion industry, he testifies that loving evangelism is the most effective pro-life tactic of all. "You don't want people to have abortions?" he asks. "Well, get them to be Christians, get them to be saved. That will cut the numbers down dramatically."[4]

12

Tolerance

Iwas on a plane to Phoenix working on this book when the woman next to me, reading what was on my laptop, offered her position on the subject. She said she had had an abortion a few months prior and had "no regrets." (Relief is a pretty common *initial* reaction—sometimes it takes as long as ten years for the gravity of the situation to set in.) I listened to her position, and then, as gently as I could, gave her mine. Her response? "I think that's great. If you believe that, that's true for you, but I have to do what is best for *me.*"

An all-too-common reaction based on the false premise that truth is whatever we want it to be. In essence, her position was, "For me, it's not a baby because that would not fit into my plans."

But you know what? There are some things that are true whether you believe them or not. Even if you've never heard of Sir Isaac Newton, or don't even believe he existed, the law of gravity still applies to you.

There is such a thing as truth. Dr. James Dobson's son, Ryan, once told me about a little experiment he uses to prove this point. He asks his audience to close their eyes and point "north." When they open their eyes, the students find that they are pointing every possible way—including up. He then asks only those who were "absolutely sure" they know which way is north to stand up and continue pointing. They find that the people standing all over the auditorium who were absolutely sure of themselves were still pointing in every direction.

He then takes out a compass. Holding it up and pointing to it, he declares, "*This* is north." I don't care how *sincere* you are, what a *good person* you are, how much *education* you have, or how *sure* of yourself you are, if you are pointing in a different direction than *this* for north, you are . . . *wrong.*"

North is north. Gravity is real. And the being in the womb *is* a human being, whether you happen to believe it or not.

But to express an absolute truth has now been declared to be "intolerant." Those who believe something to be true are increasingly silenced—for fear that those who disagree might be offended. Whether it's true or not has become irrelevant. Taken to an extreme to make my point, a common reaction to (a less universal) truth might be, "How dare you declare that gravity is real? There are *entire cultures* of people who don't believe that. Who's to say that *you* are right? Some tribal communities believe that what holds us to the earth is the result of their human sacrifices each year. I'd rather depart from your white-Eurocentric belief system that focuses on the so-called advances of people like 'Sir Isaac Newton,' and focus on a more inclusive and tolerant view that we don't really know whether gravity is real or not." Sometimes I can get a little carried away, but you get the point. It's as though they've found a right in the Constitution to be an "unoffended listener." If tolerance is the highest virtue, we must do away with things that stand in the way—even if one of them is truth.

Last year, I visited a disturbing place—the United Nations. Listen to a "Declaration on the Principles of Tolerance" resolution that the UN passed at a meeting of the Educational, Scientific and Cultural Organization in Paris in the fall of 1995: "Tolerance involves the rejection of dogmatism and absolutism."[1] Notice how "dogmatic" the UN is in its opposition to dogmatism and "absolute" in its rejection of absolutism. Rather ironic, wouldn't you say?

Don't be so "intolerant" as to declare that you happen to know "the truth." According to the UN, that is "absolutism" that must be "rejected." Now let's go a step further. In the name of "tolerance," not only are we going to reject your notion that gravity is real, we are now going to elevate to an equal level as yours all other beliefs that say otherwise. Those cultures' belief that making human sacrifices to their tree-stump "god of the roots" to ensure that we will not fall out into space is "equally as valid" as yours. Think I'm exaggerating? Listen to what the Sixth Circuit Court of Appeals had to say.

The Sixth Circuit Court of Appeals judge said that not only do "adherents of all faiths deserve equal rights as citizens," but "adherents of all faiths are *equally valid* as religions."[2] That explains why, in January 1999, CNN had a link on its website to the Church of Satan.[3] All faiths or beliefs are "equally valid"? Would that include also the "Trench Coat Mafia"? Would that include the KKK? How about pedophiles? By the way, I recently got my first hate letter because of my stand against pedophilia. I was actually called a Nazi because I said I believe that sexually molesting children is wrong. That is where this kind of "tolerance" will take you.

We are now at the point where university professor Robert Simon has said that while he has never had a student who didn't believe in the Holocaust, he is shocked at what they *are* now saying about it. He is finding that between 10 and 20 percent of his students *believe* what one student told him: "Of course I dislike the Nazis, but who is to say they are morally wrong?"[4]

Up to 20 percent of students in universities can't even say genocide is absolutely, always, morally wrong. That's a scary situation. When there are no moral truths to stand on, *anything* goes.

I believe that is how so many are able to say they are "personally opposed to abortion" but don't want to impose that belief to actually protect anyone else. One day, I was riding down the elevator in the Ohio State House with some of the folks who worked there, when they mentioned that they were going over to the YWCA to hear a speech by gubernatorial candidate, Tony Celebrezze. He had just recently adopted this position (from being pro-life). I said, *"Really?* Would you mind if I tag along?" They must have been new because they didn't really see a problem with that.

As we were walking over there, I knew I had to stay away from small-talk that included such things as, "So where do *you* work?" When asked, I simply pointed to the building, "Right over there—how about you guys?" I remember them telling me about their bosses—pro-abortion leaders in the

State House who hated my guts. "Really? You work for *them*? Great. How *nice*."

We walked into the forum and I signed my name as sloppily as I could—so no one could read it. I thanked my new friends for their kind invitation and sat down—away from them at a table in the front—so they could not get into any kind of trouble for bringing me with them. Afraid of being recognized, I avoided making eye contact until Tony started to speak and I couldn't be thrown out.

There he was making his newly-found position statement in favor of "tolerance":

"My personal position on abortion hasn't changed, but I believe that, for matters of public policy, women should make that choice for themselves—they should have the right to choose." That was met with thunderous applause from this group, of course.

A woman, gleeful at the notion of being in such close proximity to this candidate for governor, took the podium and thanked the speaker for such an inspiring message. Then she asked, "Are there any questions?"

As you might imagine, my hand was the first one up, and, for some reason she called on *me*. I saw the look of horror on Tony's face when he recognized me and realized that I was going to ask him his first question. I had just done one of those "live from the newsroom" interviews about the race—where I became a big believer in that unedited way of getting your message out, and he knew who I was.

My question? It went something like this, "Yes, I have a question for you Mr. Celebrezze. You say that your personal position on abortion hasn't changed, but your public position has. You were quoted in the *Columbus Dispatch* as saying that your personal position on abortion is that abortion is 'murder.' My question for you is: How does something you *personally* consider to be 'murder' make for a good '*public* policy'?

Of course, there is no answer for that position. He didn't have one either. The fun part came the next day when I was sitting in my office. Mark Lally, then president of Ohio Right to Life, looked up from reading the paper and scratched his head saying, "How *in the world* does a question like *this* come from a group like *that?*"

I said, "Oh, yeah, *that* was me." One person can make a difference.

It's a pretty strange position when you think about it. Can you imagine someone saying, "Well, I'm personally opposed to rape, but I don't want to impose my views on others—certainly not to pass a *law* against it or anything. After all, we can't legislate morality."

I think Martin Luther King, Jr. had the best answer for that. He said, "We hear the familiar cry that morals can't be legislated. This may be true, but behavior can be regulated. The law may not be able to make a man love me, but it can keep him from lynching me."[5]

It's not that the pro-life side is trying to "legislate morality," as much as they are working to "regulate behavior." We're not attempting to pass a law that makes the abortionist love these children; we are just trying to "stop the lynching."

The "personally opposed" position came up one day when a student approached our pro-life information table at Cleveland State University. He was aware of the "stir" we were causing on campus and decided to inquire about it. He said, "I've read your letters to the editor; just what are you all about?"

I answered, "Before I tell you what I'm all about, let me ask you— where do *you* stand on abortion?"

He started the standard "tolerant" line saying, "I'm *personally* opposed to abortion . . ."

Before he could finish, I interrupted him with another question, "Wait right there. *Why* are you personally opposed to abortion?"

He stood there for quite a while thinking. I'm guessing that he was personally opposed to abortion because abortion takes the life of innocent children. All I know is that when he thought about *why he* was opposed to abortion personally, it was a good enough reason to oppose abortion publicly as well. He actually crossed over to the other side of the information table to help us get our message out. *He* worked the table, and I went to class.

Dennis Prager made a comment in the *Wall Street Journal* following the Jewish Community Center killings explaining why the Jewish community should support Christianity, "If we continue to teach about tolerance and intolerance instead of teaching about good and evil, we will end up with tolerance of evil."[6] I think his quote summarizes the issue very well.

There are some things in society that we frankly shouldn't tolerate. That's why we have laws against such things as homicide, rape, and child abuse. If we decided everything on merely an "opinion poll," there would most likely still be some slave states today.

Imagine for a moment a group coming out and making the talk show circuits to promote their position in favor of child abuse, but they do it behind a beautiful banner that says, "THE RIGHT TO CHOOSE." What you suppose people would do then? A "tolerant pro-choice" position on child abuse doesn't quite have the same ring to it. I think they would look behind that banner to see what, exactly, was being chosen. And abusing a child is not a choice we tolerate in this country—unless, of course, we're talking about the ultimate child abuse—abortion.

By the way, accepting the choice of child abuse is becoming dangerously close to reality. Last year, the American Psychological Association (APA) floated a trial balloon that thankfully sank due to the efforts of people like Dr. Laura Schlessinger, who brought it to light. Coral Ridge Ministries (founded by Dr. D. James Kennedy) also sent 27,000 petitions to the APA urging them to repudiate the study which claimed that sex between adults and children may not always be harmful (and many thank-you cards were also sent to Dr. Laura). In fact, following the release of the study, I received my first hate letter for my stand against child molestation. I was called an intolerant Nazi because, after all, even the APA said it was OK!

APA Executive Director Raymond Fowler wrote to Dr. Kennedy in August of 1999 and told him that despite publishing a study favoring pedophilia, it remains firmly opposed to child sexual abuse. "We believe that the sexual abuse of children is a criminal act and one that is reprehensible in any context."[7] He said they also planned to "publish critiques and comments" on it in the near future. Uncontested, I'm not sure the result would have been the same.

You see, the pro-abortion crowd really didn't have to go to Madison Avenue for their "pro-choice" slogan; all they really had to do was look at the Lincoln/Douglas debates. Stephen Douglas wasn't really "pro-slavery" after all. He maintained he just believed in the slave-owners' right to choose. It's all been done before. Being "pro-choice on slavery" takes into account everyone's choice except the person it matters to the most—the slave, just as the "pro-choice" position on abortion ignores the child. Not really very tolerant when you think about it.

While dismembering human children is something we "tolerate" in society today, free speech and the expression of our freedom of religion are increasingly not tolerated.

At the Littleton funerals last year for the victims of the Columbine High School massacre, the Gospel was presented to millions as CNN aired the services. Darrel Scott, whose daughter Rachel was killed at Columbine, told me about the calls and letters he's received from people all over the country who have decided to give their lives to God and place their trust in His Son, Jesus Christ, as their Savior and Lord. "People are being saved just from seeing Rachael's funeral," he told me.

But not everyone was so happy. People were complaining that the memorial services were too Christian. One Rabbi told the *Washington Times* that these funerals reflected an ignorant, narrow-minded faith.[8]

A Presbyterian USA minister complained that it was not inclusive of all faith communities.[9] Some said it focused too much on the slain victims' faith and encouraged people to follow Christ, as if that was a horrible thing. We can't even have a *memorial service* for the people who were shot and mention what they believed without coming under condemnation? It's now too narrow-minded to even talk about Christ in church. They don't seem to understand just how inclusive Christianity really is.

John 3:16—you know that verse they hold up at football games? My grandfather, Jim Irvin, always called it the Gospel in a nutshell (I know, a lot of other people do, too, but this is my book!). It says: "For God so loved the world that He gave His only begotten son that WHOSOEVER believeth in Him shall have everlasting life." *Whosoever* is a pretty inclusive word—wouldn't you say?

But they talk about how "intolerant" it is for us to say that Christ is the ONLY way to Heaven. Well, first, it doesn't really matter so much what *we* say, the important thing is what *Christ* Himself said: "I am the way the Truth and the Life, no man cometh unto the Father except by me" (John 14:6 KJV). Pretty clear stuff. After all, if "all roads lead to Heaven," why did Christ have to die?

Secondly, as Dr. Kennedy has pointed out in his sermons, what's amazing is not that there's just "one way"—what's amazing is that there is "*A* way." If you were God and people killed *your* prophets and then killed *your* only Son—how anxious would you be to save any of them? The question we should be asking is not why is there only one way—but why is there any way at all?

Does Tolerance Have an Effect on Truth?

In 1991, and again in 1994, pollster George Barna asked a random sampling of adults, and then a sample of Christians, whether they agree with the statement, "There is no such thing as absolute truth; two people could define truth in totally conflicting ways, but both could still be correct." His results: In 1991, 67 percent of all Americans, and 52 percent of Christians agreed. In 1994, those numbers increased to 72 percent and 62 percent, respectively.[10]

What's the Solution?

Imagine one evening that you get a call from a good friend from his car phone in his newly rented convertible in Arizona. He is ecstatic as he describes the sound system and just how fast the car can go on the open road. He also reveals "how good" the beer is he's currently drinking, as well as the last five he just drank. He then points out just how "much better the stars look" when you drive with your headlights off. You inquire as to his whereabouts and, being familiar with the roads, realize that your friend is headed directly for the cliff of the Grand Canyon. What do you do?

One approach is to "not impose your morality" and to be "tolerant" and "supportive" of your friend's actions. After all, if he's enjoying himself, who are *we* to ruin his good time? Who is to say that it's wrong? Lots of people have driven drunk and recklessly and are doing *just fine.*

Maybe you try to tell him, and he says he "doesn't want to hear anything that will spoil his fun." Do you give up?

Perhaps he senses your disapproval and threatens to end the friendship if you continue to issue warnings. Now your friendship is on the line; what do you do then? Maybe you could make sure he practices "safe driving" and at least wears his seat belt.

No. If you *really* love someone, you will love them enough to tell him *the truth.* That is the difference between love and "tolerance."

Josh McDowell said it this way, "True compassionate love that seeks to provide for and protect another person's health, happiness, and spiritual growth could not comply with the cultural call: 'If you love me, you'll endorse my behavior.' Because real love—true love—grieves over the inevitable results of wrong behavior."[11]

I have talked to several people who have called themselves pro-life but are so concerned about being "tolerant" and "accepting" that they have actually driven friends (and girlfriends) to an abortion clinic to have their child killed. That kind of action is about as caring as saying: "If you'd like me to give you a lift to the Grand Canyon so you can throw your child off the cliff once we get there, while I may disagree, who am I to stand in the way?" Here's how McDowell describes the difference:

Tolerance and Love: What's the Difference?

Tolerance	Love
Seeks to be inoffensive	Takes risks
Is indifferent	Is active
Costs nothing	Costs everything[12]

The most cited Bible verse by those who advocate tolerance: "He who is without sin among you, let him throw a stone at her first" (John 8:7).

The least cited Bible verse by those who advocate tolerance: "Neither do I condemn you; go and sin no more" (John 8:11).

If You're Truly Tolerant, Anything Goes!

But what's easier than confronting people when they engage in negative behavior? "Support them" in whatever decision they make! This is what actress Sharon Stone said at a United Nations Conference on AIDS and teenage sexuality:

> No matter how much we guide our children within our families and within our churches, we are no stronger than the power of sexuality.
>
> The solution is to have parents of teens buy a box of 200 condoms, and put them at a little-used location of the house . . . but where the teens can find them. That way the kids won't be afraid to ask, and the parents won't know![13]

In my radio and television commentary I suggested that maybe we should buy a box of 200 *clean needles* and 200 *filtered cigarettes* for our kids too—because of the power of drugs and cigarettes!

In the Fall 1998 semester, Princeton University appointed Peter Singer as the Chairman of its "Center for Human Values."

Regarding traditional Christian values, he says: "Many of our moral institutions are formed for religious reasons, which were once strong but are now outdated."

Regarding disabled children: "Killing a defective infant is not morally equivalent to killing a person. Sometimes it is not wrong at all."

Regarding newborn babies: "No infant has a strong claim to life as a person."[14]

Based on Mr. Singer's stalwart stand on the rights of disabled infants, I have to wonder if he'll soon be recommending that Princeton do away with their handicapped parking spots, too. After all, if the disabled are not "morally equivalent" to other people, why should we give them a parking space at all? By the way, Mr. Singer's mother was subsequently diagnosed with

Alzheimer's disease. His reaction to the disabled now? Singer said, "It's different when it's your mother."[15]

And now the National Organization of Women, is 'tolerant' of polygamy? "We fight for lesbian families . . . I don't know why we wouldn't support this (polygamy)."[16]

Now you can sleep easy ladies—knowing that the National Organization of Women is fighting for the right of your husband to marry someone else in addition to you. I can just see their fundraising letters now: "If you contribute above and beyond your membership dues, we'll also be working for a return of 'harems.'" Wow, it's really good to know we have a women's movement we can be so proud of.

And with half of the babies aborted being female—NOW is the only movement I'm aware of that actually advocates the killing of its potential members.

Isn't tolerance grand? I could keep going, but I think you get the idea.

I have heard Dr. D. James Kennedy say, "The last virtue of a decadent society is tolerance." That is where I believe we are. The notion in which "anything goes" puts everyone, especially the most defenseless and vulnerable, in jeopardy. When the intolerable is tolerated, no one is safe. As Dennis Prager said, "If we continue to teach about tolerance and intolerance instead of teaching about good and evil, we will end up with tolerance of evil."[17]

13

Lies, Lies, Lies

Whilen I was an undergrad at Cleveland State, a woman named Carol called me from the "Students for Choice" group. She said, "I don't want you to be afraid—I'm not trying to sabotage you or anything, but I would very much like to have lunch with you."

I drove out to the East Side of town and met her in a quaint little coffee shop. I was hoping she would spot me, because I wasn't really sure who she was. She did, and waved me over to a table—a petite woman with very short black hair—and I thought she looked kind of familiar. I could tell she felt somewhat awkward when she said, "I can't really explain it, but for some reason, I just knew I had to talk to you."

She told me how she had been to Washington to march for abortion and how she and her friends used to take the literature from our pro-life table and laugh at it and have fun at our expense. Then she told me about her abortion. She had it when she was six weeks along in her pregnancy, a few weeks prior to our meeting. She had had a suction abortion, which is an early method that uses a vacuum device twenty-nine times more powerful than your vacuum at home. It sucks the tiny child apart as it removes everything in the uterus.

She said she couldn't listen to the sound of a vacuum cleaner without thinking about it—and breaking down in tears. She added, "I told some of my pro-choice friends about it, and they just laughed at me. The abortion clinic told me it was nothing more than a blob—a mass of cells," she remarked. "And then I remembered something you said—go check out a biology book in the library and see for yourself."

I hadn't remembered even talking to this woman, and here she was quoting things I had said.

"And . . . you were right," she said. "My baby had brain waves and a beating heart."

We talked for a few hours and I told her about the support groups, such as Women Exploited by Abortion (WEBA), and American Victims of Abortion, which met locally. Not really knowing much about where she was spiritually, I told her about the forgiveness of God. I'm not really sure I communicated it all that effectively, but told her that because Jesus Christ paid the penalty for our sin, God can look at us as sinless—*if* we repent, and turn to Him to save us from the consequences of our actions.

"Hard Times Pass, But Abortion Lasts Forever"

Carol told me all the reasons she had the abortion, including how she wanted to finish school, and she and her boyfriend, with whom she lived, had decided it would be best for their future. She gave a litany of other reasons, none of which were truly addressed by the abortion. She dropped out of school, and she and her boyfriend broke up. She said, "The very reasons that drove me to the abortion and that seemed so compelling mean nothing now. I had the abortion to stay in school—something that didn't even happen."

She said, "Janet, when you talk to women who are considering an abortion, I want you to tell them one thing for me." She paused as she mustered the strength to say something to someone she had considered "the enemy," and she said something none of her friends would hear: "Please tell them, 'Hard times pass, but abortion lasts forever.'"

The "very good reasons" for abortion, coupled with "it's not really a baby yet," are lies that lead to actions that cannot be undone, "because hard times pass, but abortion lasts forever." And it affects not just the baby, but the woman who has been told it's not a baby . . . and the father . . . and generations to come. Those are some pretty expensive lies.

There may be those who are reading this who are thinking, "Janet, maybe your friend Carol wasn't told the truth, but for you to suggest that the abortion movement is *built* on lies—well, that's another matter." That's *exactly* what I'm saying. I learned a long time ago that if people are going to advocate the dismemberment of a child or sucking the brains out of an infant during delivery, they don't have a problem with lying.

In fact, abortion was based on a lie from the very beginning—from the very first Supreme Court decision. It has been promoted with lies that are still being told, such as how we're not sure if it's a baby or not, and how many women they claim died as a result of illegal abortions. And when it was discovered that abortionists are killing children after partially delivering them, they simply made up a whole new set of lies. Ultimately all of these lies were admitted to by the proponents of abortion themselves.

Lie #1

Norma McCorvey, the *"Roe"* of *Roe v. Wade*, admitted <u>she lied about being gang raped</u>—a lie upon which the Supreme Court based its decision, and the lie that led many people to accept the legality of abortion. Norma McCorvey is now 100 percent pro-life.[1]

Lie #2

Doe v. Bolton, the companion decision to *Roe v. Wade*, is also based on a lie. Sandra Cano, the "Doe" of *Doe v. Bolton*, <u>never wanted an abortion, as had been alleged in that case.</u> The truth is that she was pregnant with her fourth child and was desperately trying to get her other three children out of foster care. Pro-abortion attorneys offered to help her on the condition that she would allow them to use her case to try to overturn Georgia's abortion law. She made it clear she had no intention of having an abortion, and she ended up running away to avoid keeping an abortion appointment arranged for her by her lawyers. She didn't know until 1988 that the case in which she was used as "Mary Doe" tied up the loopholes in *Roe v. Wade*, making it virtually impossible for states to prohibit abortion, even in the last three months of pregnancy, if the mother's life or "health" were endangered. Health was defined by the court in *Doe v. Bolton*, as "physical, emotional, psychological, familial and the woman's age—relevant to the well-being of the patient."[2]

Lie #3

Bernard Nathanson, the founder of the National Abortion and Reproductive Rights Action League (then the National Association for Repeal of Abortion Laws), also admitted he <u>lied about the number of women who died from illegal abortions</u> in order to repeal this country's pro-life laws.

"We spoke of 5,000-10,000 deaths a year. . . . I confess that I knew the figures were totally false. . . . It was a useful figure, widely accepted, so why go out of our way to correct it with honest statistics?"[3] Bernard Nathanson, who ran the largest abortion clinic in the world, is now 100 percent pro-life.

Lie #4

Planned Parenthood and abortion proponents lied about the scientific fact that abortion takes the life of a human being. For years they said that "no one really knows" if we're talking about a child in a womb. Yet in 1965 Planned Parenthood published a pamphlet which stated: "An abortion kills the life of a baby after it has begun." And now, Planned Parenthood reports that in 1997 it performed 165,155 abortions and made 47,550 referrals.[4]

They operate the nation's largest chain of abortion clinics, yet admitted the truth again during a weak moment on the *Phil Donahue* show, when former director Faye Wattleton responded to the statement: "It's not a frog or a ferret that's being killed. It's a baby," with, "I am fully aware of that. I am fully aware of that."[5]

Lie #5

The Executive Director of the National Coalition of Abortion Providers, Ron Fitzsimmons (he's the guy that said he "lied through his teeth" when he suggested that partial-birth abortions were "rare") now admits that as many as 5,000 of them are done each year, primarily on healthy mothers and healthy babies.[6]

As mentioned in chapter eight, the Congressional newspaper, *Roll Call* (February 27, 1997) summed it up this way: "One of the most basic rules of lobbying is 'Never lie to a Member of Congress, particularly one of your friends.' Another is, 'Never ask a member to do something that will later jeopardize his seat.' The pro-choice movement did both and will pay for it."[7]

You would think that once a lie has been confessed or proven wrong, they would stop saying it. And yet, even after Fitzsimmons admitted that he lied, abortion proponents were still making those false claims in the legislature and in debates. And I don't think I've been in a debate yet when the false claim of "thousands of women dying" hasn't come up. I love it when I'm debating someone from NARAL when it does. I then usually say something like this:

Bernard Nathanson—the *founder* of your organization said, "*We spoke of 5,000-10,000 deaths a year. . . . I confess that I knew the figures were totally false. . . . It was a useful figure, widely accepted, so why go out of our way to correct it with honest statistics?*" If the FOUNDER of your organization has already admitted that that's a lie, why do you keep saying it?

By the way, the National Centers for Disease Control in Atlanta, Georgia, says that in the last full year that abortion was illegal there were only *39* documented cases in the entire United States of women who died from illegal abortions.[8] I was talking to an Ohio state representative on the House Floor one day, and he said to me, "We can't pass a law against abortion because people will just do them anyway."

My response to him was, "Can you name ONE law that was passed in this General Assembly that has been *100 percent obeyed*? Just because not *everyone* follows the law, should we strike them from the books?" We are against illegal abortions just as much as legal abortions—both of them take the life of a child. And when women are faced with an untimely pregnancy, I think we can do better than that . . . especially with so many people standing in line who are longing to love that child.

Another fact, while I'm on the subject of illegal abortions, *The American Journal of Obstetrics and Gynecology* issued the results of a study they conducted which showed that over 90 percent of all illegal abortions were actually performed by licensed physicians. They concluded that the legalization of abortion "has had no major impact on the number of women dying from abortion."[9] It's primarily the same people doing them—only now they're going in the front door instead of the back door.

Two things I have learned that you can always count on in this battle are both seen in the partial-birth abortion debate. First, the abortion debate began with a lie and continues to be promoted with lies. Second, you can always count on the pro-abortionists' extremism. No matter how reasonable a bill is, from granting women informed consent, to protecting pregnant women from an assault that would jeopardize their unborn child, to protecting children from being killed during delivery, we can always count on them to oppose it.

The pro-abortion lobby will not give a single inch on anything that might in some way "jeopardize" their position in favor of abortion on demand—at any time for any reason whatsoever—at taxpayer expense. Apart from the fact that they are on the wrong side of human rights, their lies and their extremism are costing them the most with the American people. Even the protesters who wear the pro-abortion buttons are, in reality, not even close to the extreme positions they advocate. The good news for us is that the more the American people learn about abortion and the truth surrounding it, the more pro-life they become. That's a very good position to be in.

Now that you see the lies they've been telling the courts and the legislatures, wait until you hear what they've been telling your children.

Is Planned Parenthood drumming up abortion business in your child's school? Carol Everett, who formerly operated several abortion clinics, admits it. When speaking in schools, she had a standard protocol she'd follow that began with asking the students what names their parents gave their sexual organs. She said, "The first thing was to get the students to laugh at their parents. That way, they won't go home and tell their parents what I told them." Then she'd say, "Would your parents help you get contraception if you become sexually active? Don't worry about that. Here's a card; come to me."

Carol, who is now pro-life, says, "I knew that every time I went to a school the pregnancy rate went up sharply . . . by my own statistics and by working with Planned Parenthood and their statistics."[10] It's not very difficult to figure out—more pregnancies lead to more abortions.

Even though their own research shows that their programs fail miserably to reduce teen pregnancy (the reason they give to get into the schools in the first place), we continue to let Planned Parenthood, the nation's largest abortionist, into our schools to drum up abortion business. Bringing Planned Parenthood into the schools to lower teen pregnancy makes about as much sense as letting the cigarette industry into the schools for an anti-smoking campaign.

In fact, according to their own statistics, Planned Parenthood is failing miserably at their "goal" of preventing teen pregnancies. When Planned

Parenthood conducts their "comprehensive" sex education, students have a 50 percent higher rate of sexual activity than those who have not had the "benefit" of the Planned Parenthood sex education training.

> According to Planned Parenthood's own figures, the *annual* in-use failure rate for the 'pill' is as high as 11 percent. For the diaphragm, the normal failure rate is nearly 32 percent . . . For 'safe sex' condoms, it is over 18 percent. That means that a sexually active fourteen-year-old girl who faithfully uses the 'pill' has a 44 percent chance of getting pregnant at least once before she finishes high school. She has a 69 percent chance of getting pregnant at least once before she finishes college. She also has a 30 percent chance of getting pregnant two or more times. If she relies on 'safe sex' condoms, the likelihood of an unwanted pregnancy while she is in school rises to nearly 87 percent."[11]

Their approach of throwing condoms at the problem of teen sexuality virtually guarantees an increase in teen pregnancy and more abortion customers. And so, after pushing sure-to-fail programs to the captive audiences in the public schools, Planned Parenthood performed over 165,000 abortions in 1997. Their system is working very well for them.[12]

The Consortium of State Physicians recently released a report that says abstinence, not sex education, has lowered teen birthrates. How profound! Instead of educating children and teens on how to take great life-changing risks, we help them *avoid* them . . . and it works! As a matter of fact, this study also proved that sexually active teen birthrates have *increased!*[13]

I would like to thank this group of doctors for providing evidence of what we've known all along: If you stay away from the fire, instead of playing with it, YOU WILL NOT GET BURNED!

In 1995, the House rejected a proposal—backed by the National Right to Life Committee and other pro-life groups—to eliminate funds for the Title 10 "family planning" program. The Title 10 program, funded at $215 million per year in 1998, provides funds for about 4,000 birth-control clinics nationwide. Under Clinton Administration regulations, all of these clinics are required to counsel all pregnant women and girls regarding abortion as a "pregnancy management option" and refer them to abortion clinics upon request.

But when there are federal funds to be had, Planned Parenthood is likely to be the first in line to get them—even if they have to pretend to "teach abstinence" to do it. They will give it a passing mention to capture more funds but don't think that means they will be putting it in a positive light. Think I'm exaggerating? Listen to the approach of the Clinton/Gore Administration.

Keep in mind that the Clinton/Gore Administration gets to pick the people they want at every level, including the Centers for Disease Control. The Centers for Disease Control have put together a nifty little book to "teach your kids about abstinence" called *Reducing the Risk* that they distribute to the public schools. Sounds like the kind of thing we need in school—right? Just listen to how they present the option of abstaining from sex: ". . . you could become a hermit, or (become) so unpleasant that everyone stays clear of you. Or you could never become involved in a romantic relationship."[14]

Did you catch that? The *Reducing the Risk* program teaches that the only way kids can abstain from sex is to become a *hermit* and be *so unpleasant* that everyone stays clear of them. I can see a high school kid now thinking, "Wow. Sign me right up." With this approach, they'll probably want to have sex just to prove that they're *not* an "unpleasant hermit." This is kind of like the cigarette industry going into the schools for an anti-smoking campaign saying, "Sure. To avoid smoking, you could become a hermit and so *uncool* that no one even *offers* you a cigarette. . . ."

I remember showing this to Governor Voinovich (now in the U.S. Senate) and seeing the look of shock and disbelief. Not only does someone in the country believe such a preposterous view, they are now teaching it to children and using your tax dollars to do it. If this is not your idea of teaching abstinence, I recommend that you check with your school board and make sure *you're* not paying for your kids to be brainwashed.

In December of 1999, a coalition of Ohioans who found out that this kind of "anti-abstinence brainwashing" was being taught in their public schools placed a full-page ad in the *Columbus Dispatch* with an open letter to the governor asking that this program be withdrawn. *Reducing the Risk* sounds great until you find out that in truth it will do just the *opposite*.

An article that ran in the *Wisconsin State Journal* stated that "abstinence works, but certainly not all the time." This is the kind of nonsense that gets passed along to your children in the classroom.

The article went on to state that, "I would like you to consider that abstinence works, but certainly not all the time . . . Every contraception method entails both user and method failure. There are many groups who are likely to fail using abstinence—those who have ever been incapacitated by alcohol or another drug, or who come from drinking families . . . those who have been sexually coerced in the past. . . . Depending on abstinence with condoms alone during the holiday season is risky."[15]

A friend of mine from Wisconsin, Joleigh Little, responded to this ridiculous assertion in the best way possible—with humor:

> As an abstinent 27-year-old woman, I was shocked to read Elizabeth Karlin's guest column in the Nov. 30 *State Journal*, which states that 'abstinence works, but certainly not all the time.' . . . Imagine my amazement when I learned that, despite the fact that I am not engaging in sexual activity of any kind, I could be pregnant at this very moment! To say that this news rocked my otherwise stable world would be an understatement. There I was, living my life in relative calm with the assurance that, because of my choice not to have sex until I found (and married) the man I would spend the rest of my life with, I didn't have to worry about unintended pregnancy or sexually transmitted diseases. I was obviously deluding myself . . . never mind that centuries of medical research backed me up . . . I guess I was wrong!
>
> I will admit that since reading the column, this subject has pretty much dominated my thinking. In spite of the obvious absurdity of Karlin's claims—and the uproarious laughter the article has provoked among my family (who now wonder if they are about to become grandparents, aunts and uncles) and all of my abstinent friends (who are, as you read this, running out to purchase home pregnancy tests to rule out the possibility of abstinence-induced pregnancy), there is a serious issue at the heart of what Karlin has written.

Abstinence is not a joke; "virgin" is not a dirty word. Despite what those in the "birth-control for everyone over the age of 10" crowd may want to teach our children, abstinence does work. I know this, because I have been practicing the concept my entire life. Sure, my friends in high school and college had some fun at my expense, but I am one of the few among my group who has never had to panic over a late period, or lie awake nights wondering if I had somehow contracted a deadly STD (at least not until I read that article by Elizabeth Karlin!)

To be abstinent in the area of sexuality means to not have sex. It doesn't mean "to pretend not to have sex" or even to "intend not to have sex"; it means TO NOT HAVE SEX. Therefore, Karlin's claim that "A large minority of U. S. women seeking abortion considered themselves to be abstinent when they became pregnant" doesn't mean, as she suggests, that "abstinence works until it doesn't," it means that abstinence works <u>until you stop being abstinent.</u> The term abstinence doesn't apply to people who "consider themselves abstinent"; it applies to people who aren't having sex.

"If you're pregnant, there's a 100 percent chance that you have not been abstaining."[16]

Something I often tell teens when I speak is, "Planned Parenthood's first plan for your life was abortion—why in the world would you listen to them now?"

It's frightening to learn what is being force-fed to the children in the public schools. We must fight the propagation of these lies, but if there is a way you can avoid it, I'm not sure you want your children indoctrinated in the meantime. My strong personal recommendation to anyone considering home schooling or putting your children in a Christian private school is: do it. Many Christian schools provide scholarship opportunities and many churches are willing to help families that can't afford private schools.

The entire abortion issue has been based on lies from the very beginning. Lies like the supposed rape of Norma McCorvey and the lies that "it's not (or we don't know if it's) a baby," and "the thousands of women who have died from illegal abortions," have influenced opinions, court decisions, and legislation. Then they lied about the number of partial-birth abortions and the reasons for them. If they're going to perform them, lying about them is pretty easy to do, I would imagine.

Those lies have paved the way for the bold and blatant stance that Planned Parenthood and the abortion industry has taken today. They admit it's a baby (on rare occasions), but they just don't care about that little incidental fact. They then take their abortion advertising directly to your children where they have a captive audience in the public schools. And much of the time you are footing the bill. That's what your Title X Family Planning tax dollars are supporting.

And while I could do a complete chapter to address the lie about how "safe" abortion is supposed to be, let me just touch on it here. First, I hardly think a procedure where someone dies every time it's performed is something you can call "safe," but abortion is also very dangerous to the mother. It can leave women sterile when the abortionist breaks through the cervix (the opening to the womb) before it's ready—making it harder for it to stay "closed," when it needs to keep the baby in. A woman could also become injured or increase the likelihood of miscarriages when the abortionist, trying to cut the baby in pieces, actually takes that loop-shaped knife (curette) and cuts the woman instead. Swiping past the openings to the Fallopian tubes can create scar tissue, preventing future eggs from making it to the lining of the womb where the child can develop.

Another hidden danger of abortion is the increased likelihood of getting breast cancer. When I first heard this, I didn't get it. How would the two have anything to do with each other? Well, when a woman becomes pregnant, the hormonal changes affect the mammary glands. They start to develop new cells in preparation for milk production. When an abortion occurs, there is a dramatic shift in hormone levels. The cells in the breast, which have been developing rapidly, stop suddenly—precisely when they're at the stage most at risk for cancerous and precancerous changes.

One study, published in the *Journal of the National Cancer Institute*, November 1994, ("Risk of Breast Cancer among Young Women: Relationship to Induced Abortion," by Janet Daling, Ph.D., a supporter of legalized abortion, reported: "Among women who had been pregnant at least once, a history of induced abortion was associated with a 50 percent increased risk of breast cancer. This risk was higher (80 percent) in women who were diagnosed with cancer at a younger age (less than 35). Among women who were younger than 18 at the time of an induced abortion of a pregnancy that lasted more than eight weeks, *the risk for breat cancer was 900 percent higher.*" (emphasis added)[17]

Sounds to me like something women considering abortion should be told about. The pro-abortion mantra, "Safe and Legal," is another lie that is costing lives, and I'm not just talking about the babies. This is something to include when passing a Woman's Right to Know law in your state.

While we're on the subject of lies, I cannot end the chapter without sharing just one more letter with you. Here's a fun game, see if you can guess who it's from.

> As you know, I have strongly opposed federal funding of abortions. In my opinion, it is wrong to spend federal funds for what is arguably the taking of a human life.
>
> It is my deep personal conviction that abortion is wrong. I hope that someday we will see the current outrageously large number of abortions drop sharply.
>
> Let me assure you that I share your belief that innocent human life must be protected and I have an open mind on how to further this goal. Again, thank you for writing. Please continue to share your thoughts and concerns with me.[18]

Is it from Dr. Jack Willke, a founder of the Right to Life movement? Congressman Henry Hyde? No. This letter was written by Al Gore—now seen pounding on the podium at NARRAL events emphatically standing for a woman's right to take that innocent human life even through Partial Birth Abortion. Whether a lie or political expediency, it is just as deadly.

As I have said before, but it is worth repeating over and over again, if necessary: Abortion lasts forever, and it affects not just the baby, but the woman who's been told it's not a baby . . . and the father . . . and generations to come. Those are some pretty expensive lies.

14

Assisted Suicide

Whently the Planned Parenthood slogan, "Every child a wanted child" was used to promote the killing of human beings who were "unwanted," it was just a matter of time before that mentality was applied to the other end of the spectrum. And while "Every grandparent a wanted grandparent" hasn't proven as effective a slogan for them just yet, that same *mentality* is being used to rationalize the killing of society's other most vulnerable: the disabled and the elderly.

As predicted in 1976 by Christian philosopher Francis Schaeffer (among others), once the courts "arbitrarily separated 'aliveness' from 'personhood,'" what was to keep them from "arbitrarily do[ing] the same with the aged?"[1]

I knew it was coming, too, but I never thought I'd see it in my lifetime. I was wrong.

Jack Kevorkian

In 1990, Jack Kevorkian took the life of his first victim: a woman by the name of Janet Adkins.[2] She was described by friends as vivacious and talented. In the spring of 1990, she found she was having trouble remembering her children's birthdays. She was subsequently diagnosed with the beginning stages of Alzheimer's disease.

Just a week after beating her son at tennis, Janet sat down to watch a *Phil Donahue* show that featured, then unknown, Jack Kevorkian. He was looking for someone to try his new "suicide machine"—constructed with scraps from garage sales and flea markets.

Perhaps depressed, perhaps desperately seeking reassurance, Janet suggested to her husband that maybe she should turn to someone like that as she did "not want to be a burden" to her husband and her family. Rather than responding to his wife with love and the assurance that he wanted to honor his wedding vows of being faithful "in sickness and in health," Janet's husband ran to the phone and called the *Donahue* show.

On June 4, 1990, days after Janet Adkins first spoke with Kevorkian, she became his first so-called "mercy killing" victim in the back of his rusty Volkswagen van. Kevorkian had actually turned others down because he felt they had poor "publicity value."[3]

He later said he would have "finished Janet Adkins off" himself if his machine hadn't worked. Of course, there were no witnesses.[4]

Kevorkian had originally wanted to test his machine out on a dog, but was refused permission by the local animal shelter's policy board. Kevorkian later viewed that setback as beneficial and concluded that he should never do anything to animals when living human subjects were available.[5]

And because Ohio didn't yet have a law to protect "living, human subjects" from being victimized from this kind of treatment, Kevorkian announced that he would soon be rolling that rusty van of his across the Michigan border to my fair state. Not if we had anything to say about it! The legislature scurried around and several bills were introduced to let him know he wasn't welcome.

I called Jack Kevorkian at home one day and asked him if he wanted to be on my radio show. He agreed. Did I tell him what I did? Yeah, I told him I did a radio show. The media asked me if I told him *who I was* before he agreed. No. He didn't ask. He wouldn't debate Dr. Jack Willke, so I had him on for the second half of the show. I thought it was a good balance—Jack for life and Jack for death. When Kevorkian found out that I had actually read all his stuff—and was therefore able to call him on his misinformation, he was livid.

Kevorkian spent several minutes talking about the "extreme" and "uncontrollable" pain suffered by one of his "patients," Marjorie Wantz (victim No. 2) whom he helped kill on Oct. 23, 1991. After several attempts at avoiding my questions, he finally admitted that he had never examined Wantz. It turns out that the autopsy showed no evidence of disease. Wantz had been diagnosed as mentally ill and had been admitted to mental institutions for suffering psychosomatic pain. In other words, much of the pain this woman thought she was experiencing could have been imagined rather than real.

That didn't seem to make any difference to Kevorkian. In fact, Kevorkian admitted on the air that he wanted to "assist" in the suicides of those who are mentally disabled, as well as teenagers, and even the homeless. Nice guy!

I asked him if I were dumped by my boyfriend and feeling distraught if he would "help" me to commit suicide. His answer (at least on the air), was "no." He said he would refer me for counseling. I then asked him what if I were in a wheelchair—disabled, but depressed for the very same reason—because I felt alone and depressed—"would you assist in my suicide then?" His answer was "yes." If you're able-bodied—no. But if you're disabled—yes. Is it any wonder why the disability groups are the ones protesting suicide initiatives? They know they'll be the first to go.

Kevorkian has boldly stated that "the voluntary self-elimination of individuals who are living morally diseased or crippled lives, taken collectively, can only enhance the preservation of public health and welfare."[6] Translation: "If you're not healthy and self sufficient, do everyone a favor and die." He'll even help you, as he's helped at least one hundred and thirty (130) others. Kevorkian's reasoning is off base, but he's right about what's at stake: the lives of the sick and disabled.

You see, if the court grants one group the "right" to assisted suicide, then that right "shouldn't be denied" to others who can't make their own medical decisions. In fact, a lower court opinion on appeal in *Washington vs. Glucksberg* said, "...contrary to many press reports, this is not a narrowly drawn decision that will affect only the suicides of mentally competent, terminally ill patients. It will be immediately possible to inflict involuntary euthanasia on those deemed mentally incompetent."

You see, this would mean that people incapable of making decisions for themselves—such as children, people unable to communicate because of brain damage, and those with certain mental disabilities or illnesses—must be put to death when their guardian or "surrogate" makes this "choice" for them.

What's at stake? For starters, it is estimated that more than fifty thousand (50,000) Americans become permanently disabled each year as a result of accidents. An estimated 1.6 million people have severe dementia. Between seven hundred and fifty thousand (750,000) and one million Americans suffer from Alzheimer's disease, and an additional 7.5 million are mentally retarded. That adds up to about ten million potential guardians who would be granted the legal or statutory authority to kill the most vulnerable of our population.

Shrouded with seemingly merciful and compassionate euphemisms, many disabled would likely be put to death. Remember the other modern example of euthanasia in pre-World War II Germany: Five-year-old retarded children weren't "gassed to death"—they were "relieved from the agony of living."

You see, "physician-assisted suicide" isn't really about suicide. Someone commits suicide every 17 minutes in this country and doesn't need any "help" in doing it. It is about giving doctors the power to kill.

This is not to say that everyone should be hooked up to every piece of available technology. If people don't want medical care, they don't even have to go to the hospital. Hospices well versed in pain control and comfort care are an excellent alternative.

And there's the problem with misdiagnoses. Question: What do you call the guy who graduates last in his medical class? Answer: Doctor. Remember victim No. 33? Thirty-seven-year-old Rebecca Badger, from California, was supposedly suffering with multiple sclerosis. Kevorkian "helped" her, too. Turns out, she didn't have MS; she had been misdiagnosed. Now she's dead.[7]

All intentions may not be well meaning. Kevorkian victim No. 35: Judith Curren, age forty-two, of Massachusetts, had filed multiple complaints for spousal abuse. Then, the same person who she said had repeatedly beaten her, took her alive to Kevorkian on August 15, 1996, and brought her back dead[8]. There won't be any more of those nasty reports of abuse filed!

And even though Kevorkian was put on trial numerous times, it wasn't until he killed a man on CBS' *60 Minutes* that he was finally convicted of homicide. Ironically, the same night Kevorkian sealed his own fate, the quadriplegic actor, Christopher Reeve, starred in a TV remake of Alfred Hitchcock's *Rear Window*. (By the way, one of Kevorkian's first victims was also a quadriplegic.) It makes you wonder: If Jack Kevorkian had offered his services to Reeve just after his horse-riding accident had left him disabled, would Reeve have accepted?

Nancy Cruzan

And at the same time Kevorkian was taking the life of his first victim, we were fighting a pre-curser to this dangerous mentality in the legislature in what's referred to as "living will legislation." And the biggest push came with the 1990 Supreme Court ruling in the *Cruzan v. Missouri Department of Health* case. By 5-4 the Court ruled that Nancy Cruzan, who became severely disabled following an accident, could not be starved to death without convincing evidence that this is what she would have wanted.

This decision was a clear victory for the medically vulnerable. Disabled individuals were granted a "pardon" for the crime of being disabled and protected from the death sentence that euthanasia activists sought to force upon them. But the coverage that followed the case could have easily been mistaken for a commercial for "living wills." Playing on fear and confusion, the media gave the impression that Nancy was in a "persistent vegetative state," and needed a court ruling to "remove her from expensive state-of-the-art, highly technological machines."

None of it was true, but when you want to do away with someone, it's easier to refer to them as "a vegetable." The truth was that Nancy was not even in a coma—nurses testified that she was able to communicate with them and could feel pain. The feeding tube through which she was fed was neither high-tech nor a recent medical innovation. They've been used for over a hundred years. And the cost? The cost of tube feeding Ms. Cruzan was about $8.00 per day, usually consisting of a canned liquid formula available in most any pharmacy without a prescription.[9]

And yet the "injustice" of not being able to starve accident victim Nancy Cruzan had Ohio legislators scurrying to do something to "remedy the problem." There was a steamroller coming at us, and there was no stopping it. They were going to pass a law, no matter who it hurt. Right to Life stood alone in opposition to a "living will" bill—more appropriately named "Death with Immunity."

There are several problems with this kind of bill, but here are two. First, there is the problem with an advanced directive, in general—it doesn't allow you to make an *informed* decision. We heard testimony from a college professor who was a strong proponent of living wills and often said to his classes that he didn't want to be "hooked up to machines." He testified how one day, however, he was unable to communicate in the hospital—and was breathing through a respirator. He couldn't talk, but he was very aware of what was going on around him. When one of his students suggested that "maybe we should get him off the respirator—after all, he said that's not what he wanted," he found himself wanting to scream, "No! No! I've changed my mind—I want to live!" Thankfully, he told the committee, "I pulled out of it," and testified against the advance directives that would have killed him.

Secondly, the fear of "over treatment" is now decades outdated. The problem we have today, as well as then, is *under* treatment. If you are the patient making the decisions, you can decide to decline *any* kind of treatment you want—you don't even have to go to the hospital in the first place. Sure, you can turn down all your meals when you are competent, but the built-in safeguard is that you yourself will suffer the consequences of such a decision. To "give *that* right" to *someone else* to decide for you to stop from being fed is a pretty dangerous thing. But that was precisely what the Ohio legislature had proposed in their bill—with complete immunity—no questions asked.

If, for example, I was walking down the street with a friend and we happened to see a man who was blind, I might say, "Wow—that's rough. I would never want to be blind." That doesn't mean that if I ever became blind, I would want to be starved to death as a result. But if the accident that left me blind also left me even temporarily unable to communicate, that comment could arguably be used to remove my food and water. Get it? That is what happened to Nancy. Her parents found someone who overheard her say she wouldn't like to be in a severely disabled condition, and it was used as testimony to have her feeding tube removed—even after the victorious court ruling.

It was at this same time I heard of a 22-year-old patient named Christine who also became disabled following a car accident. She was not in as bad a shape as Nancy, yet was undergoing the same fate. She was able to get about 75 percent of her nutrition by mouth—but her father had ordered those feedings stopped. He was able to get a neurologist to declare Christine to be in a "persistent vegetative state" so he could withdraw *all* of her nutrition and hydration (that's a medical way of saying: starve the patient to death). This was exactly the kind of incident we feared would happen as a result of the Ohio legislation.

I wanted to find out more, so I called the Missouri Rehabilitation Center where Christine was being cared for—the same place where Nancy Cruzan was treated. I asked the nurse, "I understand that your patient Christine Busalacchi has been declared to be in a 'persistent vegetative state'—is that right?"

The nurse replied, "She's sitting right here eating ice cream. Maybe you should ask *her*." The nurse told me how the State of Missouri had filed suit to block the decision by Christine's father to end his daughter's life by withdrawing all of her food and water. I asked her if she was willing to testify to what she saw so we could prevent this kind of thing from happening in our state. She did, by video, but told me of another video they had taken of Christine herself. She sent it, and it showed an alert, but disabled 22-year-old who responded to those around her, laughed appropriately at jokes, and responded to those who would ask her to move and look in certain directions.

The problem was that I was forbidden, under threat of a lawsuit from the ACLU, from showing this video in a public forum. No problem. I invited the legislators on the committee to see the video in a "private setting."(Remember, "be creative.") After they saw the 13-minute video, I then played my tape recording of the medical opinion of Ron Cranford, the *same* neurologist who gave the *same* diagnosis to Nancy Cruzan: "She is in a persistent vegetative state." The chairman looked at me in horror. I asked them, "Is this what you want to happen in Ohio?" All were willing to fix the language to prevent it, with the exception of one—a woman who showed her true colors when she said "maybe the neurologist was right—after all *he* is the neurologist." And maybe that beautiful girl should be starved to death? They all just looked at her with the "you have got to be kidding" look and dismissed her input from then on.

We made remarkable changes to the bill—so many that one pro-abortion State Senator told a newspaper, that she had "never" seen any single group have so much influence over any piece of legislation. It didn't really feel like it—because there were other *necessary* changes we were forced to do without. One thing we did get was a clarification in the "advanced directive form" which had to let people know that they were, in fact, consenting to have their *nutrition and hydration withdrawn*—if they checked the box— so there would be no misunderstanding. We didn't want people to sign one of these things to prevent "high-tech" machines and end up being starved to death.

Mark Lally's foresight anticipated the need to go to a County Prosecutor, or someone who could intervene, if wrongdoing was suspected and suggested an amendment to the bill. His suggestion was dismissed as "over-reacting."

Soon after the bill we saw the first casualty of not accepting Mark's amendment: a boy in southern Ohio named Michael, who had been injured in a motorcycle accident. Michael was visited every day for seven years by his loving grandmother, but he and his mother never got along. She rarely came to see him. Yet, according to the law, his mother was the one with "standing" to make his healthcare decisions. She decided that despite the fact that he was increasingly able to eat more and more on his own, she would have the feeding tube removed and subsequently he would starve to death. Despite the valiant efforts of his grandmother, the law didn't allow for any intervention, and Michael was starved to death while his grandmother, the nurses, and pro-lifers demonstrated outside in protest. Ben Gessler of Ohio Right to Life spent days talking to and advising Michael's distraught grandmother and is to be commended for his valiant efforts on her and Michael's behalf.

Starvation and Dehydration

Now, if death is imminent and the person is unable to assimilate the food given to him or her, by all means, remove the feeding tube—it's not going to do them any good. The difference here is that the person will then die, not of starvation and dehydration, but of their actual disease or injury. In other circumstances, if you're considering taking away someone's feeding tube, this is a medical list of the kind of "dignified death" they will experience. This is what happened to Nancy Cruzan, Christine Busalacci, and to Michael.

- The mouth of a person "treated" by starvation dries out and becomes caked or coated with thick material.
- The lips become parched and cracked or fissured.
- The tongue becomes swollen and might crack.
- The eyes sink back into their orbits.
- The cheeks become hollow.
- The mucous (lining) of the nose might crack and cause the nose to bleed.
- The skin begins to hang loose on the body and become dry and scaly.
- The urine becomes highly concentrated, causing burning of the bladder.
- The lining of the stomach dries out, causing dry heaves and vomiting.
- Hyperthermia develops—a very high body temperature. The brain cells begin drying out, causing convulsions.
- The respiratory tract dries out, giving rise to very thick

secretions, which could plug the lungs and cause death.[10]

Just as with partial-birth abortions, if you did it to a dog, you would be jailed for cruelty. But that, unfortunately, is precisely what's happening to patients all across the country.

Oregon

Did you ever wonder: If Jack Kevorkian can kill 130 people in a state that *outlaws* assisted-suicide, what do you think is going to happen if doctors are given the power to kill by statute or by court decision?

Unfortunately, we found out in Oregon, where 15 patients died of a prescribed lethal injection in 1998. Of these, the main concerns that prompted their decision to die were loss of autonomy, inability to participate in activities, and loss of control of bodily functions.[11]

And this is just the beginning for Oregon. According to columnist Nat Hentoff, as of December 1, 1999, if you're poor and destitute, Oregon taxpayers begin to pay for diagnostic and counseling sessions to verify your desire to die.

But as a spokesman for the disabled community has pointed out, "the State of Oregon will not fund our [life saving treatment], yet will pay for us to die." So what message is Oregon sending? If you're young and vibrant, you live. But if you're old, poor, and destitute, the state will pay for you to die. And it's all in the name of compassion.[12]

Ellie Jenny, a member of the disability rights group "Not Dead Yet" told *The Oregonian*, "The disabled, already concerned with being labeled unproductive in a society which bases its value of a person on performance, now worry that their 'right to die' could soon become the 'duty to die,' particularly in an era of expensive health care."[13]

The "Right to Die Society of Canada" has been sending a lovely little product to people in Oregon and elsewhere that they refer to as an "exit bag." They are the folks who are always talking about "death with dignity." Just listen to how very dignified this is—it is a plastic bag to put over your head so you can suffocate yourself. It even has an optional neckband for a snug turtleneck fit— Neato! Just ask anyone with asthma how fun it is to not be able to breathe. Yeah, that's "death with dignity" all right. What planet are these people from?

The Netherlands

But can't we build in some adequate safeguards? I recently spent some time in the Netherlands, where euthanasia is commonly practiced—with a list of extensive safeguards longer than any such list proposed in assisted suicide ballot initiatives in the United States. Yet, according to their own government report, 1,040 people are killed there each year without their consent: 14 percent were fully competent; 72 percent had never given any indication [of their own preferences] regarding termination of life, yet the doctor decided for them that death was to be their "treatment."[14] And most of this has happened where assisted suicide isn't even "officially" legal—just widely practiced.

That's a thousand people a year in a country with a population not much larger than the state of Florida who are killed because someone *else* thinks their lives aren't worth living. One woman I met there told me of her brother who was in a home for the severely disabled. She said they had to hire someone to keep watch over him—so some doctor wouldn't come along and give him a lethal injection!

Another Dutch physician told me about a patient in the care of a friend of his. She had cancer, but was afraid to go to the hospital for fear someone would kill her. The doctor assured her that her fears were unfounded and, after much coaxing, talked her into checking in for some treatment. The physician checked on her that week and she was steadily improving. He saw her again on a Saturday, and she was doing better still. On Sunday, as he was making his rounds, he noticed that there was another patient in her room. He asked the nurse what happened to his patient, and she matter of factly answered, "Oh, we needed the bed." In other words, she was given a lethal injection. She was a terminal cancer patient, after all.

Certainly, good pain control is not as widely known and practiced as it needs to be. We can do better in training physicians in pain management—something seldom stressed in medical schools. But pain is manageable—we can kill pain, we don't have to kill people. A Dutch doctor told me about a patient who was in severe pain and asked to die. A colleague of his fulfilled her request and prescribed an overdose of morphine. He returned to her room expecting to find her dead body, but instead witnessed her dancing and singing—the increased dosage was what she needed all along. With her pain gone—you guessed it—she had no more interest in dying.

Not surprisingly, pain control management is almost non-existent in the Netherlands because euthanasia is the medical solution to pain and suffering. As of mid-1990, there were only two Hospice programs in operation in all of Holland.[15]

As is the case in Oregon, it doesn't end with the legalization of assisted suicide; instead, it's a slippery slope to much more dangerous laws. For example, a new law is pending in the Netherlands that would make it the first country in the world to legalize so-called "mercy killings"—even for young children. A spokesperson for the Royal Dutch Medical Association said, "If the parents don't want to cooperate, it is the doctor's duty to respect the wishes of their patient." Let's put this in plain English: Parents will have no say in the life or death of their own children. That makes perfect sense. I'm sure a twelve-year-old child who just flunked her spelling test and whose dog ran away is perfectly capable of making life and death decisions.[16]

Assisted Suicide and the American Psychological Association

Here's the bottom line: do we treat disabled people with compassion, or kill them in their moment of despair? I, for one, say we treat them with compassion. Unfortunately, some of the so-called experts disagree. In August of 1999, the *Wall Street Journal* quoted one assisted suicide advocate, James Werth, as saying that killing someone is "rational" if that person suffers from a "hopeless condition." And how does this expert define a "hopeless condition?" Well, "it includes, but is not limited to . . . a quality of life that is no longer acceptable to the individual."

In other words, assisted suicide is *always* rational. And here's the scary part: 85 percent of the American Psychological Association members agreed with him! I thought the APA was the place where you're supposed to go for help when you're feeling suicidal! You had better be careful who you call when you have someone on your ledge threatening to jump. Now the majority of APA members seem to be saying that if you're feeling "hopeless" (as suicidal people tend to feel) that's OK. The "rational" thing to do would be to jump off that ledge![17]

That was the reaction given at the news of August 17, 1996, when Lester "Joe" Cruzan, father of Nancy Cruzan, who oversaw the withdrawal of her nutrition and hydration, tragically committed suicide himself. He had been chronically depressed following Nancy's death, and the suicide came six years after the Supreme Court case that bore his daughter's name. Ron Cranford, the neurologist who declared Nancy Cruzan (as well as Christine Busalacci) to be in a "persistent vegetative state," commented on Joe Cruzan's death by hanging. He said, it was "a *rational* suicide," since he was never going to get better (emotionally).[18]

Good News

In October 1999, in an overwhelming bipartisan fashion, the House passed the Pain Relief Promotion Act, 271-156. This Act allows health care providers to prescribe and manage the necessary drugs for pain, while stopping the federal government from facilitating assisted suicide. If it also passes the Senate, this will send a strong signal that we want to kill pain and not people.

There was some more good news in November of 1998 when a whopping 71 percent of voters in Michigan—Kevorkian's home state—*rejected* assisted suicide![19] During my visit to the United Nations I had the opportunity to meet the ambassador to the Netherlands, and I quickly pointed these latest developments out to him. I also informed him that one of the reasons that voters said no to assisted suicide in Michigan was because they had heard about what was happening in his country. People weren't at all comfortable with the idea that over 1,000 deaths per year in the Netherlands were from people who were given a lethal injection without their knowledge or consent. When he expressed his doubt, I pointed out the fact that the source of these statistics was his government's records!

What to Do

So what must we do to win the battle against legalized assisted suicide? The good news is, like with abortion, the more you find out about assisted suicide, the more against it you are. We have real-world evidence to show what happens when you turn doctors into executioners, and it's not a place anyone would want to be.

I met Phillis Bowman, who founded England's Society for the Protection of Unborn Children (SPUC), at an International Anti-Euthanasia Conference in Amsterdam and she told me how they defeated an assisted suicide measure in a committee in Parliament. The committee was stacked in favor of assisted suicide, and anyone who expressed concern was kept off—since they didn't have an "open mind," she said. What they did was to pay to fly the committee members to the Netherlands to meet with doctors on both sides of the issue and find out for themselves where England would be headed if they followed suit. Afterward, the committee came back and voted *unanimously* against the suicide proposal. The more you find out, the more you're against it.

One of the most frightening things about assisted suicide is that it takes a person's last opportunity to become saved. We very often go through our lives believing ourselves to be immortal. It isn't until many of us reach our deathbeds that the afterlife is given any real consideration at all. As Christians, we should be spending a lot more of our time with those who are at this place in their life and help to prevent them from feeling so destitute and so alone that suicide seems like a positive option for them

Often, people in nursing homes have few, if any, visitors and are frightened about what lies ahead. Imagine if your church were to do more than just sing Christmas carols there once a year. Imagine if your church adopted a nursing home and befriended the people inside—people that are hungrier for God and the assurance of salvation than probably any group you will come in contact with. That's where I would like to see trained Evangelism Explosion teams go.

A friend of mine, Kim Strauch, used to go to visit her grandmother in the nursing home. She made friends with the other patients there, and when her grandmother died she wanted to find a reason to go back and visit them. She prayed about it and that day saw an ad in the newspaper where the Humane Society was offering kittens and puppies to take to nursing homes. She told me, "You wouldn't believe how people respond to them!" Nurses commented that some patients who hadn't moved in months were reaching for a kitten or puppy. "Some people are kitten lovers," she said. "Others love the puppies and would start talking about the dog they used to own when they were young. People who would never say a word to me started telling me their life stories!" Imagine if we utilized this discovery to befriend the friendless and win them over to the kingdom of God!

No. To show compassion to the terminally ill we don't need to turn doctors into executioners.

15

Thinking Big

A s I've mentioned, we serve the God of the impossible and in my life there are certain markers I look back on to remember that fact.

Charlie Brading

A few years ago there was a vacancy in the Ohio House of Representatives, and the Republican caucus was going to appoint into that office a man who was pro-abortion and pro-euthanasia. I knew about him because I had seen him testify in the Senate in favor of starving patients to death. This was not someone we wanted to become a legislator, but we were told his appointment was a "done deal."

I remember tracking down a pro-life member of the Republican leadership at home to try to prevent the appointment, which was likely to occur that week. I told him we had a pro-life alternative—but before I could finish my appeal, he interrupted, "Janet, if your credibility means anything to you, I wouldn't try it." Those were words I have never forgotten.

Well, apparently, my credibility didn't mean much to me at that time, because we tried it.

The pro-abortion man they were ready to appoint was a doctor *and* a lawyer and, as a result, a very attractive appointee to the committee hearing our bill. If he were appointed, he would swing the vote on the committee, and that would kill our legislation. This made our involvement even more critical. He was also a county coroner—which, under the circumstances, seemed appropriate.

My good friend Linda Theis, who lived in the House district where the vacancy existed, came down to help out. She brought with her Noreen Moss, who had worked in this doctor's office and could personally testify that he was pro-abortion. We spent the day lobbying for our pro-life alternative, Charlie Brading. He was a mayor from a county that made up a fraction of the district—but it was in the district—and we wanted him appointed.

It was a tough road, especially since the outgoing "pro-life" legislator had recommended his pro-abortion buddy to replace him. We tried everything we knew to make our case, but we were up against some pretty tough odds. The House leadership's strong-arm tactics, and an outgoing pro-lifer's recommendation carried a lot of weight with the pro-life Republicans, and the pro-abortion Republicans were all too happy to comply. Noreen (who wasn't known by the legislators) even tried to lobby the pro-abortion legislators on the issue of taxes. I remember hiding behind a beam—so the opposition wouldn't know we were together. Being seen with me would have ruined *her* credibility with the legislators on the other side of the issue!

While the legislators met for their vote, we went for coffee. "Well, we tried," Linda said, exasperated. "Judging by the reactions of the people we talked to, I don't think we have a chance." At least we did what we needed to do—we told them the facts—something we had a responsibility to do.

When the caucus came back from their secret ballot, we prepared ourselves for the worst. Larry Manahan, a senior pro-life state representative was the first person we saw. He announced the results with, "I don't know how you ladies did it. I have been in the legislature for over thirty years, and this is the *first time* I have ever seen *anything* like this happen. We bucked the system. A pro-lifer got in against all odds that anyone would ever give you." I was told that Charlie was so shocked when they announced the results that he had tears in his eyes.

Ed Kasputis, who had just been elected, said, "I just thought cool stuff like this happened all the time!"

To give you an idea of the commotion this upset made, afterwards I was called into the office of Representative Bob Corbin who informed me that I had "no business interfering" in "inter-caucus politics." He said I had "overstepped my bounds," and as a result I was "no longer welcome in his office." I explained to him that I merely informed the legislators where the two candidates stood on abortion—something that as a lobbyist I was compelled to do. I told him, "Look, it's not like we were going to print the roll-call of the votes—it was a *secret* ballot! I just let the caucus know the facts, and let them come to their own conclusion. Is that something I should be forbidden from doing?" Yeah, he thought so.

For years the newspapers wrote about that little encounter as if I had said or done something so terrible as to be "banned from a legislator's office!" Over time the reports became plural (even though it wasn't true), giving the impression that I must really be obnoxious to have warranted such a sanction! What I had done was affect the outcome of the vote—something I was hired to do. Representative Bill Batchelder, now a judge, was all excited to read the news. "I'd wear that as a badge of honor!" he exclaimed. Somehow it just doesn't quite read that way in print.

The same "pro-lifer" in Republican leadership who said that my credibility was going to be jeopardized issued the warning, "You just bought yourself a primary." It was going to be a bloody battle, but we were going to give it our all. Linda Theis headed up the effort for the re-election and literally bused people into the district to go door to door for Charlie. We had tried everything we knew how to do, but we were working against a well-funded party machine working for their candidate who, incidentally, was from the county that made up 90 percent of the district.

It didn't look good. In fact, it looked downright awful—so bad that when Charlie came to his election party, he brought with him only a *concession* speech—thankfully, something he didn't need. When his opponent called to concede the election, Charlie didn't tell anyone—thinking it might be a cruel joke. And the man I risked my "credibility" for and got kicked out of an office for is still in the Ohio legislature to this day—a pro-life vote we can count on. It was well worth it.

The next day I ran into a member of the House leadership who had sided with us. He was crossing the street with former Congressman Bob

McEwen and all they could say was, "It was YOU GUYS! There is no other way to explain it—you guys won that race! Congratulations!"

So when I face a situation where someone tells me "that's impossible," I think about being told the same thing with the Charlie Brading appointment. And I think about the "discharge petition" (that I talked about in chapter eight) when I was told, "Janet, it's never been done—somebody tried it in the 1970s, and couldn't get enough signatures." And yet we had more then half the Ohio House of Representatives on that discharge petition in less then twenty-four hours. You see, it doesn't matter if it's never been done. It doesn't matter if your credibility is at risk. It doesn't matter if "it's impossible"—because with God all things are possible.

Running for the Central Committee

While the CENTER FOR RECLAIMING AMERICA is non-partisan, on the issue of life, the platforms of the two major political parties could not be more at odds, and I, as an individual, have made a choice.

While the right to life is just a "single issue," as I've mentioned before, it is a prerequisite to every other right we have. And so I made my choice about which party to belong to based upon where they stand on *the* inalienable human right: the right to life.

The 1996 Democratic Party Platform (the latest) states, "We will . . . provide for the full range of reproductive choice—education, counseling, access to contraceptives, and the right to a safe, legal abortion."

In contrast, the 1996 Republican Platform states, "The unborn child has a fundamental individual right to life which cannot be infringed. We support a human life amendment to the Constitution, and we endorse legislation to make clear that the Fourteenth Amendment's protections apply to unborn children. Our purpose is to have legislative and judicial protection of that right against those who perform abortions. We oppose using public revenues for abortion and will not fund organizations which advocate it. We support the appointment of judges who respect traditional family values and the sanctity of innocent human life."

The choice is clear. I am a Republican because I believe in what the

Republican Party stands for. I've been asked about those who are jumping ship to go to the Taxpayer's Party or the Reform Party. My thought is that *I* will cease to be a Republican when the Republican party ceases to stand for what I believe—not sooner. I think we can be more effective from within the major parties.

I also believe that the third parties present a very significant danger to the pro-life cause. In fact, I tend to agree with those who argue that it was Ross Perot and the Reform Party that paved the way for the election of Bill Clinton and Al Gore. One of my biggest fears is that the third parties will once again drain votes from the pro-life Republican presidential candidate and not from the pro-abortion Democratic candidate (based on the announced candidates for the 2000 Presidential election), paving the way for another pro-life defeat.

However, I have to say that I know many strong pro-life Democrats who are fighting for the unborn from within their party. A prime example is former Pennsylvania Governor Bob Casey, who unfortunately was excluded from speaking at his own party's convention because of his pro-life stand. Nevertheless, many of our pro-life bills would not have passed without Democratic support. In fact, I believe we will not return protection to unborn children *without* the support of pro-lifers from within the Democratic Party. We simply cannot win with the support of one party alone.

I became a Republican (by declaring my party in the primary elections); however, I was frequently unhappy with the stands of Republicans who ended up on the ballot. My solution was simple. I voted for the pro-life Democratic candidate (if there was one) instead of a pro-abortion Republican. After all, *life is the priority*, prerequisite issue.

In March of 1996 I decided to run for a seat on the Republican Party State Central Committee, which is the governing board of the Ohio Republican Party. Involvement in your state and county party (of your choice) is critical because then, instead of just casting your vote for those who are running for election, you get a "say" in *who* will actually be placed on that ballot. The problem is that far too many Republicans whose stands are inconsistent with their party's platform are the very ones who end up on the ballot. I wanted to have a say in that.

The State Central Committee seat in my district was open as a result of redistricting. I got wind of the fact that the pro-abortion secretary of the Republican Party was moving down to run in my district. I decided to go for it and started rounding up support early—before anyone else talked to the main political players like the governor, U.S. senator, U.S. congressman, state representatives, mayors and county commissioners. By the time my opponent talked to them, almost everyone had already committed to me.

But then I had to face the interview with the *County* Central Committee. The interview was by a panel, including the pro-abortion speaker of the Ohio House, and the pro-abortion county party chairman—both of whom were less than thrilled with the prospect of my running. I was able to get them to go neutral in the race when I said, "You guys keep talking about the 'big tent' in the party—I just hope that tent is big enough to include people who *actually agree* with the Republican Party Platform."

But they spent an incredible amount of money. My opponent told the *Dayton Daily News* (May 5, 1996), "You can elect a House representative for what we put in."[1] And I can believe it. People in the district were getting two and three phone calls each with lovely messages like, "Which of the following things do you find *most* alarming about Janet Folger: the fact that she's a special interest anti-abortion lobbyist..." Then they sent out four oversized, full-color brochures to every Republican in the district. I have to admit it didn't look good. Congressman John Kasich told me, "My opponents don't even do this much against me in my election for *Congress!*"

By most estimates we didn't have a chance. Even some of my campaign workers agreed that it was hopeless. Yet for the next six weeks, on Saturday mornings at 8:00 A.M., at least fifty people would come to my house and then go door to door and put up yard signs for me—sometimes in the snow. I would feed them donuts, go over our battle plan, and meet them back for lunch. My parents made the two and a half-hour drive down from Cleveland every single week. My dad and pro-lifer Paul Imhoff divided the district into zones and we put together packets with literature, yard signs, and a map for each carload of campaign workers. My mom made Sloppy Joes and prayed before we all went out each day. One of the campaign workers wasn't a Christian and he would chide my mom about how her prayers were going up against a campaign with "*a lot* of money." My mom told him *we would see* which one was more powerful.

The opposition had significantly more money than we would ever have, but we didn't give up. We held our own fundraisers in an effort to compete. One of our fundraiser flyers that got a bit of attention invited people for pizza at $35 a person. On the bottom of the flyer I had a little fun and wrote in small print:

> This is a chain flyer. Send it out to ten (10) friends within the next ten (10) days and you will have good luck and the party will prosper. Congressman John Kasich (who, incidentally, endorses Janet) sent this flyer to ten friends, took the majority of the U.S. House, was appointed Chairman of the Budget Committee, and became a national celebrity (he may also win the lottery). On October 28, 1992, Lenny Miller did not send this flyer to ten of his friends. Ten days later, Bill Clinton was elected. Mike DeWine (who also endorses Janet) was treasurer of his seventh grade student council. Later, he sent out this flyer to ten friends. Now he is a United States Senator. Do not break the chain. (This is a joke. No laws, election or otherwise, have been violated.) (Breaking the chain *may* not harm you in any way. However it would jeopardize our Party, our Posterity, and these United States of America).

Some folks from my opponent's camp made a big stink about this, and circulated rumors about filing an election complaint—which just gave me more publicity and showed that they had no sense of humor!

The Stoke family, who helped in my campaign each week, is among the most talented families I have ever met. This is a tribute to home schooling. They actually designed and created human coffee cans (my last name's Folger—get it?) for people to wear in the St. Patrick's day parade and to hand out literature. The youngest in their family wore Folger "coffee singles" and handed out little coffee single packets all along the parade route. During our "get out the vote" calls, someone actually told me they were voting for me because the cutest kids they ever saw gave them a Folger's coffee single in the parade. You never know what moves people.

We worked the polls in the rain that day—which worked to our advantage—only the really committed come out to vote in the rain. And those who are the most committed (thinking that maybe they *should be* committed) are standing out in the rain to hand them literature. That wins big points. My mom handed literature to people as they went in to vote with an enthusiastic recommendation, "She's done a lot of really great stuff—but, best of all . . . she's my daughter!"

When the polls were closed, we all returned to my house to prepare

I think human coffee cans were a first for the St. Patrick's Day Parade. My parents are wearing the campaign ball-caps. Next to me is my campaign manager, Chuck Mifsud (who would kill me if his name wasn't mentioned).

for our election "party." Reminiscent of the Brading appointment, many of the loyal individuals who had been working tirelessly on my campaign came to the party that night saying, "Well, we tried." "We gave it our best shot—but you just can't beat that kind of money." Exhausted, we looked at each other saying, "At least we gave it our best." We couldn't think of anything we had left undone.

As the results started pouring in, we called into headquarters for regular updates. The preliminary results were 60-40. When I relayed these numbers to my state representative friend, Pat Tiberi, he offered his condolences and said, I'm really sorry Jan—you gave it a good shot—but there was simply no way to go up against that kind of money."

Coffee kids Mark and Abby Stoke were little vote-getters handing out coffee-single packets.

My response really shocked him, "No, Pat, 60-40 *us*." We had won!

It turned out that this dinky little race for a seat that most people didn't even know *existed*, received more calls at both the county and *state* parties than *any* other race on the ballot. The *Dayton Daily News* reported the story of my surprise landslide victory with the headline "It's GOP's portable target." They went on to report that,

> Janet Folger put an army of grass-roots workers out in full force knocking on doors, calling voters, and flooding churches with literature. Folger's supporters delivered. She trounced (her opponent) for a central committee seat with 60 percent of the vote in a race some say illustrates how divisive the abortion issue is in the Republican Party.

Here's my favorite part, "'If Right to Life targets you, they can knock you right out,'" said Mary Ann Christie, state coordinator for Ohio Republicans for Choice."[2]

You may not believe this (I had a tough time myself), but Mrs. Becky Stoke, whose family helped on my campaign, was a poll-worker and witnessed just how dedicated pro-life people really are. One woman had accidentally slammed her hand in her car door as she was getting out to vote. She had her kids with her and was bleeding on the floor as she signed in. Mrs. Stoke noticed that she *looked* pale and suggested that she go to the hospital. The lady said she was going to, but "first she had to vote for the pro-lifer in that Central Committee race." I can't say that everyone will be quite *that* committed.

Think about it: for those who call themselves "pro-choice," abortion is just a means to have sex without consequences, but to a pro-lifer, abortion is legal child dismemberment.

God can overcome impossible hurdles if you just trust Him. As Dr. D. James Kennedy has said, "All of life can be summarized with two words: Trust God."

This is the verse I wrote in my journal:

> He sent from above, He took me; He drew me out of many waters. He delivered me from my strong enemy, from those who hated me, for they were too strong for me. They confronted me in the day of my calamity, but the Lord was my support. He also brought me out into a broad place; He delivered me because He delighted in me.
>
> —Psalm 18:16-19

At the first Central Committee meeting after the election, the decision was made that my opponent would remain on the committee for an additional year as secretary. There was a clause that permitted lame-duck officers to serve for half of the next term, even if they were defeated in the preceding election. And while outgoing members where given commendations and framed resolutions for their years of service, it was moved that those who chose to stay on for another year of service should not receive their awards—inasmuch as they weren't leaving office yet.

My first motion as a member of the committee was to speak against that decision. I moved that since the officers (my opponent and another officer) had given years of faithful service to the committee, they should not be denied their commendations and framed resolutions for that service, regardless of whether or not they stayed on the committee for another year. My motion passed unanimously, and that day my opponent became my friend. This same woman who had spent thousands of dollars trying to malign me as a "right-wing-extremist" called me at home to thank me for standing up for her. That was a very good day.

It's amazing to see what God can do. I've seen so many "done deals" come undone, and so many "impossible" things happen, that I have come to expect it. It's gotten to the point that when I hear the word "impossible," I just wait for God to make it happen.

Yes, I Believe in God

I saw God moving through a local pastor of a small church. Reverend James Cox, of West Lauderdale Baptist Church. He spent his own money to produce and distribute hundreds of T-shirts with the words, "Yes, I Believe in God"—the final words of Cassie Bernall, Rachael Scott, and others at Columbine High School in Littleton, Colorado.

Barbara Collier, the field director for the CENTER FOR RECLAIMING AMERICA, and I met with him and soon realized that we were speaking to a man of faith *and action*. Not only did he start this campaign on a shoestring budget, but he also had plans to fill one of Ft. Lauderdale's stadiums with kids in just a few weeks. I, for one, didn't have a lot of confidence that he could pull off a rally of that magnitude in such a short time, but we said we would help anyway.

We sat and brainstormed on how we might take his idea and implement it on a national level. It went something like this:

"We could put together these kits!"

"Yeah, 'Yes Kits' that could equip kids to take God back into their schools!"

"And an 'I believe in God' song!" I added enthusiastically. "We need a song by a famous artist to play on Christian stations all across the country!"

And with this conversation our "Yes, I Believe in God" campaign was under way.

Pastor Cox's rally turned out to be a huge success, with hundreds of teens rededicating their lives to Christ and scores coming to know Christ for the first time. I met some of the kids from Littleton at the Ft. Lauderdale rally and then flew out to Colorado to meet with the rest of their group.

For several hours we brainstormed about ways to help students to share their faith. I showed them "Cartoon Guy"— a drawing that Jonathan Loerop, one of our interns at the CENTER FOR RECLAIMING AMERICA and Evangelism Explosion (EE) trainers had worked on to help lead students through the Gospel presentation. They liked it—and we went ahead with it. Not only is it in our kit, but E.E. International—Dr. Kennedy's worldwide evangelism ministry—has decided to translate the Cartoon Guy into two other languages for use overseas! So thanks to Jonathan's artwork and input from the students, more kids will be reached for the Lord in other countries as well!

But that was just the beginning. We wanted a New Testament (with Psalms and Proverbs), but were told that it was going to cost us $4.00 each. If, on the other hand, we wanted a Bible with *our logo* on the cover, including customized inside pages with a salvation message and a list of "student freedoms," it was going to cost us only $1.28 apiece. Some decisions aren't hard to make.

Then there was the *Book of Hope*. We had decided against including it in the kit until one of our consultants told me he had done over $45,000 worth of research on this little book and found it worked better at reaching unsaved teens than anything else they had tested. Since it worked, I wanted it, but we were closing in on the deadline, and it didn't look like Marilyn Baughman, the woman in charge of the *Book of Hope* project, was going to call us back in time.

As it turned out, I went to speak at an Assembly of God church in Boca Raton later that week. This speaking engagement had been on my calendar for over a year. At the end of my speech a lady came up to me and introduced herself as Marilyn Baughman, suggesting she would like to help! Two days later she had the president and CEO of the *Book of Hope* in my office giving us a *below* cost rate to include it in our packets! I was seeing the hand of God at work all around me.

A Piano Phone and Faith

The packets were coming along nicely, thanks to a lot of overtime from our staff and interns, but we still needed a song. It's hard to imagine, but the big names in Christian contemporary music weren't returning my calls. One of the artist's agents told me to send him what I had. I didn't really have much, but I faxed him my ideas. I met with some of my musically talented friends, Allison and Romeo DeMarco, one morning at 7:00 A.M. in my office and played what I was thinking about on my *piano phone*. They looked horrified.

"Oh, come on guys," I told them smiling, "For the refrain we can just hit re-dial!"

We had a song, albeit a very rough song. We were joined by Lisa Velazquez (a roller-blading friend who has actually recorded her own CD) and spent a Saturday over at Allison and Romeo's house making the song presentable enough to play for some people in the industry. I then spent an extended lunch hour with Lisa and some guys from the church who "happened" to have guitars with them that day, producing "the song" in one of Coral Ridge's studios, along with another friend, Steve Vollmann.

We took the tape around and asked for advice. Everyone we asked seemed to say the same thing: "Rebecca. You guys really need Rebecca St. James."

So we tried—many times—not just for her, but for anyone else we thought could do what we were looking for. Barry Kase, our Director of Media Relations, was getting tired of trying. He said to himself, "Just one more call." And that was when he reached David Smallbone, Rebecca St. James' father and agent. He just "happened" to be a big D. James Kennedy fan, and Barry said he sounded interested in getting involved.

But in a meeting with people in the music industry the next day we were told, "I've been in the music business a long time, and this simply isn't going to happen." That was reinforced with a clarification from the former president of the Christian Music Association: "*Short of God appearing here Himself*, this simply isn't going to happen."

As I've said before, when someone says "never" or "impossible," I just look for God to make it happen. In fact, I had seen Him work so many times already, I simply asked, "Would you mind if I write that down? Because when it happens, I want to make sure I quote you correctly," I said in my most *respectful* smart-alecky voice. Then I proceeded to write down their words right in front of them.

And guess what? Our "Yes, I Believe in God" song, produced and sung by Christian contemporary artist Rebecca St. James, made the top ten! And as of this writing, it went to number one on the Adult Contemporary Christian Music Charts! She also agreed to be our "Yes, I Believe in God" campaign spokesperson, and her public service announcements promoting the campaign are running on stations across the country![3]

Someone asked me, "Can you *believe* this? Can you believe that we got *Rebecca St. James?*"

"Yes, I can believe it. God is God, after all." And when you have the faith of even a mustard seed, you better stand back, because mountains are going to move!

As of this writing, thousands of "Yes" kits have been put into the hands of school kids, with more orders coming in every day. Youth pastors and churches are ordering them by the hundreds, equipping kids nationwide to stand up and say, "Yes, I believe in God. God can do incredible things if you only look for Him to work and trust Him. He can and will do *God-sized* things.

16

Where We're Headed

I've talked about the pro-abortion movement's goal to keep the truth from reaching people. It is the only way they can win. They have used lies from the beginning, and they continue to promote abortion with lies. And they have fought every single effort of the pro-life movement—no matter how reasonable. You have seen how the word "tolerance" is being misused to condemn anyone who claims to speak the truth in a society where truth has become relative and subjective.

I have also talked about the inactive church living in a "separate society," being neither salt nor light to our dark and dying world. In the next chapter I will expound further on how the lie of "separation of church and state" has shoved the church "into the closet" while our secular society removes any vestiges of Christianity from the public square.

While we sit behind the four walls of our church, our rights are being chiseled away one by one. In this chapter I will tell you how, if Christians choose to stay within that closet, separate from the rest of society, they will very soon wake up with a padlock on the outside of the door. I am not merely talking about being prohibited from engaging in pro-life work. I am talking about even being able *to share our faith*. What happens if we don't act is a very frightening prospect, and I base that on what our inaction has already cost.

> *The only thing necessary for evil to triumph is for good men to do nothing.*
>
> —Edmund Burke[1]

That is my favorite non-biblical quote and this chapter gives a pretty good indication of just how true it is, and where we'll be if we continue to do nothing. If you are an active pro-life Christian, you are among those labeled "politically incorrect" and are fair game for ridicule. That is the first step in a movement to silence us.

Let me begin by saying that the assault on pro-lifers and Christians has become so commonplace that many of us have become desensitized to it. It happens so often that most of the time we don't even recognize it. Because they appear everywhere we are quoted, it is as if the labels "radical," "right-wing," and "extremist" were part of our names. But imagine for a moment that you picked up *The Washington Post* and read this:

African Americans are largely poor, uneducated and easy to lead.

There would be outrage! Something like that would never be tolerated, nor should it be. To characterize a whole race of people in such a negative way is racist. However, if you do it to Christians, it's completely acceptable. Here's what was *really* said:

[Pat Robertson's and Jerry Falwell's] followers are largely poor, uneducated, and easy to lead.[2]

By the way, this is from a "news article." The attack on Christians was so blatant that the *Post* was forced to run a correction the following day admitting they had no factual basis for the statement. However, there was no apology forthcoming from the writer, Michael Weisskopf, because he "[tries] not to . . . attribute every point in the story if it appears to be universally true."[3]

What if something like *this* were said, "Jewish people are 'bozos' and Judaism is a religion for losers." Same reaction—universal outrage. The Anti-Defamation League would be calling for the job of anyone who said such a thing. Such a person could never be trusted with fair news treatment! The person whose job they would be calling for would be Ted Turner—the owner of CNN. But what he really said was, "*Christians* are 'bozos' and *Christianity* is a religion 'for losers.'"[4]

By the way, in a stunning and ironic twist, Ted Turner's wife, Jane Fonda, has reportedly become a Christian. Insiders say that her spiritual faith has grown so much, her entire worldview is affected. Recently, for example, she refused to "meditate" at an environmental conference, suggesting to those involved that they would be well advised instead to "pray to Jesus Christ."[5]

In his interview with *Playboy* magazine, Minnesota Governor Jesse Ventura said, "Organized religion is a sham and a crutch for weak-minded people who need strength in numbers. It tells people to go out and stick their noses in other people's business." "Religion is a sham?" Kind of makes you wonder what Jesse "The Body" Ventura (an ex-professional wrestler) thinks of professional wrestling—doesn't it? But because he slammed *all* organized religion, a spokesman later tried to CLARIFY that Ventura only really meant "evangelical Christians." He said that the governor was just referring to those "members of the religious right, who are intolerant, and the governor hates intolerance."[6]

It's only the *Christians* (referred to in the less than affectionate term) that are weak-minded and in need of a crutch. Wow. I feel better already. I'm glad the governor is such a tolerant guy!

Incidentally, a *Minneapolis Star-Tribune* poll found that three-quarters of those polled said they disagreed with his recent comments on religion. And his approval rating fell from 73 percent in July to 54 percent.[7]

Ridicule then moves to demonization. Imagine for a moment that Reverend Jesse Jackson said *this:*

> The National Organization for Women was a strong force in [Nazi] Germany. It laid down a subtle scientific, theological rationale for the tragedy in Germany. NOW was very much in evidence there.

Now you're looking at that ridiculous quote, and you're probably thinking, "What a stretch—The National Organization for Women wasn't even *around* during the *time* of Nazi Germany—let alone was it a "force" there. Neither was the Christian Coalition. Here's what Jesse Jackson *really* said:

> The *Christian Coalition* was a strong force in [Nazi]

Germany. It laid down a subtle scientific, theological rationale for the tragedy in Germany. The *Christian Coalition* was very much in evidence there.[8]

Listen to what *else* is being said about us, keeping in mind, as with any political campaign, if something goes unanswered it is assumed to be true:

"Comedy"

You know what else I can't stand, is them [sic] people that are anti-abortion. F--- them; I hate them. They're horrible; they're hideous people. They're ugly, old, geeky, hideous men... They just don't want nobody to have an abortion 'cause they want you to keep spitting out kids so they can f---ing molest them.[9]

"News"

The story of Oklahoma City [bombing] and the militias should not make us forget that the main form of political terrorism in the United States today is perpetrated by right-wing opponents of abortion.[10]

Syndicated columnist Ellen Goodman . . . wrote that "radical anti-abortion groups like Operation Rescue and Rescue America have to be dealt with as <u>domestic terrorists as deadly as the ones who blew up the World Trade Center and as fanatic as the cultists in Waco</u>.[11]

It's just that their religion is so narrow, and it's so mean, and it's so ugly, and it's so intolerant, and it's so un-Christian.[12]

—Bill Press, CNN *Crossfire* Co-Host

"Education"

At its annual conventions, the National Education Association distributed flyers and packets decrying "the radical right." Why? Because Christians are in favor of the freedom of choice over where to send your children to school—and not the freedom to kill tomorrow's students.[13]

The Ohio Educational Association (a division of the National

Educational Association) was looking to find out some information in an official survey. Imagine if *this* was what they asked: *"Are any of the school board members in your school district known or suspected to be Jews?"*

You can immediately recognize the first question as a frightening parallel to pre-World War II Germany. Here's what they *really* asked: *"Are any of the school board members in your school district known or suspected to be proponents of the Radical Right?"* [14]

> Watching religious conservatives is like people in the 18th century going to asylums to watch lunatics chew on their own wrists. They are a fringe, and people who take them seriously aren't engaging in some disinterested dialogue. They're looking at a spectacle. [15]

"Entertainment"

Here's what syndicated radio host Howard Stern told a pro-life caller on November 11, 1999: [16]

> Howard Stern: . . . And the unborn is a blob. It's a blob.
>
> Lisa: What about the partial-birth abortion?
>
> Stern: I'm all for it. Any time a woman is in pain and can't get through life, I don't need her to bring another painful life into this world that will be neglected and rejected and raised to be a criminal, so that you idiots can electrocute it, if I commit this crime.
>
> Lisa: It won't be a criminal.
>
> Stern: Of course they will be and worse.
>
> Lisa: That is so ridiculous.
>
> Stern: Okay, honey. You've got all the answers. You piece of garbage. I hate you more than anything on this planet.
>
> Lisa: I love you, too.
>
> Stern: No, I hate you. I hate you.
>
> Lisa: Howard.
>
> Stern: I hate you. You're an idiot. I can't stand dumb people. If I was president, I would have you gassed. I would march you into the ovens.

Stern: I don't care. I'm telling you that as soon as you take away abortion, this society will be ruined. It's already ruined. It's going to be worse. And don't let any religious freak tell you anything different.

Lisa: And you believe it's a blob?

Stern: It's a blob. It's soulless. There's nothing in there.

Lisa: A partial-birth abortion.

Stern: That's right. Women should be able to abort up to nine months.

Lisa: Seven months.

Stern: Nine months. I said nine months.

Lisa: A slit to the head.

Stern: I said nine months.

Lisa: Up to nine months.

Stern: That's right. I know you should have been aborted. You weren't, you unloved piece of garbage. Do you know what it's like to see the world clearly? Through clear eyes? You don't even know what it's like. It's painful because I see the obvious answer.

. . . .

Stern: All right, listen. I'm not going to argue abortion. Guess what. Na na na. Abortion's legal. F--- you. We will kill as many babies as we want. And you can't stop it.

Stern: Birth control. I'll tell you when I ran for governor I said we'll fill all the pot holes with fetuses. And I meant every word of it.

. . . .

Brian: This woman on here with you is an idiot.

Stern: Of course.

Brian: I believe that maybe her parents would have thought about an abortion when they would have saw in the future what they were going to have.

Stern: Of course we wish we could abort her.

Brian: Do you think it would be too late to abort her right now?

Stern: No. It wouldn't.

Brian: I'm ready.

Stern: If she came down here right now, I'd put a coat hanger in her head.

Brian: HO. HO.

Howard Stern, heard all across this nation on radio and TV stations, is suggesting that he would "march pro-lifers to the ovens." Why in the world would we sit idly by and let him?

According to Bill Johnson, of the American Decency Association, over 9,700 advertisers have stopped advertising on Stern's show since 1996. Until 1999, he had added his show to between nine and twelve radio stations a year. But in 1999, he had "a net gain of negative one."[17]

The Movement to Silence Us

As ridicule moves to demonization, demonization moves to censorship. Now that you've felt the tolerance for our diverse viewpoint and the warmth from the outside world, take a look at the specific movement to silence us. While it was happening earlier, I first noticed it in the early '90s when the assault against pro-life Christians moved into the mainstream. A few examples:

. . . The "fire-breathing Christian radical right". . . is about to take over the Republican Party.[18]

—Vic Fazio, Democratic Congressional Campaign Chairman

They are what the American people fear the most.[19]

—Vic Fazio, Democratic Congressional Campaign Chairman

Ralph Reed put it into perspective when he said:

Murder is the leading cause of death for African-American males aged eighteen to thirty-four, and a minority adolescent male living in our nation's capital has a higher likelihood of being killed than an American soldier did in Vietnam. Yet people of faith getting involved in public life is what the American people fear most.[20]

Saying that people fear them—that should keep them quiet. Maybe we can prevent the President's impeachment by name-calling too:

> A vote against impeachment is a vote against bigotry. It's a vote against fundamentalism, the right-to-life movement, and the radical right. And if this president is impeached, it will be a great victory for the forces of genuine evil, evil, genuine evil.[21]
>
> —Alan Dershowitz, December 16, 1998

And, heaven forbid, we find a newspaper that's not blatantly pro-abortion:

> The *Daily Oklahoman* is the worst paper in America because it "demonizes feminists and Planned Parenthood . . . the only 'research' you'll find here comes filtered through the anti-abortion zealotry of the *Family Research Council, Eagle Forum,* the *Christian Coalition,* and the *American Family Association*." [22]
>
> —*Columbia Journalism Review,* Jan/Feb 1999

Call Them Murderers

And then there's the call from the abortion leaders to prevent us from speaking the truth by calling us all murderers. Kind of ironic—isn't it?

> Those in the leadership of the other side must acknowledge and admit that their words drive unrestrained factions of their own movement to commit these horrific acts . . . Denials and condemnations no longer suffice. They must stop referring to abortion as murder and to doctors who perform them as murderers.[23]
>
> —Kate Michelman, President of NARAL, December 19, 1998

No, *truth* doesn't kill. Abortion does. The National Conference of Catholic Bishops ran a full page ad in *The New York Times* (January 22) in 1995 that said it best: "Abortion policy must be debated. Without violence. But with truth."

And then Planned Parenthood joined NARAL in the movement to silence us by blaming people that speak the truth about abortion murder:

That word game has turned out deadly. It is time to
point the finger where the blame belongs—at the doors
of people who spew hate from radio and TV talk shows,
WEB sites, and pulpits.[24]
—Gloria Feldt, President of Planned Parenthood,
December 19, 1998

That's the way to keep the churches quiet, call them murderers.
Good one, Gloria.

Calling people murderers who happen to disagree with you isn't just
limited to the abortion debate. During the Truth in Love campaign that
expressed hope for change to those struggling with homosexuality, that
approach became the latest fad.

Katie Couric said on *The Today Show* that saying homosexuals can
change prompts people to say: "If I met someone who was homosexual, I'm
going to take action to try to convince them or try to harm them."[25]

I was on the *Today Show* the next day when the homosexual lobby
tried the same approach.

If I had it to do over again, I would simply say:

I would like to address what you said yesterday, Katie: There
is a very big difference between trying to convince someone and
killing them. And to accuse peaceful people who express hope for
change with the murder of Matthew Shepard or anyone else, is
irresponsible journalism.

I think I should have demanded an apology as well. Hindsight is
20-20.

Most of the organizations that joined with us in that campaign experienced the same kind of "tolerance": everything from vulgar, harassing
phone calls to death threats. When professional football player Reggie White
spoke on the issue, he experienced that kind of "open-minded" appreciation
for the diversity of his views, too. He said, "I've been called homophobic; I've
been called stupid. I've been called unintelligent and I've been called a nig-
ger by so-called gay activists." Why is it that tolerance is a one-way street?

Before I tell you who else called us murderers, let me give you a sample of one of the full-page "Truth-in-Love" campaign ads that caused all the commotion. One featured a picture of hundreds of ex-homosexuals (there were 850, but they couldn't all fit in the picture) with the headline, "We're standing for the truth that homosexuals can change." Brace yourself for the "hateful," "bigoted," "intolerant" speech they say is responsible for murder (Note: if you're under 18, you may want to ask your parents before reading it): "We believe every human being is precious to God and is entitled to respect. But when we see great suffering among homosexuals, it's an inherent Christian calling to show compassion and concern." Wow! I guess now you can see what all the fuss is about.

You can understand why the city of San Francisco would be prompted to accuse us of murder:

> It's not an exaggeration to say that there's a direct correlation between these acts of discrimination, like Matthew Shepard, such as when gays and lesbians are called sinful, and when major religious organizations say they can change if they try, and the horrible crimes committed against gays and lesbians.[26]

I did a radio show during the campaign where I was also accused of murder for holding to the traditional biblical view of homosexuality. The host said, "Well, if *you're* not responsible for the murder of (homosexual) Matthew Shepard, then *who* is?"

My answer was, "How about the people who actually killed him?" It's kind of crazy, I know. I can see why it wouldn't readily occur to anyone.

Incidentally, it really wasn't the homosexual issue that sparked that campaign—it was the freedom of speech and the freedom of religion. Not only had Reggie White undergone assault for his biblical beliefs (that homosexuality is a sin, like other sins for which you can find forgiveness), Senate Majority Leader Trent Lott had also come under fire for expressing the same thing.

Former White House spokesperson, Mike McCurry decided to join in on the fun when he said that *anyone* who believed (what the Bible had to say about homosexuality) was "backward thinking." A spokesperson for the White House had just slapped millions of American families in the face. And in any campaign, if an attack goes unanswered, it is assumed to be true. That was the spark that started the Truth in Love campaign. In the midst of all the hostility, those who worked on the campaign felt it important to advocate that the freedom of speech also applies to those who disagree.

Do you see a trend here? Label them. Ridicule them. Even blame them for murder. But what if they still won't keep quiet? The next logical step is *make them keep quiet.*

San Diego Judge

I first noticed this dangerous trend when I heard about a judge in San Diego in April of 1994. This judge had ordered pro-life pregnancy center workers to "announce themselves" to callers and identify themselves as "pro-life." They were also ordered to inform everyone that they give their information from a "biblical perspective."[27] Think about this for a moment. The judge did not order the abortion center workers to "announce themselves" to all their callers and to inform them that their information is given from a "pro-abortion, secular perspective."

Like lepers shouting, "Unclean!"—only the pro-lifers had to announce themselves with a pro-life label to everyone they talked to. What next? Here's a time-saving idea: Perhaps we should sew little yellow crosses on our sleeves so people will know just by looking at us that we're pro-life Christians—and eliminate the need to announce it to people!

FACE

Then there was the so-called "Freedom of Access to Clinic Entrances" (FACE) legislation targeting the peaceful pro-life demonstrations of civil disobedience. While I always believed in fighting abortion within only legal means, peaceful civil disobedience has long played a part in our country's battle for civil rights. I'm told that the restaurant where Martin Luther King, Jr. held his first sit-in is being made into a museum. At the same time, pro-lifers who wish to use the exact same means to stand for the civil rights of the unborn are declared to be felons.

To get an idea of how this law specifically targets the *thoughts* of the pro-life protester, imagine three people sitting in front of the door of a medical building where they perform abortions *and* do animal research. The first offender is engaging in civil disobedience because she works at the abortion facility in the building and thinks she doesn't get paid enough. The second protester is an animal-rights activist. He is upset because they are using rabbits for cancer research down the hall. And the third civil-disobedient citizen is a pro-lifer. She is upset about the fact that they are performing partial-birth abortions inside the building, and is trespassing, like the others, to make her point.

All three are blocking the building's entrance and, under equal justice laws prior to FACE, all three would be equally in violation of the trespass law. FACE, however makes one of them a felon. Guess which one?

The first one is involved in a labor dispute—she'll probably be asked to leave, and if she doesn't, she'll likely get a slap on the wrist for trespassing before getting her raise. The animal-rights activist? Most likely the news media will come out and film the action—especially if a Hollywood star is involved—and the cameras will zoom in on the mean police officer for carrying away this noble defender of rabbits.

The third protester? Not because of her actions—she was doing the exact action as the other two—but because of her belief that it is wrong to pull an infant out of the womb four-fifths of the way before sucking the living child's brains out, she is a felon. That's right. FACE says she will now lose her right to vote, her right to bear arms and run for office . . . and spend hard time in a *federal* penitentiary (one year for the first offense, three years for repeat offenses). That's called a *thought crime*, and it targets the pro-lifer not for his or her actions, but for having a *pro-life motivation*.

Madsen

In *Madsen v. Women's Health Center, Inc.*, the U.S. Supreme Court ruling upheld "bubble laws" that said that no one could come within 36 feet of a clinic entrance and driveway of an abortion facility. Even on a *public side-*

walk—that is, if you are pro-life.

Unlike FACE, we're not talking about trespassing or blocking anything—we're talking about the First Amendment rights of pro-life citizens to legally demonstrate on a public sidewalk near an abortion mill.

There are other parallels as well. Hitler reinterpreted Christmas and Easter into pagan holidays. Christmas was turned into a pagan festival and, at least for the SS troops, its date was changed to December 21, the date for winter solstice. Carols and Nativity plays were banned from the schools in 1938, and even the name Christmas was changed to "Yuletide." Crucifixes were eliminated from classrooms, and Easter was turned into a holiday that heralded the arrival of spring.[28] But we would never do anything like that. Compare signs and ads posted saying, "Jews are not wanted," to an ad that ran in the *Village Voice* that specifically stated "NO CHRISTIANS."[29]

The seemingly "harmless" beginnings of the Holocaust started with negative depictions of Jewish people in such things as political cartoons depicting Jews as rats (making it easier to "exterminate" them). Now

CHRISTIANS AS RATS.
(Oliphant © 1993 Universal Press Syndicate. Reprinted with permission. All rights reserved.)

Christians are the subject of such negativity. A political cartoon pictures Christians as rats pulling the Republican elephant into the "faith mission" with the quote, "You're being saved, like it or not." If only those pesky Christian rats would leave the Republican party alone. Serves them right—just what do they think they are *doing* trying to influence public policy like that?

And then, along with censorship, comes discrimination.

Michelle Shocks

Michelle Shocks of Seattle, Washington, was riding home on a bus one day when another passenger boarded saying, "Praise the Lord!" He was happy to be out of the pouring rain. Michelle asked the passenger where he went to church, and they started to privately discuss religion across the aisle. But then the driver asked them to stop. He ordered them to refrain from their discussion because it might "offend" the other passengers.

Michelle then moved to a seat next to the other passenger and they continued their discussion in hushed tones so as not to offend anyone. The bus driver pulled the bus to the side of the road and demanded that both passengers leave the bus. Michelle, who was 25 years old and 5 months pregnant, was forced to walk her last mile home—in the rain![30]

Are Christians being told to go to the back of the bus? No, they're now being *thrown off* the bus.

John Reyes and 150 other college students held a peaceful, pro-life demonstration in front of a high school in Lynchburg, Virginia. But school officials called the police. When asked to leave, John promptly complied, but that wasn't good enough. He was later indicted for trespassing and sentenced to six months in jail. The judge, who sentenced John to the six-months, has allowed criminals convicted of grand larceny, possession of cocaine, and assault and battery to serve no jail time at all. The prosecutors said that John's six-month jail sentence sent the "correct message" to future protesters. And what might that message be? Sell deadly cocaine or hurt others and you receive a "get out of jail free" card; share a pro-life message and you "go directly to jail."

Samuel Kent

Never mind the protesting. If you are a student, you can forget about praying. Apparently, when you walk through the doors of a public school, you check your First Amendment rights at the door.

Samuel Kent is a federal judge. He ruled in a 1995 graduation prayer case that any student violating his order against praying in the name of Jesus would be sentenced to a six-month jail term. Here is what he said in court:

> And make no mistake, the court is going to have a United States marshal in attendance at the graduation. If any student offends this Court, that student will be summarily arrested and will face up to six months incarceration in the Galveston County Jail for contempt of Court. Anyone who thinks I'm kidding about this better think again.
>
> . . . .
>
> Anyone who violates these orders, no kidding, is going to wish that he or she had died as a child when this court gets through with it.[31]

This is the United States of America, ladies and gentlemen. And now they want to silence us from talking to God.

Antonio Peck

Five-year-old Antonio Peck was told that he was supposed to make a poster on how to "save the world." So little Antonio drew a picture of Jesus and printed the words: "The only way to save our world." When he showed his picture to the teacher, he was punished and told that it was "unacceptable." It was supposed to be about the environment. So he drew another poster of people taking out trash, and put Jesus on the side praying. When they displayed Antonio's picture on the bulletin board, they folded over that part. After all, Jesus is not someone you are allowed to see in school.

Discrimination leads to legislation and court mandates. It has to be enforced, after all. In the Holocaust museum in Washington, D.C., one of the things that struck me was how the laws that were passed would come up on video screens, one after the other, next to the date they were passed. In a book I bought there by Michael Berebaum, called *The World Must Know,* he described the first of these laws:

> On April 7, 1933, it dismissed all non-Aryans from civil serv-ice, including notaries and teachers in state schools. It was the first of 400 separate pieces of legislation enacted between 1933 and 1939 that defined, isolated, excluded, segregated, and impover-ished German Jews.[32]

Historically, after ridicule, demonization, censorship, and discrimina-tion, comes persecution. In Germany, the call came for a **final solution.** Reggie Rivers, who writes for the *Rocky Mountain Times* wrote:

> I can periodically understand the frustration and general fatigue that compelled the Romans to throw select Christians to the lions. It's not just that the lions were hungry; it was that the Romans were tired of listening to the self-righteous babbling of Christians who claimed to be experts on everything and had egos the size of . . . well, God."[33]

In 1996, evolutionist Richard Dawkins was named "Humanist of the Year" by the American Humanist Association. (Just to give you an idea of where they stand, other past winners include Faye Wattleton and Ted Turner.) In his acceptance speech, he compared the threat of AIDS and "mad cow disease" to the threat posed by faith. So faith is now compared to a dis-ease? According to Dawkins, faith is "one of the world's great evils, compa-rable to the smallpox virus but harder to eradicate." Dawkins made this quote three years ago, and he has yet to be admonished by his fellow humanists.[34] "Eradicate." That's an interesting word. Kind of like "exterminate" and "eliminate." Excuse me, but I thought humanists preached tolerance.

I visited Greg Cunningham, a friend who came to a university in Miami with his Genocide Awareness Project (GAP) that depicts huge posters of forms of genocide throughout history next to pictures of another set of vic-tims—unborn babies. He has to put barricades around his displays because students have tried to cut, mangle, and destroy them. Here's a quote from the school paper I just happened to pick up while I was there:

"Whoever these people are, they should be shot . . . "[35]

It's good to see that the university campus is still about the free exchange of ideas. Statements like that would never be tolerated against any other group of people. Neither should they be tolerated against Christians.

Want to know where this is going?

In France, where only one half of one percent is evangelical Protestant, the government has now defined evangelicals as "representing extreme factions of the traditional Reformed church." One man seeking appointment to a high office was told by government officials that he would not get the post as long as his children remained in a Christian school.[36]

According to Michael Horowitz, of the Hudson Institute, Canadian Christians already suffer the most quasi-official bigotry of any religion in the developed world.[37] For example, in January 1998, a symposium on legal and religious issues at the University of Toronto Law School heard a Department of Finance official declare, "modern society has gone beyond the need to consider religion a charity," and the panel of legal experts unanimously agreed.[38]

In British Columbia, the Court of Appeals denied Surrey School Board the right to remove homosexual propaganda from first grade classrooms. According to the Court, the board's earlier decision to remove the pro-homosexual literature was found to be illegitimate because it was "influenced" by the religious beliefs of parents in that school district.[39] You see, only atheists and agnostics are allowed to do that.

In Quebec, anti-Christian bigotry has now reached into homes. A government employee removed a child from her Baptist family there because she thinks Baptists "might have unusual beliefs regarding child rearing."[40]

One World Church

UN member Robert Mueller, who has served as the right-hand man to past UN Secretaries General U Thant, Kurt Waldheim, and Javier Perez de Cuellar, is working on a project of his own. His dream is a one-world church —something he would like to see implemented this year. He said, "My dream is to get a tremendous alliance between all the major religions and the UN."

In 1999, representatives from every religion all over the world put the finishing touches on the United Religions Charter. If ratified in June of 2000, this will become the World Church.

There's just one little problem standing in the way of his dream—those darned Christians. In his book *New Genesis*, Mueller points out that "Peace will only be possible through the taming of fundamentalism. . . ."[41]

The bottom line is that fundamentalism must be "tamed" to make way for tolerance. If you believe the Bible, that "taming" is aimed at you.

Inaction has consequences. If our freedoms mean anything to us at all, we had better start using them—while we still can. While persecution of Christians is not happening here yet, the idea is not all that far-fetched when you look at what is happening around the globe. In Sudan, Christians are being sold as slaves, tortured, and killed routinely. In China, Christians are shot on sight (not to mention being forced to undergo abortions). Christians are persecuted in Iran, Pakistan, North Korea and a host of other countries around the globe.

The trend toward silencing the pro-life Christian is real. Label them. Ridicule them. Even blame them for murder. And if they still won't keep quiet? The next logical step is *make them* keep quiet through court orders and legislation . . . and then tolerate those who call for them to be killed. That is how far we've come.

I don't know about you, but I would rather use my freedoms to speak out about where this trend is going, than wait until those rights get taken away.

We must never forget the warning from Pastor Martin Niemoller (1892-1984), a survivor of a Nazi concentration camp:

> In Germany they came first for the Communists, and I didn't speak up because I wasn't a Communist. Then they came for the Jews, and I didn't speak up because I wasn't a Jew. Then they came for the trade unionists, and I didn't speak up because I wasn't a trade unionist. Then they came for the Catholics, and I didn't speak up because I was a Protestant. Then they came for me, and by that time no one was left to speak up.[42]

17

Taking Action

Some Christians don't believe they should be involved in the fight to end abortion. What does the Bible say?

> Deliver those who are being taken away to death,
> And those who are staggering to slaughter, O hold them back.
> If you say, "See, we did not know this,
> Does He not consider it who weighs the hearts?
> And does He not know it who keeps your soul?
> And will He not render to man according to his work?"
>   —Proverbs 24:11 (NASB)

> If you love me, you will obey what I command.
>   —John 14:15 (NIV)

What about the Christians in Germany in the days that preceded World War II—what were *they* doing when the innocent were "being taken away to death?" The following poem was written about that.

> *I found myself in danger, I cried out in despair*
> *I prayed, "Lord let them hear me! Let just one person care!"*
> *I raised my voice to heaven as the train kept moving on*
> *As we passed behind the church yard I could hear the Worship songs.*
> *I cried out all the louder to the Christians there inside*
> *But they raised the chorus louder not hearing me outside.*
> *I knew they heard the whistle and the clacking of the tracks.*
> *They knew that I was going to die and still they turned their backs.*
> *I said, "Father in heaven how can your people be so very hard of hearing,*
> *To the cry of one like me?"*

I shouted, "Please have mercy! Just a prayer before I die?!"
But they sang a little louder to the Holy One on high.
They raised their hands to heaven but blood was dripping down.
The blood of all the innocent their voices tried to drown.
They have devotions daily, they function in my name
And they never even realized it was I upon that train.

—Penny Lea

This poem is based on a conversation Penny had with an old man. Here is his story:

> I lived in Germany during the Nazi holocaust. I considered myself a Christian. I had attended church since I was a small boy. We had heard the stories of what was happening to the Jews, but like most people today in this country, we tried to distance ourselves from the reality of what was really taking place. A railroad track ran behind our small church, and each Sunday morning we would hear the whistle from a distance and then the clacking of the wheels moving over the track.
>
> We became disturbed when one Sunday we noticed cries coming from the train as it passed by. We grimly realized that the train was carrying Jews. They were like cattle in those cars . . . their screams tormented us. We knew exactly at what time that whistle would blow, and we decided the only way to keep from being so disturbed by the cries was to start singing our hymns. By the time that train came rumbling past the church yard, we were singing at the top of our voices. If some of the screams reached our ears, we'd just sing a little louder until we could hear them no more. I can still hear them crying out for help. God forgive all of us who called ourselves Christians, yet did nothing to intervene.[1]

It's a lot easier to do when the screams are silent.

In 1909, Teddy Roosevelt said, "I believe that the next half century will determine if we will advance the cause of Christian civilization, or revert to the horrors of brutal paganism."[2]

If you're not sure whether we've advanced the cause of Christian civilization or reverted to the horrors of brutal paganism, go back and have a glance at Chapter 8 about partial-birth abortion.

How did we get here? Former abortionist Bernard Nathanson, who founded NARAL (back when the letters stood for the National Association for Repeal of Abortion Laws) shared some of his insight in his book, *Aborting America.*[3] He talked about how he stirred up "anti-Catholic prejudices and pontificated about the necessity for 'separation of church and state.'" He adds, "As if we did not welcome the embrace of liberal Protestants and Jews!" He also mentions his former NARAL colleague, Larry Lader, who was "upset greatly by religious activity against abortion but was full of praise for church activism on the slavery issue."

Nathanson said, "All of this religious line was, of course, *necessary political strategy.*" He also gave insight as to how he was able to accomplish his goal of legalizing abortion: "A more general argument is that abortion laws are a threat to American 'pluralism,' or that 'one religious group' ought not to 'impose' its views on others in our society."

In other words, Nathanson and the other pro-aborts sought to silence the Christian opposition by demonizing them by using the old myth of "separation of church and state."[4]

Nathanson now admits that "under the First Amendment . . . any group has a right to express its views and to try to persuade others of its stand on a moral issue."[5]

What the Constitution Really Says

The First Amendment agrees—it is *Congress* that can't impose on our rights of free exercise of our religion: "*Congress* shall make no law respecting an establishment of religion, or prohibiting the free exercise thereof."

As George Washington so eloquently stated, "If I could entertain the slightest apprehension that the Constitution framed in the Convention, where I had the honor to preside, might possibly endanger the religious rights of any ecclesiastical Society, certainly I would never have placed my signature to it."[6] Washington happens to be fairly knowledgeable about the Constitution, considering the fact that he presided over the entire

Constitutional Convention, thereby overseeing the whole process from beginning to end. If he thought it was a threat to any rights at all—any religious freedoms, he wouldn't have even signed the thing!

James Madison was the chief architect of the Constitution. Here's what he said on July 12, 1788, to the Virginia Convention: "There is not a shadow of a right in the federal government to intermeddle with religion."[7] Incidentally, Madison also declared, "Religion [is] the basis and foundation of Government."[8]

Wow! The ACLU better hope *that* never gets out!

OK. So there's no "separation of church and state" in the Constitution. The First Amendment tells us that it is Congress that can't infringe on our religious freedoms. So where does this "Constitutional separation" come from? Maybe from Fisher Ames, the guy who was responsible for and introduced the original wording of the First Amendment in the House of Representatives. It must have been him—right? Otherwise our nation might end up with something as horrible as Bibles in the public schools!

History reveals, however, that Fisher Ames actually spent a good portion of his life fighting to make the Bible a prominent book in the public schools. He feared that the Bible was losing prominence in the schools. In 1801 he gave us some clear insight into his position when he said, "Should not the Bible regain the place it once held as a school book? Its morals are pure, its examples captivating and noble."[9] Fearing that the Bible was losing prominence in the schools, he spent years fighting to make sure the Bible was first and foremost the book that was read in the public school system. Unless he was schizophrenic, that pretty much rules him out as the originator of the so-called doctrine of separation of church and state!

Wait a minute, I've got it! Let's go to the ACLU's *favorite* place to look for the "Constitutional separation of church and state"—the courts. Let's start at the top. How about the first Supreme Court? And the first Chief Justice of the U.S. Supreme Court? That was John Jay, and surely he could put an end to this great debate and shed some light on this flagrant disregard of the "real meaning" behind it all. Surely he would tell those Christians to keep their views to themselves—separate from the state. Here's what John Jay actually had to say, "Unto Him who is the author and giver of all good, I render sincere and humble thanks for His manifold and unmerited blessings, and especially for our redemption and salvation by His beloved Son." Hardly sounds like he believed in separation of church and state.

OK. Maybe those early members of the Supreme Court were like that, but what about the Court a hundred years later? The Supreme Court of the United States, in their 1892 decision, *Holy Trinity v. United States,* cited 87 precedents from the Founding Fathers, acts of the Founding Fathers, acts of Congress and state governments, proving that this nation was founded upon Christian principles. They could have cited a whole bunch more, but they thought 87 precedents were enough.

The Court's unanimous opinion stated, "These, and many other matters which might be noticed, add a volume of unofficial declarations to the mass of organic utterances that this is a Christian nation."[10]

That could really hurt an ACLU fundraising letter.

OK, if we've checked the Constitution itself, the president of the Constitutional Convention, the chief architect of the Constitution, the congressman who wrote and introduced the specific language of the First Amendment, the first Supreme Court, the Supreme Court 100 years later, it looks like we're running out of places to look. Maybe we can see if some prominent people who were out of town had anything to say. Yeah, that's what we should base our national policies on.

Thomas Jefferson was in France at the time the Constitution was ratified and had nothing to do with it. But if you snoop around in his private letters, maybe he said something that might be construed as a means to keep those Christians quiet.

The Danbury Baptists had heard some troubling rumors that there might be a "national denomination" selected. They wanted to make sure the government wasn't intending to get involved in matters of religion, particularly the establishment of a national denomination.

In his private response to the Danbury Baptists, Jefferson wrote: "I contemplate in solemn reverence the act of the whole American people which declared that their legislature should make no law respecting the establishment of religion or prohibiting free exercise thereof, thus building a wall of separation between the church and state."[11]

It is clear by the context that Jefferson's "wall of separation" referred to a one-directional wall to protect the Church from the State. This is the same guy who said, "No power over the freedom of religion [is] delegated to the United States by the Constitution,"[12] in the Kentucky Resolutions of 1798.

Did you catch that? The United States has NO POWER over the freedom of religion. No power. Maybe the pro-aborts and the ACLU would do better to understand their "separation" hero, Thomas Jefferson, better if they read more than one private letter taken out of context.

I don't know how it could be any more clear (although I didn't check anyone else who was out of town that day). You have the freedom to exercise your religious beliefs and speak out as you see fit, and there's nothing the government can do about it—at least not according to the original intent of the Founding Fathers, the Constitution, the First Amendment and the Supreme Court for the first 170 years after the birth of this nation.

Supreme Court Justice Antonin Scalia shed some light on why the current courts seem to have such a problem with this issue:

> Church and state would not be such a difficult subject if religion were, as the Court apparently thinks it to be, some purely personal avocation that can be indulged entirely in secret, like pornography, in the privacy of one's room. For most believers it is not that and has never been.[13]

Rest assured, anything they can do to keep you on the sidelines will be tried. If the "constitutional separation of church and state" doesn't do the trick, they will try something else—like shutting out half the nation's population (males) from ever speaking up.

But you're a man—or—you've never had children. What makes you think you can talk about abortion?

Just because I'm not Jewish does that mean that I can't talk about the Holocaust? Just because I'm white, does that mean I can't talk about racism? Half the babies aborted were boys. Every single one of them had a father. Men not only have a right to speak to this issue, they have a responsibility to do so!

"Why Do We Need to Change the Law?"

I was speaking at a luncheon at a Baptist church in downtown Ft. Lauderdale, and the senior pastor asked me, "Isn't it enough that we *change hearts?* Why do we need to change the law?"

My answer was that the law acts as a teacher—it influences behavior. The best example I can think of is the Minnesota Parental Notice law. Both the Ohio and Minnesota parental notice laws were passed around the same time. Both were challenged and went to the Supreme Court.[14] But there was one difference. Our Ohio law was enjoined as the cases traveled up through the courts, while Minnesota's law remained in effect. So what have we learned from this?

For one thing, since Minnesota's parental notice law went into effect in 1981, the abortion rate has dropped 61 percent! (2,327 teen abortions in 1981 down to only 899 in 1995.) You would expect a drop in the abortion rate, but 61 percent is pretty remarkable.[15] When parents are notified, teens find out that their parents aren't "going to kill them" when they find out they're pregnant. The result: A child is born that otherwise would have been aborted in an effort to cover it up.

The abortion rate went down, but that's not my only point. Another thing we learned from Minnesota (and other states with similar laws) is that the *teen pregnancy rate* dropped as well! It went from 4,360 teen pregnancies in 1981 to only 2,922 in 1995—a 33 percent drop![16]

This clearly demonstrates that when teens are no longer able to obtain an abortion without their parents knowing about it, they are much more responsible about their sexual behavior. Yes, laws change behavior. Even though the homicide rate is high—imagine what it would be like if the laws and the penalties were removed!

I cannot tell you how many women I have talked to who chose abortion because they felt, "Well, greater minds than mine have determined that it's legal. Who am I to question it?" No, the law is very much a teacher. It changes attitudes . . . and it changes behavior!

Everything is Up for Grabs in the 2000 Election

As I write this, we are facing what is arguably the most important election in our nation's history. As many as three Supreme Court justices could be appointed by the next president. They're the ones who have the power to overturn even a partial-birth abortion ban *and* the power to overturn *Roe v. Wade*—and it's the president who makes these appointments!

That means that this next election will determine whether or not we will return protection to unborn children in my lifetime. That is how critical it is that you do everything within your power to register pro-lifers to vote, inform them, and get them to the polls. If you are in a place where this is possible, I would ask you right now to get on your knees and pray like you have never prayed before for the churches to wake up and make this happen.

"In 1988 only 18 percent of those who voted were evangelical born-again Christians, according to an exit poll by the National Research Institute. That was '88. By '92 that figure had risen to 24 percent. By 1994, just six years later, that figure had risen to 33 percent—making that group of "evangelical born-again Christians" the largest single voting block in America—larger than any one of the five sought-after, highly touted voting blocks of America."[17] Yet many Christians are not even registered and others still are voting for pro-abortion candidates like Bill Clinton.

What You Can Do

As I've said before, actions are what you believe. Everything else is just religious talk. If you believe that abortion takes the life of an innocent human being, here's a place to start:

- Register to vote
- Register your church members to vote
- Get informed about where the candidates stand (with

candidate surveys and with voter guides)
- Inform your church where the candidates stand
- Vote
- Get your church members to vote (that's what those directories are for!)
- Get involved in the pro-life movement and become a liaison to your church
- Start a social issues group in your congregation to keep the others informed
- Actively seek candidates to run
- Support them
- Run yourself!

Awhile back the pro-abortion lobby printed buttons, "I'm Pro-Choice and I vote." As I've heard Mrs. Barbara Willke say, "How much better it is to say, 'I'm Pro-Life and I walk a precinct!'"

Contrast this with an article by American Family Association President, Don Wildmon, who describes what Christians are *currently* doing to respond to what's happening around them.

That's What Christians Do Now

In 1973 the Supreme Court said it was OK to kill unborn babies. Since then, we have killed more than the entire population of Canada. And it continues. A woman's choice? Half of those who have died in their mothers' wombs would have become women. They didn't have a choice. It is called abortion.

Me? I go to church, the minister preaches, I go home. That's what Christians do now.

First it was in dingy theaters. Then convenience stores. Then grocery stores. Then on television. Now it is in the homes of millions via the Internet. It is called pornography. Me? I go to church, the minister preaches, I go home. That's what Christians do now.

They called it no-fault. Why should we blame anyone when something so tragic happens. Haven't they already suffered enough? Half of the marriages in America end this way. The children suffered. The family broke down. It's called divorce.

Me? I go to church, the minister preaches, I go home. That's what Christians do now.

At one time it was a perversion. We kept it secret. We secured help and hope for those who practiced it. Now it is praised. We have parades celebrating it, and elected officials give it their blessing. Now it is endowed with special privileges and protected by special laws. Even some Christian leaders and denominations praise it. It is called homosexuality.

Me? I go to church, the minister preaches, I go home. That's what Christians do now.

It used to be an embarrassment. A shame. Now a third of all births are to mothers who aren't married. Two-thirds of all African-American children are born into a home without a father. The state usually pays the tab. That is why we pay our taxes, so that government can take the place of parents. After all, government bureaucrats know much better how to raise children than parents do. It is called illegitimacy.

Me? I go to church, the minister preaches, I go home. That's what Christians do now.

At one time it was wrong. But then the state decided to legalize it, promote it, and tax it. It has ripped apart families and destroyed lives. But just look at all the money the state has raised. No longer do we have to teach our children to study and work hard. Now we teach them they can get something for nothing. We spend millions encouraging people to join the fun and excitement. Just look at the big sums people are winning. They will never have to work again! It's called gambling.

Me? I go to church, the minister preaches, I go home. That's what Christians do now.

Not long ago, Christians were the good guys. But now any positive image of Christians in movies or on TV is gone. We are now depicted as the bad guys—greedy, narrow-minded hypocrites. The teacher can't have a Bible on her desk, but can have *Playboy*. We don't have Christmas and Easter holidays—just "winter" and "spring" break. We can't pray in school, but can use foul language. It's called being tolerant.

Me? I go to church, the minister preaches, I go home. That's what Christians do now.

Yes, all these things came to pass within 30 years. Where were the Christians? Why, they were in church. All these things are for someone else to deal with. Times have changed. Involvement has been replaced with apathy.

But don't blame me. I didn't do anything. I go to church, the minister preaches, I go home. That's what Christians do now.[18]

Maybe that's what Christians do *now*, but it doesn't have to be what they'll do tomorrow.

Now that you know there is no "constitutional separation of church and state," and now that you know that you've been commanded by the God of the Universe to rescue "those who are being taken away to death," there should be nothing stopping you from getting involved . . . and involving your church.

We don't have to be a church that sings "a little louder" to cover the screams of the innocent. We can join together—yes, even with different denominations, to make a difference and bring to an end the modern-day Auschwitz, Treblinka, and Dachau's in our cities. The starting place is prayer. But that is just the starting place! If we joined together in this effort, imagine what we could do! One would say, we could even . . . "reclaim America!"

I don't know about you, but I think that has kind of a nice ring to it!

18

God-Sized Ideas

In December 1986, Ronda was 20 years old and living with her boyfriend. They were planning to get married when she found out she was pregnant. Quite a surprising discovery, since doctors had told her that wasn't possible. Her boyfriend was furious. His parents advised that she "take care of this problem" right away. After all, that wasn't the way to start off a marriage. They should get to know each other and travel first, they said.

Ronda agreed to have an abortion. But that night she couldn't help but think about her best friend who had an abortion in high school and was filled with regret. Her friend cried constantly, repeating the words, "I can't believe I killed my baby . . . I just can't believe it." Ronda was haunted by those words and just couldn't go through with it. Her fiancé argued with her, but when he realized her mind was made up, he agreed to move up the wedding date and give it a try.

The marital problems and stress took its toll on Ronda; she was given medication to prevent contractions, and the doctor ordered her to immediate and complete bed rest to prevent a miscarriage. Rather than stay and help her with meals, her husband went on a ski trip. When Ronda went into premature labor she called her mother.

Her mother advised Ronda not to take her medication—that premature labor was "God's way of getting rid of a deformed baby," and she should just "let nature take its course."

Her husband didn't want her to have the baby. Her mother didn't want her to have the baby. Her in-laws didn't want the baby, and

Ronda didn't want it either, but something within her made her take that medication. The baby was born prematurely, and her husband left six weeks later.

Ronda then met and later married a Christian man who led her to the Lord and taught her little girl all about God. That little girl, Emily, who was almost aborted, who was almost born too early to survive, turned seven years old and invited Norma McCorvey, the "Roe" of *Roe v. Wade,* to church where Norma became a Christian and turned pro-life.

Satan wanted Emily dead, but God had bigger plans—plans that pro-lifers could only dream about, plans that most would have never in their wildest imagination have even entertained: the poster child for abortion, the one who started it all, the Roe of *Roe v. Wade,* now a pro-life Christian. That's what God can do through a seven-year-old. What can He do through *you?*

> *Now to Him who is able to do exceedingly abundantly above*
> *all that we ask or think, according to the power that works in us.*
> —Ephesians 3:20

What would you do if you *knew* you couldn't fail? What kind of things would you accomplish for God?

I met Brenda Geiger at one of my presentations when, for some reason, rather than going to hear another speaker, she sat through my presentation *twice*—something only my parents would be inclined to do.

She came up and told me how she agreed with me but felt overwhelmed with all she had to do. Maybe that's where you are in this book. Maybe she said what you're already thinking.

"Janet, we're busy," she exclaimed. "We've got kids that need help with their homework , who need to go to soccer practice . . . and then we've got to make dinner. I know I'm speaking for a lot of people—we want to make a difference but how can we?"

My second favorite Edmund Burke quote is this one: "Nobody

made a greater mistake than he who did nothing because he could only do a little."

"Who do I write to? What do I say? And where are my stamps?" I know some of you can relate. We met for lunch and discussed her idea to put together a package for moms like her who could do something very easily and very quickly—something that would only take three minutes a month.

It's called the "Three Minute Impact," and provides everything you need to influence public policy in just three minutes—a congressional directory, fact sheets, stationery, stamps, and a subscription to *Impact* newsletter—which features an issue each month with one action step. Make an impact in three minutes.

This is from our "game show" at the Reclaiming America for Christ Conference in February 1999. You too can win cash and prizes when you "Make an Impact" in three minutes or less!

We presented her idea at the Reclaiming America for Christ Conference in February of 1999 in a game show format in front of about 1,800 people. Contestants tried to beat the clock to write their note to Congress asking them to support the partial-birth abortion ban.

In *under a minute*—my mom and dad were *tied* as they ran to the opposite side of the stage to put their note in the mailbox—it was cheesy, but it really *wasn't* fixed! Several hundred people rushed to get their "Three Minute Impact" folders and are still making an impact—all because of one woman's idea.

"Nobody made a greater mistake than he who did nothing because he could only do a little."

With God all things are possible. All things. Overcoming a fear of public speaking. Dealing with the media. Electing and appointing pro-life people who never had a chance. Changing hearts of opposition leaders. Passing laws in ways that have never been done. And bringing an end to abortion. With God *all* things are possible.

What would you do if you *knew* you couldn't fail? Forget about the money it takes, forget about the obstacles—we're dealing with God here. That means our ideas can be God-sized!

If there were no limits, what kind of God-sized ideas would you undertake?

Michigan Right to Life asked that question. They said they would like to run television commercials statewide with a toll-free number that connects women contemplating abortion with a pregnancy center right where they live. And they have. Because of that, their educational, political, and legislative efforts over time, they have effectively lowered the abortion rate by over 43 percent in their state!

One woman came home from college in a southern state to visit her parents in Michigan and taped her favorite program while she was there. What no one knew was that she was pregnant and scheduled to have an abortion when she returned to school. When she got back, however, she watched her video tape, and on it was one of the Michigan Right to Life commercials with the 800 number for pregnant women to call. She called, and even though she was out of state, they scrambled and got her the help she needed—help that helped save a life.

What kind of things do I dream about? What if, instead of

being an "incidental" occurrence, that was what happened nationwide? What if we put the best commercials available (along with others we could create) on in all 50 states? If not with a nationwide 800 number, with the number of the pregnancy centers in the local areas?

Coral Ridge Ministries has produced an award-winning ad that Dr. Willke has said is "the best pro-life ad I have ever seen." When a pregnancy center ran the ads we produced in El Paso, Texas, their caseload increased by 75 percent! Many of these women would have otherwise had abortions. Want to use these ads in your state? They're yours— free for the asking. And we can work with Michigan and the other groups already doing this. When I was at Ohio Right to Life, we joined with groups like the Caring Foundation to run our television campaign. We also asked Michigan Right to Life to join us in a little known pro-life ad featuring Mother Teresa! Imagine what we could do if we all worked together in a unified way, completely determined to return protection to unborn children. It would happen; that's what. Forget about whose "turf" you're on and just do it.

Michigan has also produced ads to create a more positive image—rather than abide by the image that has already been created for us—something critical if we are to win (see chapter 11 on debate). There are also ads directed at men—typically forgotten in this tragedy— and women who've already had abortions, and people who would be inclined to support assisted suicide.

If the message you want isn't already out there, we can create it! When 50 states join together, that cuts way down on production costs per viewer! By the way, cable channels are very inexpensive—and maybe that's a good place to start. But I have to believe that there are people willing to join together to make this happen—and I have to think that there would even be people willing to put some "matching money" forward for a project of this magnitude.

Now let's talk about *real* God-sized ideas! What if we had our *own* television network—that would not just have quality Christian and family-friendly programming, but also have shows on the current issues. And real news—reliable news that people could turn to find out what's really going on—without people who are 97 percent against us putting it together—news that even non-Christians would watch because it was so truthful, reliable, and relevant. While the rest of the country was focused on such things as the O.J. Simpson trial, Princess Diana, and Elian Gonzalez, we could be finding out what's really going on. I'll bet you didn't know (before reading chapter 16), for example, that the U.N. is looking to ratify a "one-world church" in June of 2000—did you? That might have deserved a mention on the evening news!

I dream about a Church that seeks an active role in society and pastors that aren't afraid to speak out. The reason the other side hates it so much is because it's so effective! I think they know that more than we do.

I have a dream . . . OK, now I'm getting a little carried away: What if we had a training school that taught pro-lifers how they could oversee the organization and recruitment of pro-lifers to serve in every level of government? A friend of mine in Columbus, Ohio, took on the responsibility of filling in every vacancy in the Republican and Democratic county central committees. They, again, are the groups that decide who will be on the ballots before they're ever printed! Wouldn't that be a good place for pro-lifers to start? Other counties have done that too, starting with the open seats and then moving to challenge others—and now have a pro-life majority overseeing who gets elected! Imagine what it would be like to have each candidate planning to run for office have an interview before a completely pro-life screening committee! We would have different counties, different states, and a different nation.

We need to take advantage of the fact that most people don't ·care about the local offices enough to vote for them. That means that our organized effort could deliver pro-life Christian majorities on everything from school boards to city councils to the county commissions. What if we had a place to train these candidates to run and win . . . and to train our people already in office how to address pro-life issues? As I'm sure you are aware, it's a whole lot easier to say you're "pro-choice" and "don't want to impose your beliefs on anyone" than it is to stand and defend human life. By the way, if these folks don't want to "impose their beliefs," maybe they shouldn't vote on anything! And maybe those with their finger in the air constantly checking opinion polls should be replaced with a machine that votes the latest opinion poll, while we're at it!

There *is* a better way, and if we all work together, we become a far more powerful force than we already are.

What would you dream if you knew you couldn't fail? With God all things are possible. All things. Overcoming a fear of public speaking. Dealing with the media. Electing and appointing pro-life people who never had a chance. Changing the hearts of opposition leaders. Passing laws in ways that have never been done. And bringing an end to abortion. With God *all* things are possible.

If you make yourself available, God will use you. God doesn't discriminate against age either—you can even be seven years old, like Emily! We have a dark and dying world out there. It is crumbling around us, and if we don't exercise our First Amendment rights, not only are we going to lose them, but evil will continue to triumph—at an accelerated rate.

God is the One who says that we are to rescue those being led to slaughter. God wants us to choose life so we and our descendants will live. God is the One who told us to be salt and light in this dark and dying world. I don't know about your worldview, but in mine, what God, the Creator of the universe, says, matters! The good news is that He will empower you to do all of it.

How do you get to the Promised Land? You keep walking—but you also need to look at the map!

We *will* win this because we have the Truth that will not return void. The Truth prevails. We will win because we have persistence—and persistence wins. And we will win because we have love—and love conquers all. In fact, we are already making an incredible difference! On January 6, 2000, the Centers for Disease Control (CDC) released the 1997 figures on abortion in the United States. They are now lower than any number the CDC has reported since 1978! (1,184,758 abortions— 20 per 1,000 women, ages 15 to 44).[1] This is down from 1.6 million in 1990.[2]

And we will win this sooner if we turn to God and let Him work through us. We will win sooner if we activate the Church—first by registering Christians to vote and informing them of where the candidates stand on abortion, and then getting them to actually cast their pro-life ballots on election day. We will win sooner if we utilize creativity and humor to make a difference in everything we do, from dealing with the media to electing pro-life candidates and passing pro-life legislation. We will win if we work together—and share with each other what we have learned.

And finally, I believe we will win because if even a two-year-old child can recognize the truth—that the being in the crossfire of this debate is . . . a baby, it is only a matter of time before the rest of the country does too.

One day the rest of the nation will learn that there has been an American Holocaust going on while they've been singing in church and they will join us and rise up and help us stop it.

I believe with all my heart that one day, when the nation sees the truth, just like in Germany, our children will be taught about what happened in *our* nation. They will learn in school about the American Holocaust. And I believe that when this happens, our children and grandchildren will come home from school one day with a very important question for *us*—a very simple, straightforward question. That question is: "Where were *you* when they were killing babies?"

I want to be able to answer, "I was doing everything I could to stop it."

Glory Be to the God of the Impossible!!

Endnotes

Chapter 1: Why Read This Book?
1. The Alan Guttmacher Institute, "Facts in Brief," 1996.
2. Alsa Torres & J. D. Forrest, "Why Do Women Have Abortions?" *Family Planning Perspectives.*, Vol. 20. No. 4, July/August 1988, 170.
3. Lynn Vincent, "The Harvest of Abortion," *World*, 23 October 1999, 16.
4. D. James Kennedy, Jerry Newcombe, *The Gates of Hell Shall Not Prevail* (Nashville: Thomas Nelson Publishers, 1996), 89.
5. Mimi Hall, "Polls: Shift in support for abortion," *USA Today*, 21 January 1998, 1A.
6. Bob Sipchen, "Cause and Effect," *Los Angeles Times*, 3 April 1997, 1E.
7. "Wirthlin Poll," National Right to Life, 5 November, 1996.
8. "L.A. Times Exit Poll," National Right to Life, 5 November 1996.

Chapter 2: Getting Out of the Desert
1. Daniel E. Troy, "Electing the Supreme Court," *The Weekly Standard*, 10 May 1999, 26.

Chapter 3: A Simple Issue
1. "Life Before Birth," *Life Magazine*, 30 April 1965.
2. *Donahue*: Transcript #3288, 6 September 1991.
3. From a speech at a Ohio Congressional Breakfast on 22 January 1992.
4. William Brennan, *Dehumanizing the Vulnerable: When Word Games Take Lives* (Chicago: University of Chicago Press, 1995), 67.

Chapter 4: The Beginning
1. Fannie Weinstein, "Controversy," *People*, 30 November 1998, 117.

Chapter 5: My Worldview
1. William Bennett, *The Index of Leading Cultural Indicators: Facts and Figures on the State of American Society* (New York: Simon & Schuster, 1994).
2. U.S. Bureau of the Census, Statistical Abstract of the United States: 1987, (117th edition), Washington, D.C., 1987, 769; and also Eugene Martin

Christiansen, "A New Entitlement," *International Gaming and Wagering Business,* August 1998, 3.

3.   Wickelgren, Ingrid: "Male Homosexuality Absence of Linkage to Micro Satellite Markets at XQ28," *Science Journal,* Volume 284, 23 April 1999.

4.   U. S. Department of Health and Human Services, Public Health Service, Center for Disease Control and Prevention, *Center for Disease Control HIV/AID Surveillance Report 1998,* Vol. 9, No. 2, May 1998.

5.   U. S. Department of Health and Human Services, Public Health Service, Center for Disease Control and Prevention, *Sexually Transmitted Disease Surveillance 1997* (Atlanta 1997), Gonorrhea 2.

6.   Simopekka Virkkula, "One Man's War," *Books from Finland,* 24 (1990), 45-50.

Chapter 6: God Intervenes
1.   Mac Powell, Tai Anderson, Mark Lee, Brad Avery, David Carr, "Love Song," 1996 New Spring Publishing, Big Man Little Man Publishing/Gray Dot Songs (ASCAP) (all rights admin. by Brentwood-Benson Music Publishing, Inc.) All rights reserved. Used by Permission.

2.   Sipchen, Bob, "Cause and Effect," *Los Angeles Times,* 3 April 1997, 1E.

3.   Ibid.

4.   *Doe v. Bolton,* 410 U.S.179, (1973), Chapter 7.

Chapter 7: Creativity for the Cause
1.   Jim Underwood, "Not a referendum on abortion," *The Plain Dealer,* 18 November 1990, A10.

2.   Janet Folger, "Right: He was wrong, wrong, wrong," *The Plain Dealer,* 1 December 1990.

Chapter 8: Partial-Birth Abortion
1.   Congress, House, Subcommittee on the Constitution of the Committee on the Judiciary, "Partial Birth Abortion Hearing before the Subcommittee on the Constitution of the Committee on the Judiciary," 104th Congress, First Session, 15 June 1995, Serial No. 31.

2.   Letter of Martin Haskell, M.D., to Congressman Charles D. Canady, Chairman, Subcommittee on the Subcommittee of the Constitution, dated, 27 June 1995.

3.   Henry Hyde, "Henry Hyde's Plea to Override the President's Veto of the Partial-Birth Abortion Ban." Taken from the Congressional Record, 19 September

Notes to Pages 85-135

1998. available from http://law.gonzaga.edu/people/dewolf /hyde.htm.

4. Janet Folger, "Partial-birth abortion too common, never necessary to protect women," *Columbus Dispatch*, 25 November 1996, p. 11A.

5. Charles E. Cook, "Partial-Birth Betrayal: Democrats Seething As Activist Admits Lie," *Congressional Roll Call*, 8 February 1997.

6. Michelle Morgan, "Abortion advocates admit they have been lying to public now reveal most partial-birth abortions are performed on healthy mothers of healthy babies," Representative Charles Canady Press Release, 26 February 1997.

Chapter 9: More Legislative Lessons
1. Paul Imhoff, "The Battle of the Rallies—We Won!" *Ohio Right to Life Society News*, December 1989.

2. Lee Leonard, "Bill to protect fetuses could be abortion ploy," *Columbus Dispatch*, 22 April 1996, 9A.

Chapter 10: The Media
1. D. James Kennedy, Jerry Newcombe, *The Gates of Hell Shall Not Prevail* (Nashville: Thomas Nelson Publishers, 1996), 87.

2. Ibid.

3. Department of Health and Human Services, Public Health Service, Center for Disease Control, *HIV/AIDS Surveillance Report*, Vol. 9, No. 2, (Atlanta 1998).

4. Michael Heaton, "Onward Christian Folger," *The Plain Dealer Sunday Magazine*, 8 November 1998, 9.

5. Ibid.

6. Media Research Center, "The Clinton Boom Begins?" *Media Watch*, December 1992.

Chapter 11: The Debate
1. J.C. Willke, *Abortion Questions and Answers* (Cincinnati: Hayes Publishing Company, Inc., 1985), 46, 47.

2. Chris Skurkey, "Take Off Those Gags and Blindfolds," *The Daily Kent Stater*, 9 October 1992.

3. Alda Torres, J.D. Forrest. "Why Do Women Have Abortions?" *Family Planning Perspectives*, Vol. 20, No. 4 (July/August 1988).

4. Interview with Eric Harrah appeared on *The Coral Ridge Hour*, the weekly television broadcast of Coral Ridge Ministries, on 8 December, 1998.

Notes to Pages 138-146

Chapter 12: Tolerance
1. "Declaration of Principles on Tolerance," The Member States of the United Nations Educational, Scientific and Cultural Organization, meeting in Paris at the twenty-eighth session of the General Conference, from 25 October to 16 November 1995.

2. Josh McDowell, Bob Hostetler, *The New Tolerance—How a cultural movement threatens to destroy you, your faith, and your children* (Tyndale House: Wheaton, Illinois, 1998), 19.

3. Reuters, "Has Church of Satan Gone to Hell?" CNN Custom News – World, 26 January, 1999 [Journal on-line] available from http://customnews /cnews/pna.show_story?p_art_id=3373001&p_section_name=World. (Accessed 27 January 1999).

4. Josh McDowell, Bob Hostetler, *The New Tolerance—How a cultural movement threatens to destroy you, your faith, and your children* (Tyndale House: Wheaton, Illinois, 1998), 25.

5. Martin Luther King Jr. *Wall Street Journal, 13* November 1962, from "A Collection of Quotes by Martin Luther King Jr.," available from http://www.geocities.com/~wwwin/mlking.htm (Accessed 5 January 2000).

6. Dennis Prager, "Anti-Semitism in America," *Wall Street Journal,* 26 August 1999, 14A.

7. "APA, Dr. Laura Respond," *Impact,* November 1999, 2.

8. Valerie Richardson, "Evangelical Tone of Memorial Spurs Backlash," PropheZine, *The Washington Times,* Littleton, Colorado, (Journal on-line) from [RTF bookmark start: http://www.prophezine.com/search/database/ Issue77/ is/77.9.html (Accessed 31 December 1999).

9. Ibid.

10. Chuck Colson, "Why Christians Are Losing the Culture War," *Christian Research Journal,* Summer 1996.

11. Josh McDowell, Bob Hostetler, *The New Tolerance* (Tyndale House: Wheaton, Illinois, 1998), 92.

12. Ibid., 95.

13. Associated Press, "Sharon Stone Says Keep Condoms Near," *Washington Post,* 2 December 1998 (Newspaper on-line) available from http://search.washingtonpost.com (Accessed 7 December 1998).

14. Don Feder, "Professor of Death Will Fit Right in at Princeton," *Jewish World Review,* 28 October 1998 (Newspaper on-line) Internet accessed 1 January 2000.

Endnotes

15. Robert Reiger, "Funeral Singer Changes Tune," *Culture Facts*, 15 September 1999, Family Research Council.

16. Julie Ann Kessler, "Choose Polygamy, Choose NOW," *Washington Times*, 22 August 1998, (article on-line) available from http://www.claremont. org/KesslerNOWchoose.htm (Accessed 4 November 1998).

17. Dennis Prager, "Anti-Semitism in America," *Wall Street Journal*, 26 August 1999, 14A.

Chapter 13: Lies, Lies, Lies

1. "An Interview with Norma McCorvey The 'Roe' of *Roe v. Wade* and Sandra Cano, the 'Doe' *of Doe v. Bolton,"* Ann Scheidler, Chicago Pro-Life Action League, 20 April 1996.

2. *Doe v. Bolton*, 410 U.S. 179 (1973).

3. Bernard Nathanson, M.D., *Aborting America* (New York: Doubleday, 1979), 193.

4. *National Right to Life Fast Facts on Planned Parenthood 1999.*

5. *Donahue:* Transcript #3288, 6 September 1991.

6. Michelle Morgan, "Abortion advocates admit they have been lying to public. Now reveal most partial-birth abortions are performed on healthy mothers of healthy babies," Representative Charles Canady Press Release, 26 February 1997.

7. Charles Cook, "Partial-Birth Betrayal: Democrats Seething As Activist Admits Lie," *Roll Call*, 27 February 1997.

8. Dr. and Mrs. J.C. Willke, *Abortion: Questions and Answers* (Cincinnati: Hayes Publishing Company, 1985), 104.

9. Ibid., 105.

10. *New American,* "Wages of Sex Ed" 22 November 1999.

11. George Grant, *Grand Illusions, The Legacy of Planned Parenthood* (Franklin, Tennessee: Adroit Press, 1988), 32.

12. *National Right to Life Fast Facts on Planned Parenthood 1999.*

13. Robert Regier, "Abstinence Ed Lowers Illegitimate Births," *Culture Facts,* 17 February 1999, Family Research Council.

14. Tony Snow, "Subsidizing the Condom Cult," *Jewish World Review,* 18 October 1999, available from www.Jewishworldreview.com/tony/snow1018199.asp (Accessed December 1999).

15. Elizabeth Karlin, "Abstinence among least reliable birth control methods," *Wisconsin State Journal,* 30 November 1997.

16. Joleigh Little, letter to the editor, response to Elizabeth Karlin (unpublished).

17. *Respect Life Newsletter*, "Is There an Abortion-Breast Cancer Connection?" June, 1995.

18. Congressman Albert Gore, Jr., letter to contituent, August 22, 1984.

Chapter 14: Assisted Suicide

1. Michael S. Hamilton, "The Dissatisfaction of Francis Schaeffer," *Christianity Today*, 3 March 1997.

2. Jack Kevorkian, *Prescription Medicine*, (Prometheus Books 1991), 219.

3. Ibid.

4. Mike Williams, "If machine failed, Doctor was set to help death," *Detroit Free Press*, 13 December 1990.

5. Jack Kevorkian, *Prescription Medicine*, (Prometheus Books 1991), 209-210.

6. Statement of Jack Kevorkian in response to complaint for Injunctive Relief and Motion for Temporary Restraining Order, at 11, NO 90-390963 – AZ (Oakland County Circuit Court, 17 August 1990).

7. "Kevorkian, A Predator on the Loose," *IATEF Update*, available from http://www.iaetf.org/iua4.htm#2; (Internet accessed 3 Janurary 2000).

8. Ibid.

9. "Questions About Artificial Feeding," *International Anti-Euthanasia Task Force*, available from http://www.iaetf.org/fctaf.htm (Accessed 3 January 2000).

10. Rita Marker, *Deadly Compassion—The Death of Ann Humphry and the Truth About Euthanasia* (New York: Avon Books, 1995), 92.

11. Wesley Smith, "Oregon Releases Information on Reported Assisted Suicide Deaths," *International Anti-Euthanasia Task Force*, available from http:www.iaetf.org/orr299.htm (Accessed 3 January 2000).

12. Nat Henthoff, "Free Ticket to Eternity," *Washington Post*, 8 February 1999, 21A.

13. Statement of Ellie Jenny, member of Not Dead Yet as reported in *The Oregonian*, "Laws separate euthanasia and assisted suicide," April 14, 1999.

14. "Medical Decisions About the End of Life I," "Report of the Committee to Study the Medical Practice Concerning Euthanasia. II," *The Study for the Committee on Medical Practice Concerning Euthanasia* (2 vols.), (The Hague, 19 September 1991).

15. Rita Marker, *Deadly Compassion—The Death of Ann Humphry and the Truth About Euthanasia* (New York: Avon Books, 1995), 157.

16. Mike Corder, "Dutch Government moves to become first country to legalize mercy killing," Associated Press, 10 August 1999.

17. Wesley Smith, "Don't Rationalize Suicide," *Wall Street Journal*, 3 August 1999.

18. Tragedy Compounded: Joe Cruzan Commits Suicide," *International Anti-Euthanasia Task Force*, available from http://www.iaetf.org/iua4.htm (Accessed 3 January 2000).

19. Citizens for Compassionate Care, "Citizens for Compassionate Care Statement on Proposal B," Press Release, PRN Newswire, 3 November 1998.

Chapter 15: Thinking Big
1. Debra Jasper, "It's GOP's portable target," *Dayton Daily News*, 5 May 1996.

2. Ibid.

3. The Christian Research Report (CRR), January 4, 2000.

Chapter 16: Where We're Headed
1. William J. Federer, *America's God and Country Encyclopedia of Quotations* (Coppell, Texas: FAME Publishing, Inc., 1994), 82

2. Michael Weisskopf, "Energized by Pulpit or Passion, the Public is Calling," *Washington Post*, 1 February 1993, A1.

3. "Christians: Easy Targets for the Media," *Impact*, May 1993.

4. "Ted's Latest Insults," *The Cincinnati Enquirer*, 2 March 1999, A16.

5. Joseph Farah, "Fonda becomes born-again Christian; Split with Ted has spirtual roots, say friends," *World Net Daily*, 6 January 2000

6. Rochelle Olson, "Ventura Talks to *Playboy* Magazine," Associated Press, 30 September 1999.

7. Ibid.

8. D. James Kennedy, Jerry Newcombe, *The Gates of Hell Shall Not Prevail* (Nashville, Tenn.: Thomas Nelson Publishers, 1996), 114.

9. Ibid., 88.

10. Michael Lind, "Understanding Oklahoma Scofflaw Conservatism Beyond the Hyperbole, Ideas Have Consequences," *Washington Post*, 30 April 1995, C1.

11. John Leo, "Not the way to stop abortions," *U.S. News & World Report*, 29 March 1993, 17.

12. *Culture Facts*, Family Research Council, 11 November 1998.

13. Charlene K. Haar, "NEA Delegates Debate Change?" Capital Research Institute, September 1997, www.capitalresearch.org/trends/ot-0997.html.

14. From Ohio Human and Civil Rights Commission questionnaire, published

by Ohio Education Association, December 1994 Representative Assembly.

15. Regina Barecca, English professor at the University of Connecticut, as quoted in *The Federalist*, Vol. No. 99-05, 4 February 1999, 5.

16. Bill Johnson, "Howard Stern Information Action Page," www.american-decency.org/stern/main.htm.

17. Ibid.

18. John Wheeler, "Assault on Faith," *Christian American*, 15 September 1994, 4.

19. Ibid.

20. Ralph Reed, *Mainstream Values are No Longer Politically Incorrect* (Dallas, Texas: Word Publishing, 1994), 10.

21. The Washington Update "The 'Left' Melts Down," *American Renewal*, 16 December 1998.

22. Bruce Selcraig, "The Worst Newspaper in America," *Columbia Journalism Review*, January/February 1999.

23. Bob Jones IV, "Shouting Down Christians?," *World*, Vol. 13, No. 49, (Article on-line from http://www.worldmag.com/world/issue/12-19-98/ cover 1. asp (Accessed 3 January 2000).

24. Ibid.

25. Katie Couric, *The Today Show*, 12 October 1998.

26. From a letter from City of San Francisco Board of Supervisors written to Coral Ridge Ministries in response to the release of the Truth in Love Campaign, 19 October 1998.

27. The Washington Update, *American Renewal*, 22 April 1994

28. Erwin W. Lutzer, *Hitler's Cross: The revealing story of how the Cross of Christ was used as a symbol of the Nazi agenda* (Chicago: Moody Press, 1995), 115.

29. Advertisement, *Village Voice*, 7 February 1998, 147.

30. Diane Brooks, "Religious Talk is a Bus-Stopper, Woman Says," *Seattle Times*, 7 April 1999.

31. Transcript of Excerpt of Proceedings Before the Honorable Samuel B. Kent, U.S. District Court for the Southern District of Texas, C.A. No., G-95-176, 5 May 1995, 3-4.

32. Michael Berenbaum, *The World Must Know* (Boston: Little, Brown Company, 1993), 22.

33. Reggie Rivers, *Rocky Mountain Times*, 4 August 1998, A-6.

34. Richard Dawkins, "Is Science a Religion?" *The Humanist*, January/February 1997.

Notes to Pages 207-214

35. Letter to editor by Brad Bauman, *The Beacon,* responding to a pro-life group that displayed photos depicting the reality of abortion, 9 February 1999.

36. Jodi Veenker, "Christian Group Labeled 'Cultic,'" *Christianity Today,* 6 September 1999, 26.

37. Joseph Woodard, "Ideas," *Calgary Herald,* 14 August 1999.

38. Ibid.

39. Ibid.

40. Ibid.

41. *Discerning the Times,* "The One World Church," Volume 1, Issue 6, July 1999.

42. Jack Nelson, *TERROR IN THE NIGHT* (New York: Simon and Schuster, 1993), 9.

Chapter 17: Taking Action

1. Penny Lea, "Singing a Little Louder" pamphlet, *I Believe in Life Ministry.*

2. William J. Federer, *America's God and Country Encyclopedia of Quotations* (Coppell, Texas: FAME Publishing, Inc., 1994), 540.

3. Bernard Nathanson, *Aborting America* (Toronto, Ontario: Life Cycle Books, 1979).

4. Ibid., 172, 173.

5. Ibid., 172, 173.

6. George Washington. May 10, 1789, in addressing the General Committee of the United Baptist Churches of Virginia. From: William J. Federer, *America's God and Country Encyclopedia of Quotations* (Coppell, Texas: FAME Publishing, Inc., 1994), 653.

7. John Eidsmoe, *Christianity and the Constitution: The Faith of our Founding Fathers* (Grand Rapids: Baker Books, 1987), 108.

8. James Madison. 20 June 1785, Robert Rutland, ed., The Papers of James Madison (Chicago: University of Chicago Press, 1973), Vol. VIII, 299, 304. From: William J. Federer, *America's God and Country Encyclopedia of Quotations* (Coppell, Texas: FAME Publishing, Inc., 1994), 410.

9. William J. Federer, *America's God and Country Encyclopedia of Quotations* (Coppell, Texas: FAME Publishing, Inc., 1994), 26.

10. U.S. Supreme Court, *Church of the Holy Trinity v. United States,* Argued and submitted 7 January 1892, decided 29 February 1892.

11. Thomas Jefferson. January 1, 1802, in a personal letter to Nehemiah Dodge, Ephraim Robbins, and Stephen Nelson of the Danbury Baptist Association,

Notes to Pages 214-228

Danbury, Connecticut. From: William J. Federer, *America's God and Country Encyclopedia of Quotations* (Coppell, Texas: FAME Publishing, Inc., 1994), 325.

12. Thomas Jefferson. 16 November 1798, in the *Kentucky Resolutions of 1789, Article III*. From: William J. Federer, *America's God and Country Encyclopedia of Quotations* (Coppell, Texas: FAME Publishing, Inc., 1994), 323.

13. Justice Antonin Scalia, Dissent in *Lee v. Weisman*, 505 U.S. 577 (1992).

14. *Ohio v. Akron Center for Reproductive Health*, 497 U.S. 502 (1990).

15. Minnesota Department of Health, "Minnesota Abortion Statistics,"1995

16. Ibid.

17. D. James Kennedy, *Spiritual State of the Union* (Fort Lauderdale, Florida: Coral Ridge Ministries, 1995).

18. Donald E. Wildmon, "That's What Christians Do Now," *American Family Journal*, August 1999, 2.

Chapter 18: God-Sized Ideas

1. National Right to Life, "National Right to Life Applauds Sustained Drop in U.S. Abortion Rate, Lowest Abortion Rate Since 1975," *National Right to Life Press Release*, 6 January 2000.

2. The Allan Guttmacher Institute, "Facts in Brief," New York / Washington, DC, 1996.